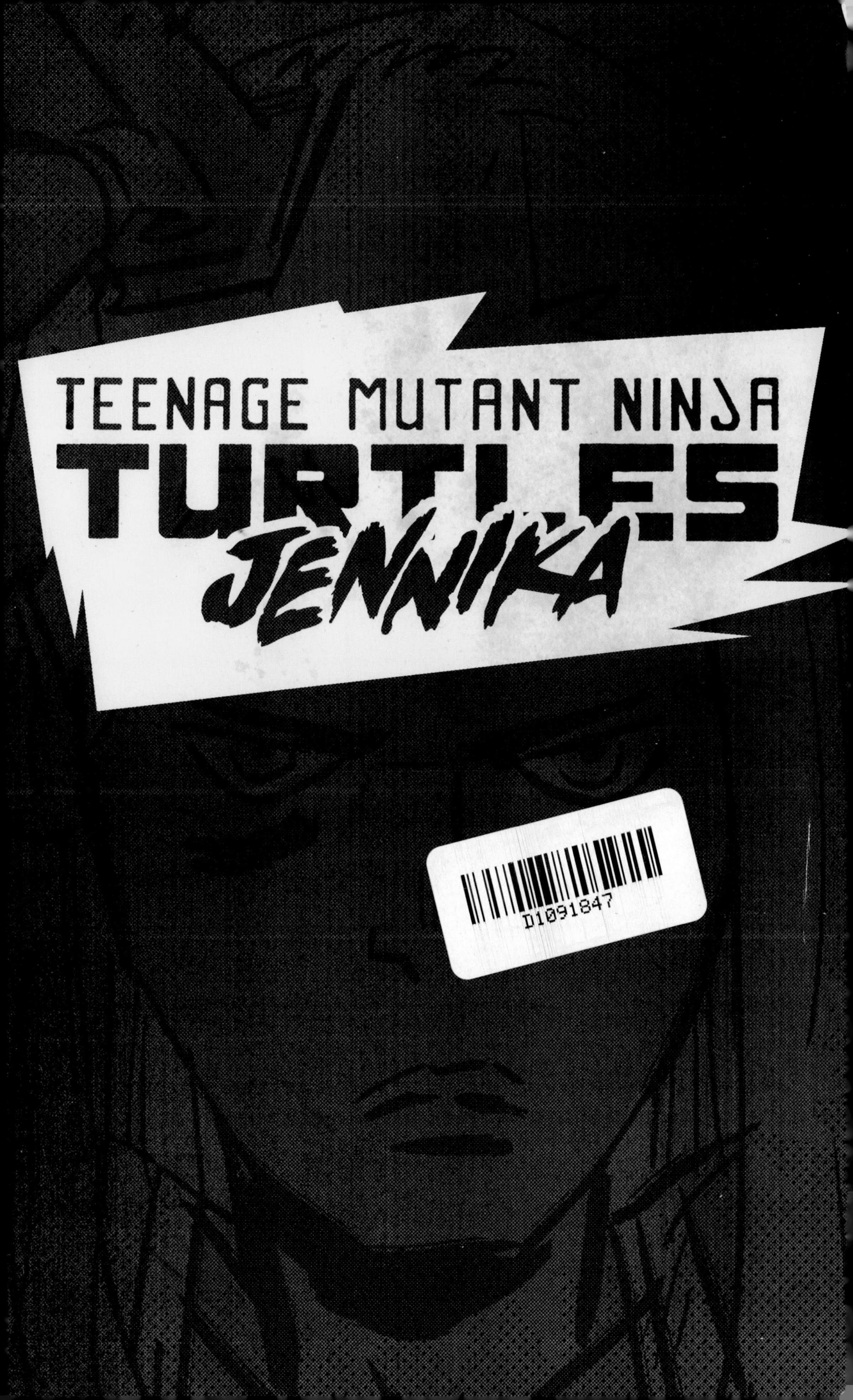
TEENAGE MUTANT NINJA
TURTLES
JENNIKA

nickelodeon.

Special thanks to Joan Hilty & Linda Lee
for their invaluable assistance.

Cover Artist: **Brahm Revel**
Series Editor: **Bobby Curnow**
Collection Editors: **Alonzo Simon** and **Zac Boone**
Collection Designer: **Shawn Lee**

Chris Ryall, President & Publisher/CCO • Cara Morrison, Chief Financial Officer
Matthew Ruzicka, Chief Accounting Officer • John Barber, Editor-in-Chief • Justin Eisinger,
Editorial Director, Graphic Novels and Collections • Scott Dunbier, Director, Special Projects
Jerry Bennington, VP of New Product Development • Lorelei Bunjes, VP of Technology &
Information Services • Jud Meyers, Sales Director • Anna Morrow, Marketing Director
Tara McCrillis, Director of Design & Production • Mike Ford, Director of Operations
Shauna Monteforte, Manufacturing Operations Director • Rebekah Cahalin, General Manager

Ted Adams and Robbie Robbins, IDW Founders

www.idwpublishing.com • Facebook: facebook.com/idwpublishing • Twitter: @idwpublishing
Tumblr: tumblr.idwpublishing.com • Instagram: instagram.com/idwpublishing
YouTube: youtube.com/idwpublishing

Originally published in TEENAGE MUTANT NINJA TURTLES UNIVERSE issues #6–9
and as TEENAGE MUTANT NINJA TURTLES: JENNIKA issues #1–3.

ISBN: 978-1-68405-716-0   23 22 21 20   1 2 3 4

WHAT IS NINJA?
Story & Art by Brahm Revel
Letters by Shawn Lee

THE CURE FOR YOU
story, art & letters
BRAHM REVEL

TIME AND AGAIN
Story & Colors by Ronda Pattison
Art by Jodi Nishijima
Letters by Shawn Lee

WRECKREATION
Story & Colors by Ronda Pattison
Art by Megan Huang
Letters by Shawn Lee

WHAT IF?
Story & Colors by Ronda Pattison
Art by Jodi Nishijima
Letters by Shawn Lee

Art by Jodi Nishijima

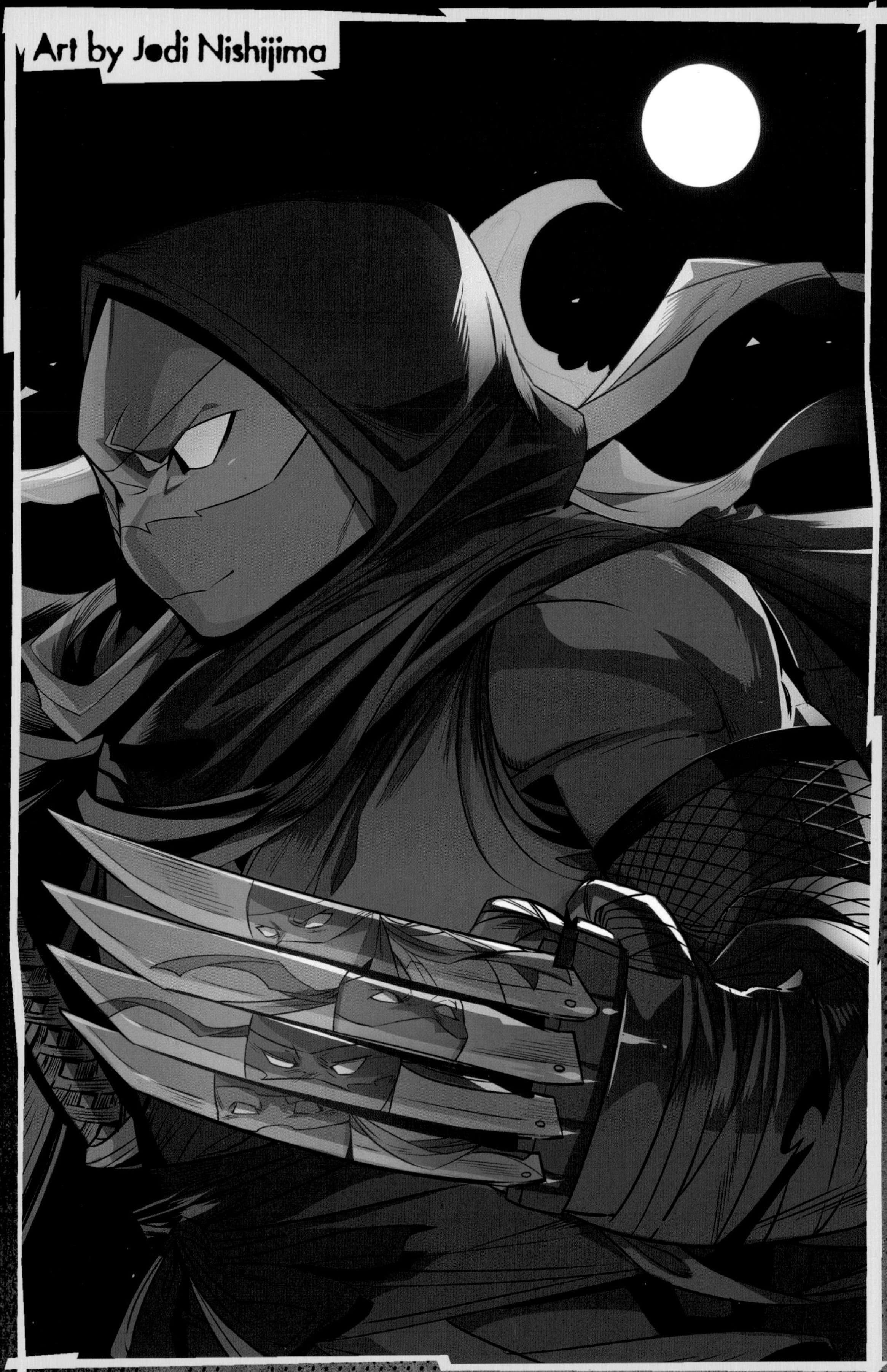

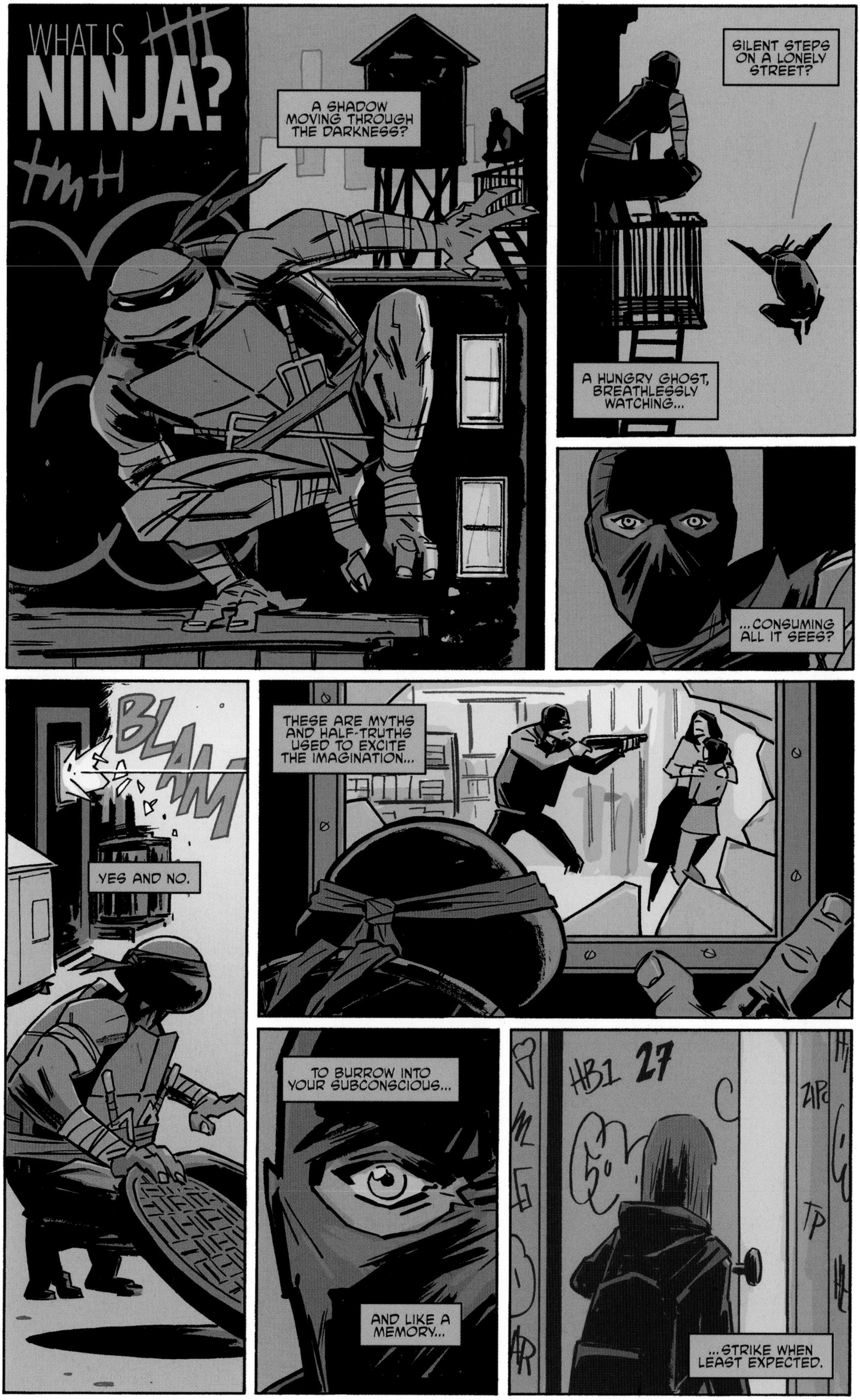
WHAT IS
NINJA?
A SHADOW MOVING THROUGH THE DARKNESS?
SILENT STEPS ON A LONELY STREET?
A HUNGRY GHOST, BREATHLESSLY WATCHING...
...CONSUMING ALL IT SEES?
BLAM
YES AND NO.
THESE ARE MYTHS AND HALF-TRUTHS USED TO EXCITE THE IMAGINATION...
TO BURROW INTO YOUR SUBCONSCIOUS...
AND LIKE A MEMORY...
HB1 27
...STRIKE WHEN LEAST EXPECTED.

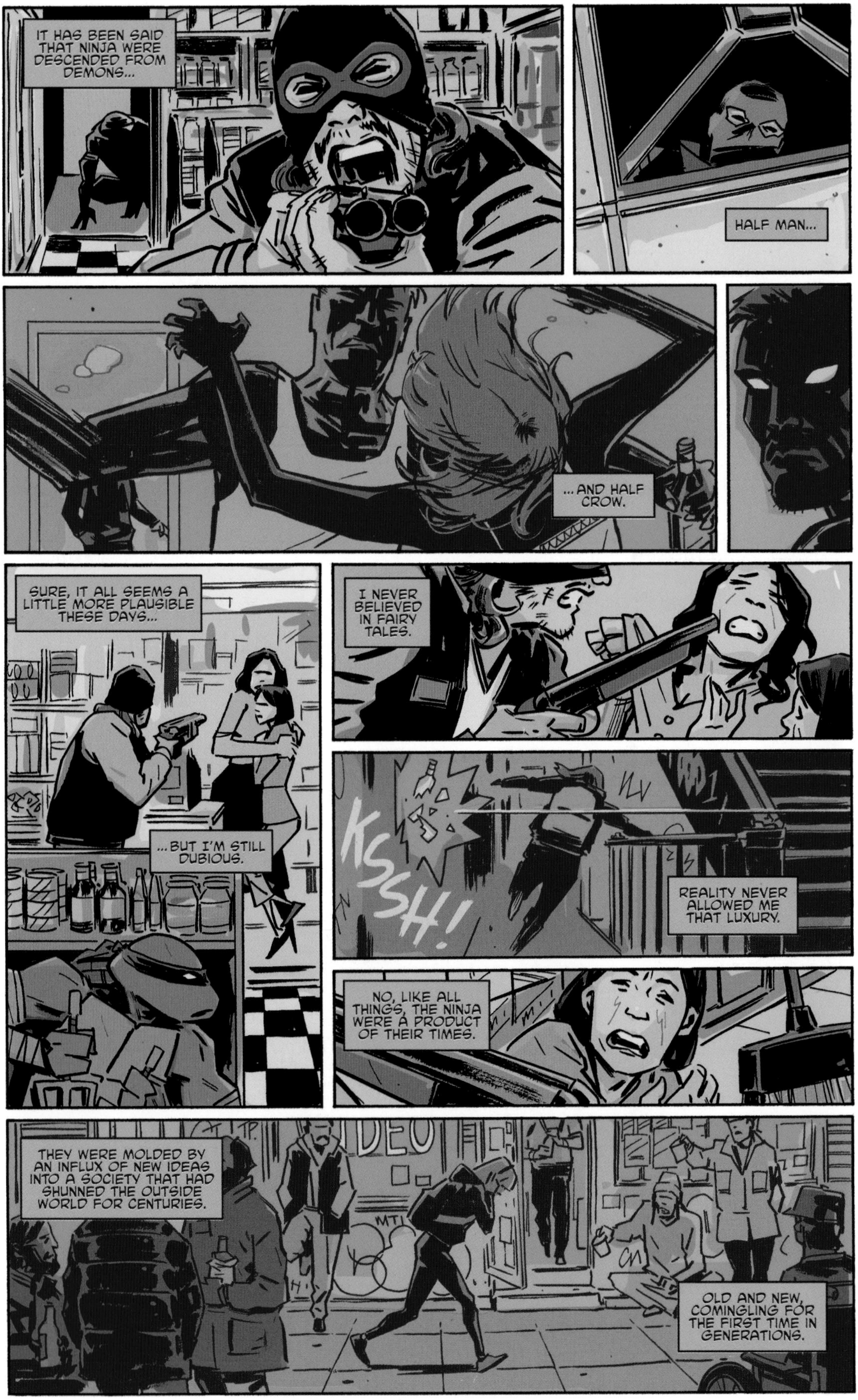
IT HAS BEEN SAID THAT NINJA WERE DESCENDED FROM DEMONS...
HALF MAN...
...AND HALF CROW.
SURE, IT ALL SEEMS A LITTLE MORE PLAUSIBLE THESE DAYS...
...BUT I'M STILL DUBIOUS.
I NEVER BELIEVED IN FAIRY TALES.
KSSH!
REALITY NEVER ALLOWED ME THAT LUXURY.
NO, LIKE ALL THINGS, THE NINJA WERE A PRODUCT OF THEIR TIMES.
THEY WERE MOLDED BY AN INFLUX OF NEW IDEAS INTO A SOCIETY THAT HAD SHUNNED THE OUTSIDE WORLD FOR CENTURIES.
OLD AND NEW, COMINGLING FOR THE FIRST TIME IN GENERATIONS.

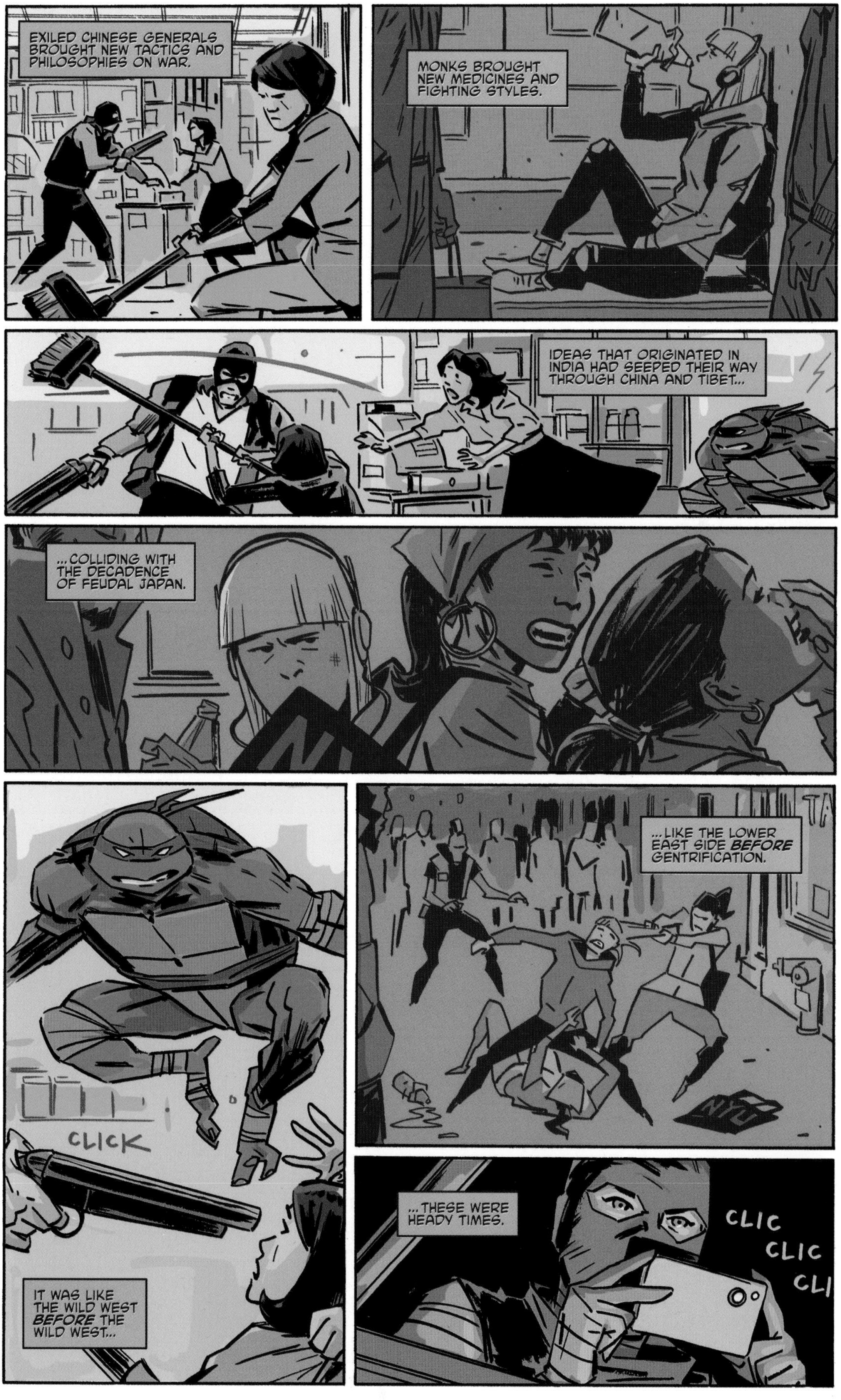
EXILED CHINESE GENERALS BROUGHT NEW TACTICS AND PHILOSOPHIES ON WAR.
MONKS BROUGHT NEW MEDICINES AND FIGHTING STYLES.
IDEAS THAT ORIGINATED IN INDIA HAD SEEPED THEIR WAY THROUGH CHINA AND TIBET...
...COLLIDING WITH THE DECADENCE OF FEUDAL JAPAN.
CLICK
IT WAS LIKE THE WILD WEST *BEFORE* THE WILD WEST...
...LIKE THE LOWER EAST SIDE *BEFORE* GENTRIFICATION.
...THESE WERE HEADY TIMES.
CLIC
CLIC
CLI

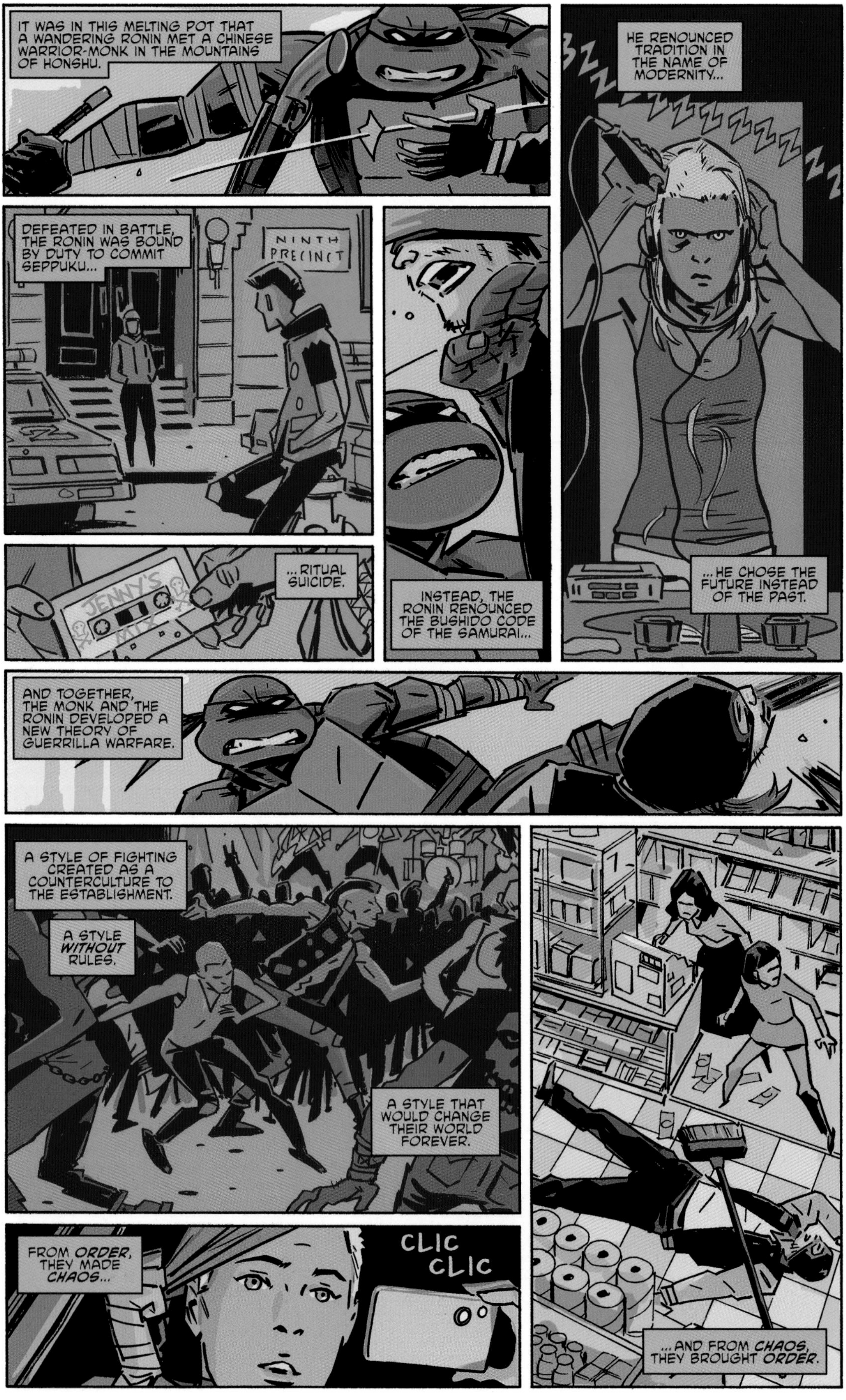
IT WAS IN THIS MELTING POT THAT A WANDERING RONIN MET A CHINESE WARRIOR-MONK IN THE MOUNTAINS OF HONSHU.
DEFEATED IN BATTLE, THE RONIN WAS BOUND BY DUTY TO COMMIT SEPPUKU...
NINTH PRECINCT
...RITUAL SUICIDE.
JENNY'S MIX
INSTEAD, THE RONIN RENOUNCED THE BUSHIDO CODE OF THE SAMURAI...
HE RENOUNCED TRADITION IN THE NAME OF MODERNITY...
ZZZZZZZZZZZZZ
...HE CHOSE THE FUTURE INSTEAD OF THE PAST.
AND TOGETHER, THE MONK AND THE RONIN DEVELOPED A NEW THEORY OF GUERRILLA WARFARE.
A STYLE OF FIGHTING CREATED AS A COUNTERCULTURE TO THE ESTABLISHMENT.
A STYLE *WITHOUT* RULES.
A STYLE THAT WOULD CHANGE THEIR WORLD FOREVER.
FROM *ORDER*, THEY MADE *CHAOS*...
CLIC
CLIC
...AND FROM *CHAOS*, THEY BROUGHT *ORDER*.

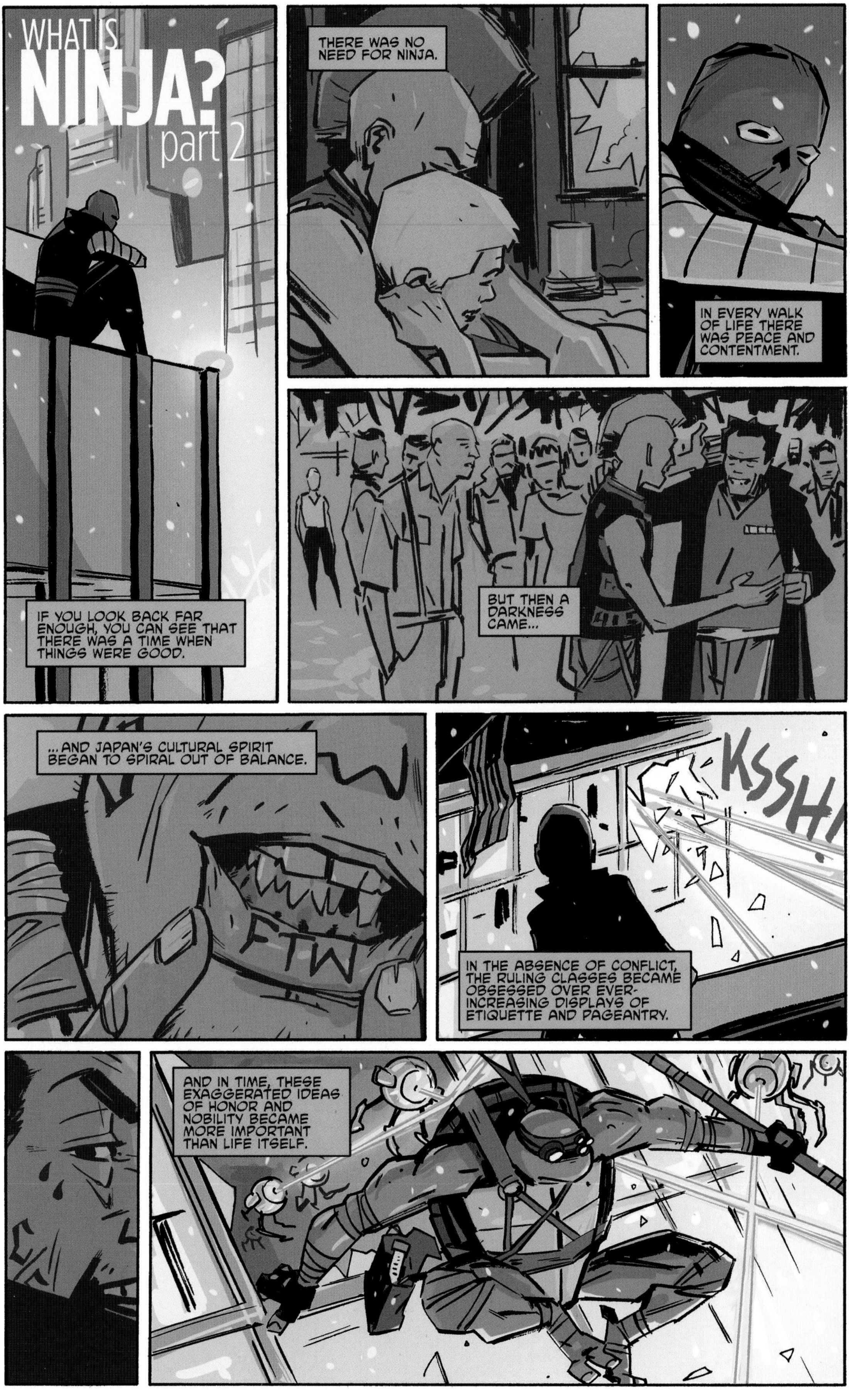
WHAT IS NINJA? part 2
IF YOU LOOK BACK FAR ENOUGH, YOU CAN SEE THAT THERE WAS A TIME WHEN THINGS WERE GOOD.
THERE WAS NO NEED FOR NINJA.
IN EVERY WALK OF LIFE THERE WAS PEACE AND CONTENTMENT.
BUT THEN A DARKNESS CAME...
...AND JAPAN'S CULTURAL SPIRIT BEGAN TO SPIRAL OUT OF BALANCE.
FTW
KSSH!
IN THE ABSENCE OF CONFLICT, THE RULING CLASSES BECAME OBSESSED OVER EVER-INCREASING DISPLAYS OF ETIQUETTE AND PAGEANTRY.
AND IN TIME, THESE EXAGGERATED IDEAS OF HONOR AND NOBILITY BECAME MORE IMPORTANT THAN LIFE ITSELF.

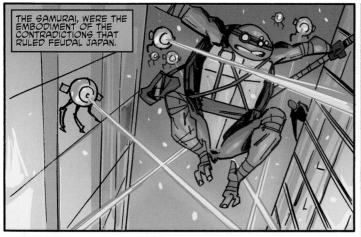

THE SAMURAI, WERE THE EMBODIMENT OF THE CONTRADICTIONS THAT RULED FEUDAL JAPAN.

STEEPED IN A HIGHLY STYLIZED NOBILITY, THE SAMURAI PLEDGED COMPLETE DEVOTION TO THEIR MASTERS...

...WHO IN TURN WOULD UNLEASH THEIR SAMURAI WARRIORS WITH RECKLESS ABANDON OVER THE SLIGHTEST OF PERCEIVED INSULTS.

THE *BUSHIDO CODE*, HOWEVER, REQUIRED THAT THE SAMURAI ADHERE TO A STRICT SET OF ETHICS WHILE ON THE FIELD OF BATTLE.

THE HONOR THAT SAMURAI GAVE THEIR ENEMIES MADE THEM NOBLE ADVERSARIES, BUT ALSO LIMITED THE TACTICAL ADVANTAGES THEY COULD ACHIEVE.

THIS COULD EASILY TURN SKIRMISHES INTO QUAGMIRES.

IN EFFECT, THE SAMURAI WERE GOOD AT STARTING WARS, BUT INEFFECTUAL AT ENDING THEM.

AS SUCH, NINJUTSU DEVELOPED IN THE VOIDS CREATED BY HONOR AND LOYALTY.

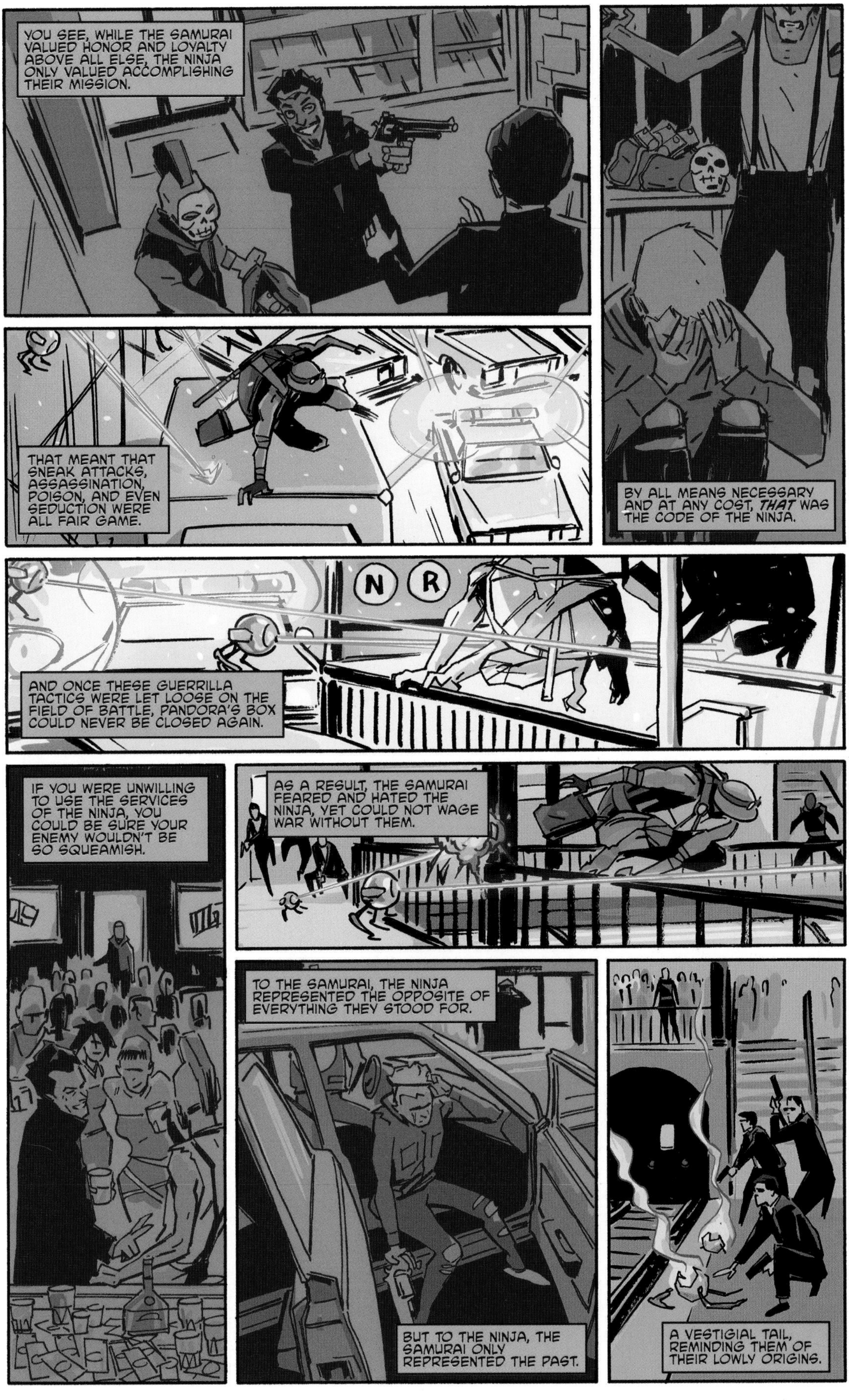
YOU SEE, WHILE THE SAMURAI VALUED HONOR AND LOYALTY ABOVE ALL ELSE, THE NINJA ONLY VALUED ACCOMPLISHING THEIR MISSION.
THAT MEANT THAT SNEAK ATTACKS, ASSASSINATION, POISON, AND EVEN SEDUCTION WERE ALL FAIR GAME.
BY ALL MEANS NECESSARY AND AT ANY COST, *THAT* WAS THE CODE OF THE NINJA.
N
R
AND ONCE THESE GUERRILLA TACTICS WERE LET LOOSE ON THE FIELD OF BATTLE, PANDORA'S BOX COULD NEVER BE CLOSED AGAIN.
IF YOU WERE UNWILLING TO USE THE SERVICES OF THE NINJA, YOU COULD BE SURE YOUR ENEMY WOULDN'T BE SO SQUEAMISH.
AS A RESULT, THE SAMURAI FEARED AND HATED THE NINJA, YET COULD NOT WAGE WAR WITHOUT THEM.
TO THE SAMURAI, THE NINJA REPRESENTED THE OPPOSITE OF EVERYTHING THEY STOOD FOR.
BUT TO THE NINJA, THE SAMURAI ONLY REPRESENTED THE PAST.
A VESTIGIAL TAIL, REMINDING THEM OF THEIR LOWLY ORIGINS.

BUSHIDO, HOWEVER, *DID* GIVE THE SAMURAI A CODE TO HIDE BEHIND, ALLOWING THEIR VIOLENT EXISTENCE TO BE TEMPERED BY A CERTAIN SENSE OF WISDOM AND SERENITY...

...THE NINJA WERE GIVEN NO SUCH REPRIEVE.

THEIR WORKMAN-LIKE DEDICATION TO GETTING THE JOB DONE SOMETIMES MEANT DOING THE UNTHINKABLE.

NO...

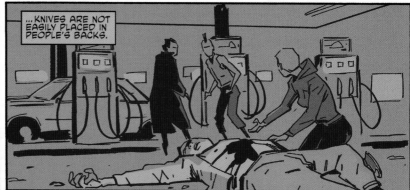

...KNIVES ARE NOT EASILY PLACED IN PEOPLE'S BACKS.

AND ONCE THERE, THEY CANNOT EASILY BE TAKEN OUT AGAIN.

CLIC!

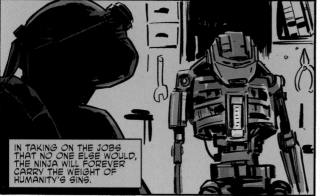

IN TAKING ON THE JOBS THAT NO ONE ELSE WOULD, THE NINJA WILL FOREVER CARRY THE WEIGHT OF HUMANITY'S SINS.

THEY CAME FROM THE VOID TO RETURN BALANCE...

...AND TO THE VOID THEY MUST RETURN.

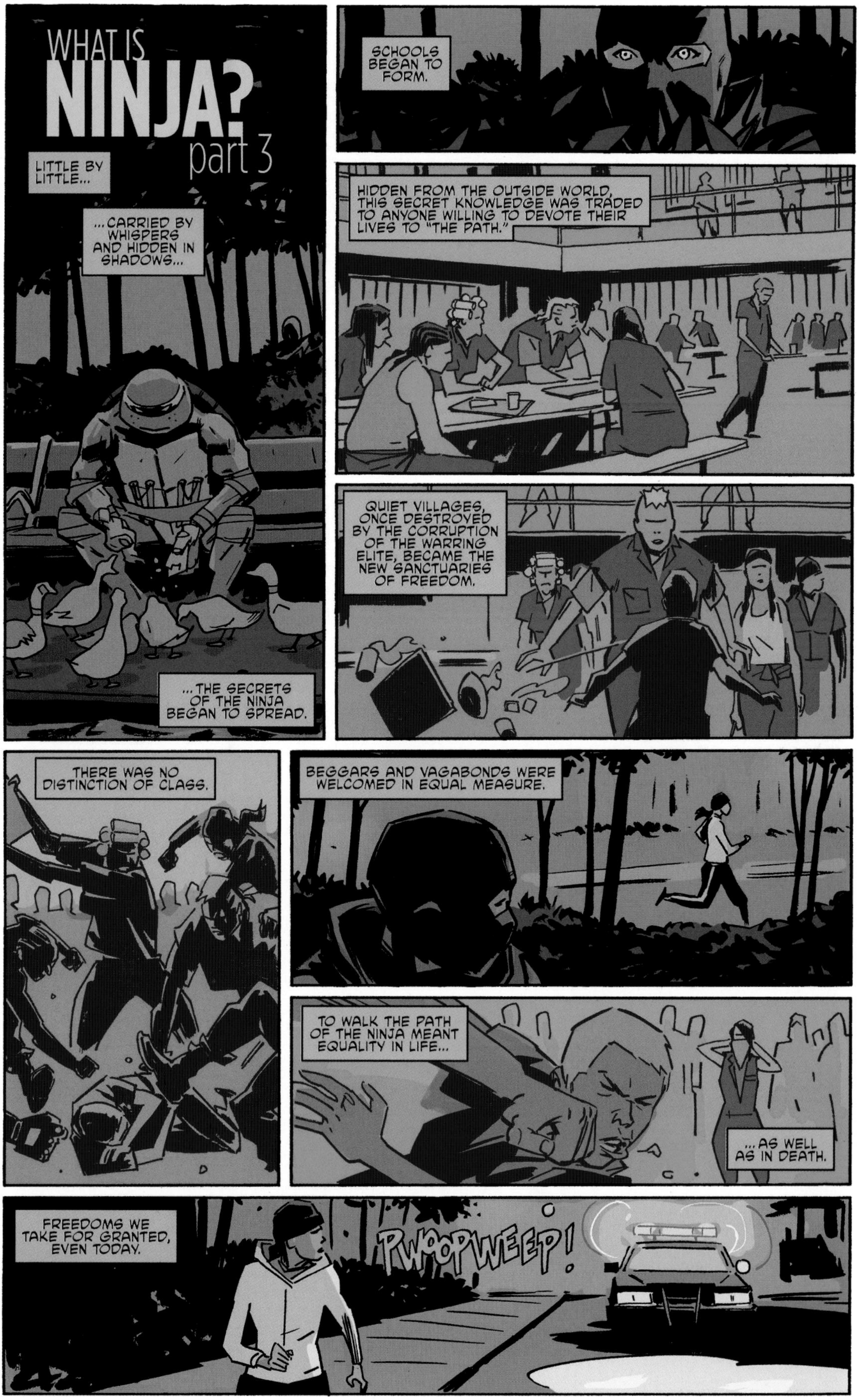
WHAT IS
NINJA?
part 3
LITTLE BY LITTLE...
...CARRIED BY WHISPERS AND HIDDEN IN SHADOWS...
...THE SECRETS OF THE NINJA BEGAN TO SPREAD.
SCHOOLS BEGAN TO FORM.
HIDDEN FROM THE OUTSIDE WORLD, THIS SECRET KNOWLEDGE WAS TRADED TO ANYONE WILLING TO DEVOTE THEIR LIVES TO "THE PATH."
QUIET VILLAGES, ONCE DESTROYED BY THE CORRUPTION OF THE WARRING ELITE, BECAME THE NEW SANCTUARIES OF FREEDOM.
THERE WAS NO DISTINCTION OF CLASS.
BEGGARS AND VAGABONDS WERE WELCOMED IN EQUAL MEASURE.
TO WALK THE PATH OF THE NINJA MEANT EQUALITY IN LIFE...
...AS WELL AS IN DEATH.
FREEDOMS WE TAKE FOR GRANTED, EVEN TODAY.
PWOOPWEEP!

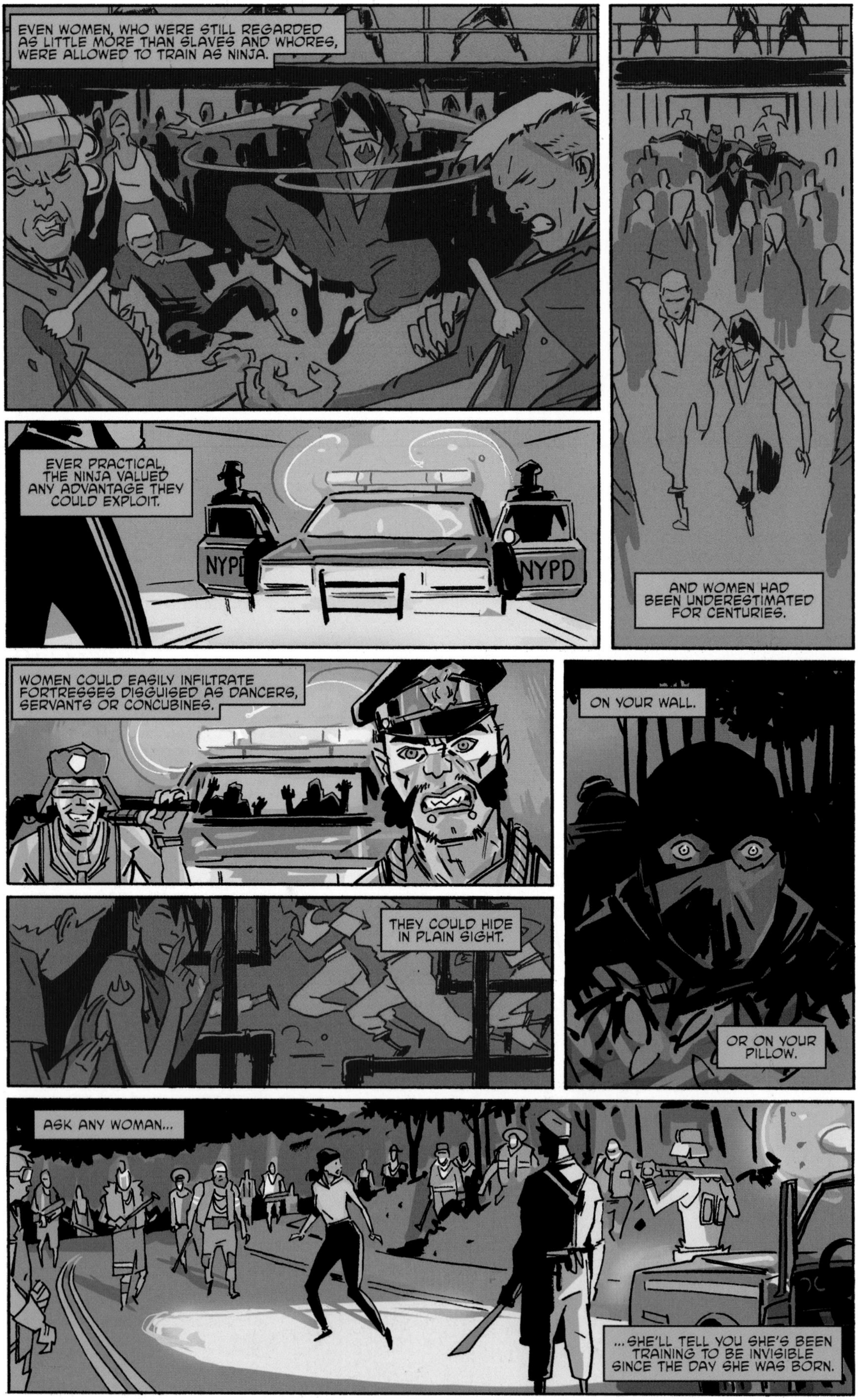
EVEN WOMEN, WHO WERE STILL REGARDED AS LITTLE MORE THAN SLAVES AND WHORES, WERE ALLOWED TO TRAIN AS NINJA.
EVER PRACTICAL, THE NINJA VALUED ANY ADVANTAGE THEY COULD EXPLOIT.
NYPD
NYPD
AND WOMEN HAD BEEN UNDERESTIMATED FOR CENTURIES.
WOMEN COULD EASILY INFILTRATE FORTRESSES DISGUISED AS DANCERS, SERVANTS OR CONCUBINES.
ON YOUR WALL.
THEY COULD HIDE IN PLAIN SIGHT.
OR ON YOUR PILLOW.
ASK ANY WOMAN...
...SHE'LL TELL YOU SHE'S BEEN TRAINING TO BE INVISIBLE SINCE THE DAY SHE WAS BORN.

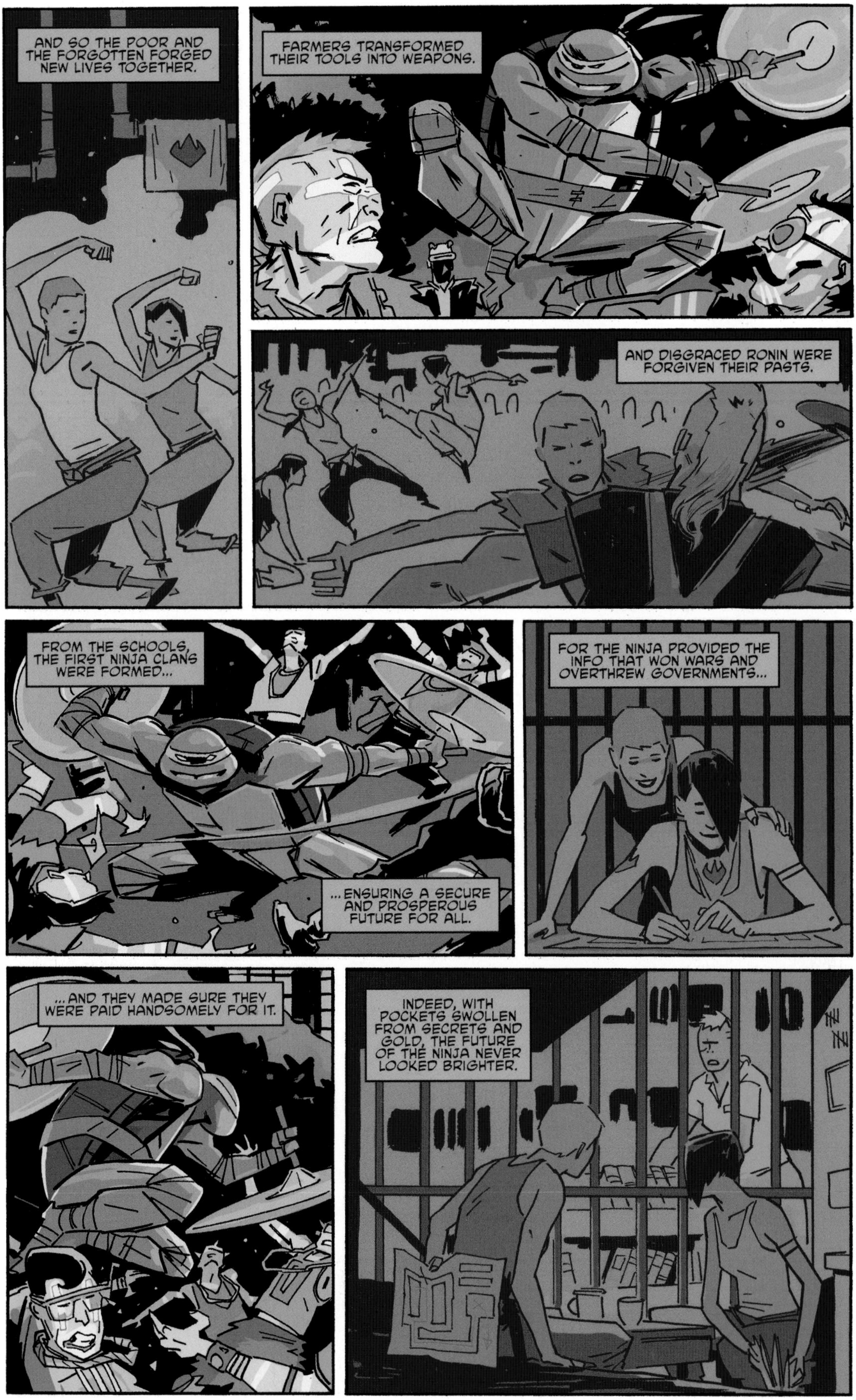
AND SO THE POOR AND THE FORGOTTEN FORGED NEW LIVES TOGETHER.
FARMERS TRANSFORMED THEIR TOOLS INTO WEAPONS.
AND DISGRACED RONIN WERE FORGIVEN THEIR PASTS.
FROM THE SCHOOLS, THE FIRST NINJA CLANS WERE FORMED...
...ENSURING A SECURE AND PROSPEROUS FUTURE FOR ALL.
FOR THE NINJA PROVIDED THE INFO THAT WON WARS AND OVERTHREW GOVERNMENTS...
...AND THEY MADE SURE THEY WERE PAID HANDSOMELY FOR IT.
INDEED, WITH POCKETS SWOLLEN FROM SECRETS AND GOLD, THE FUTURE OF THE NINJA NEVER LOOKED BRIGHTER.

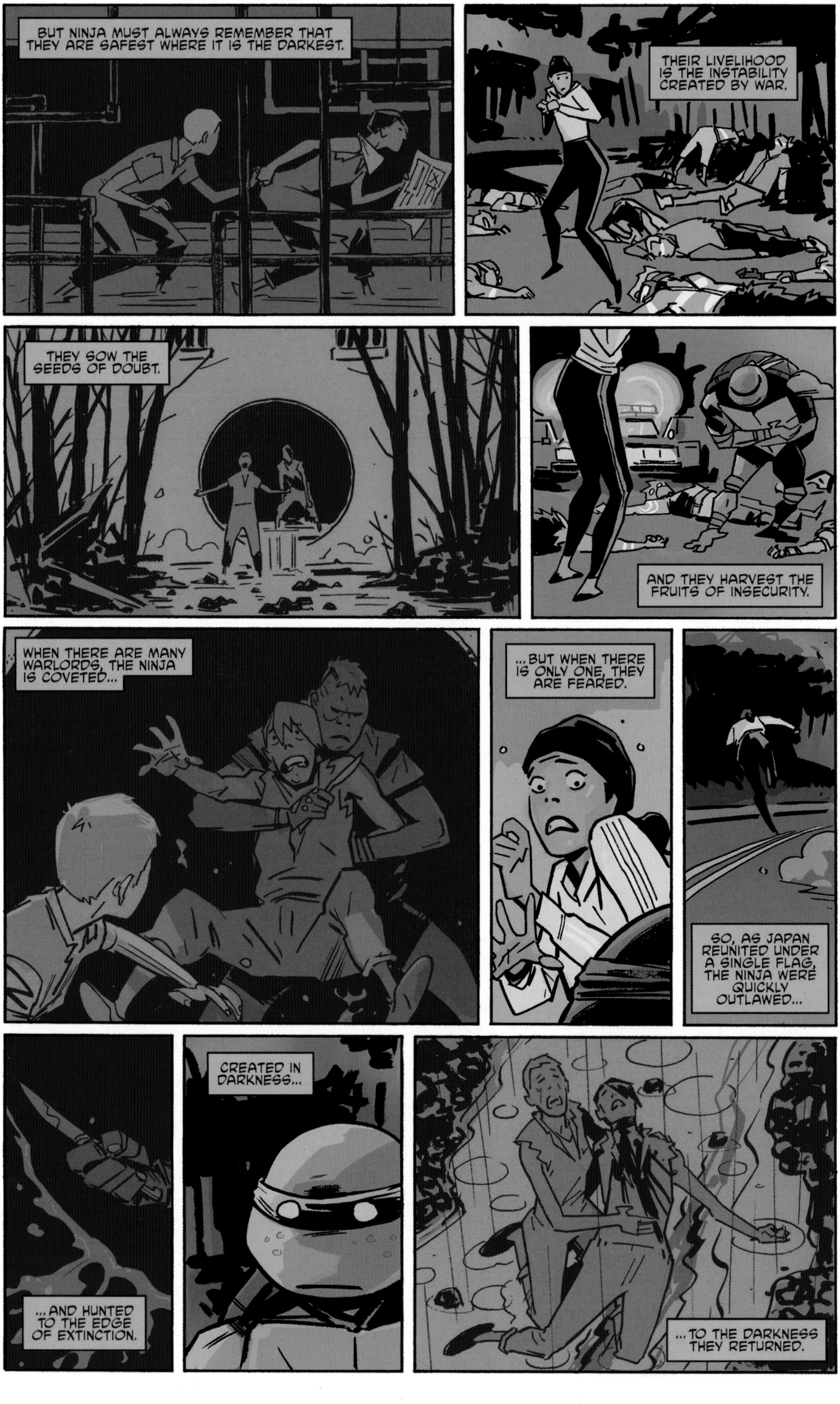
BUT NINJA MUST ALWAYS REMEMBER THAT THEY ARE SAFEST WHERE IT IS THE DARKEST.
THEIR LIVELIHOOD IS THE INSTABILITY CREATED BY WAR.
THEY SOW THE SEEDS OF DOUBT.
AND THEY HARVEST THE FRUITS OF INSECURITY.
WHEN THERE ARE MANY WARLORDS, THE NINJA IS COVETED...
...BUT WHEN THERE IS ONLY ONE, THEY ARE FEARED.
SO, AS JAPAN REUNITED UNDER A SINGLE FLAG, THE NINJA WERE QUICKLY OUTLAWED...
...AND HUNTED TO THE EDGE OF EXTINCTION.
CREATED IN DARKNESS...
...TO THE DARKNESS THEY RETURNED.

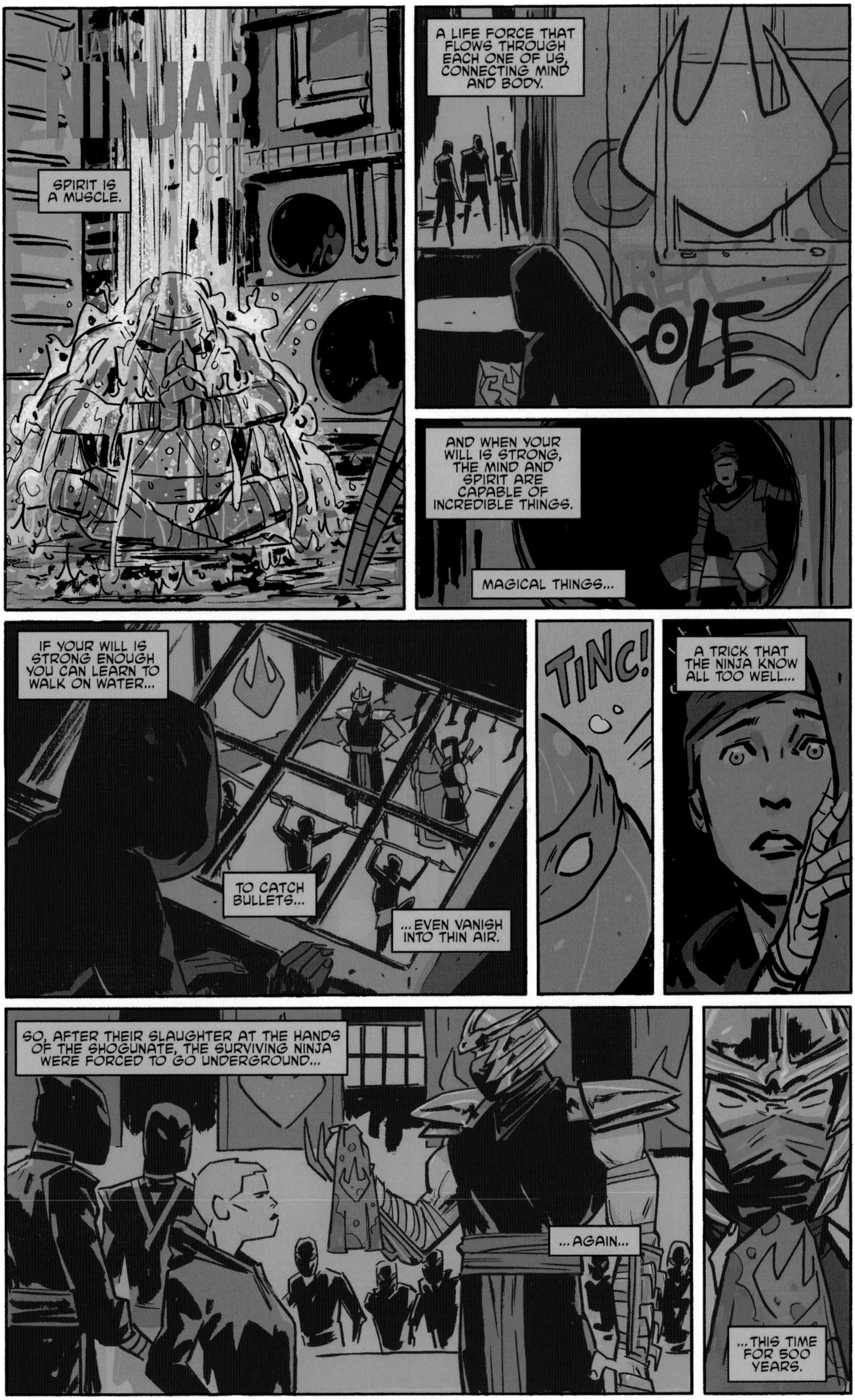
WHAT IS
NINJA?
part 4
SPIRIT IS A MUSCLE.
A LIFE FORCE THAT FLOWS THROUGH EACH ONE OF US, CONNECTING MIND AND BODY.
COLE
AND WHEN YOUR WILL IS STRONG, THE MIND AND SPIRIT ARE CAPABLE OF INCREDIBLE THINGS.
MAGICAL THINGS...
IF YOUR WILL IS STRONG ENOUGH YOU CAN LEARN TO WALK ON WATER...
TO CATCH BULLETS...
...EVEN VANISH INTO THIN AIR.
TINC!
A TRICK THAT THE NINJA KNOW ALL TOO WELL...
SO, AFTER THEIR SLAUGHTER AT THE HANDS OF THE SHOGUNATE, THE SURVIVING NINJA WERE FORCED TO GO UNDERGROUND...
...AGAIN...
...THIS TIME FOR 500 YEARS.

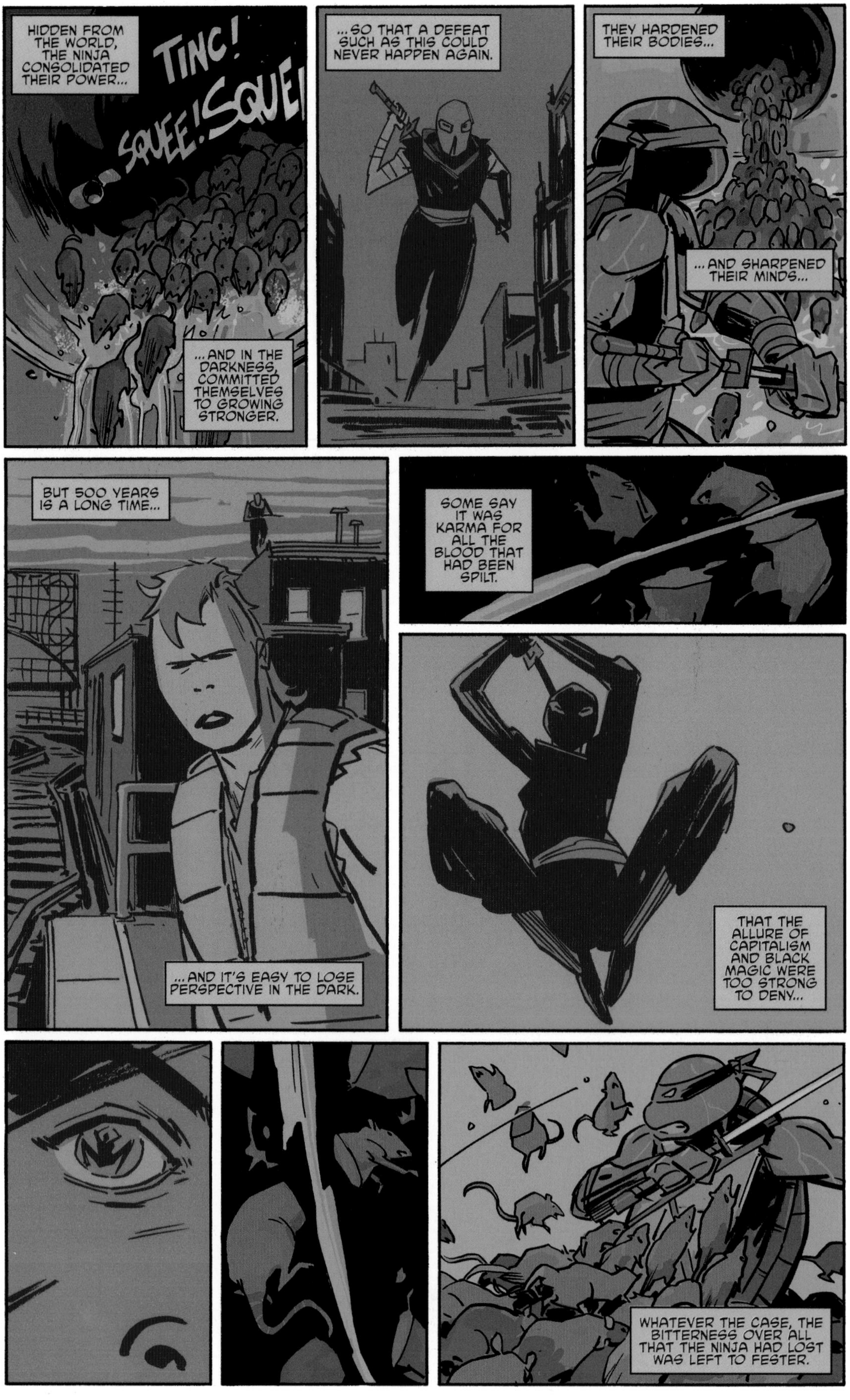
HIDDEN FROM THE WORLD, THE NINJA CONSOLIDATED THEIR POWER...
TINC!
SQUEE! SQUEE
...AND IN THE DARKNESS, COMMITTED THEMSELVES TO GROWING STRONGER.
...SO THAT A DEFEAT SUCH AS THIS COULD NEVER HAPPEN AGAIN.
THEY HARDENED THEIR BODIES...
...AND SHARPENED THEIR MINDS...
BUT 500 YEARS IS A LONG TIME...
...AND IT'S EASY TO LOSE PERSPECTIVE IN THE DARK.
SOME SAY IT WAS KARMA FOR ALL THE BLOOD THAT HAD BEEN SPILT.
THAT THE ALLURE OF CAPITALISM AND BLACK MAGIC WERE TOO STRONG TO DENY...
WHATEVER THE CASE, THE BITTERNESS OVER ALL THAT THE NINJA HAD LOST WAS LEFT TO FESTER.

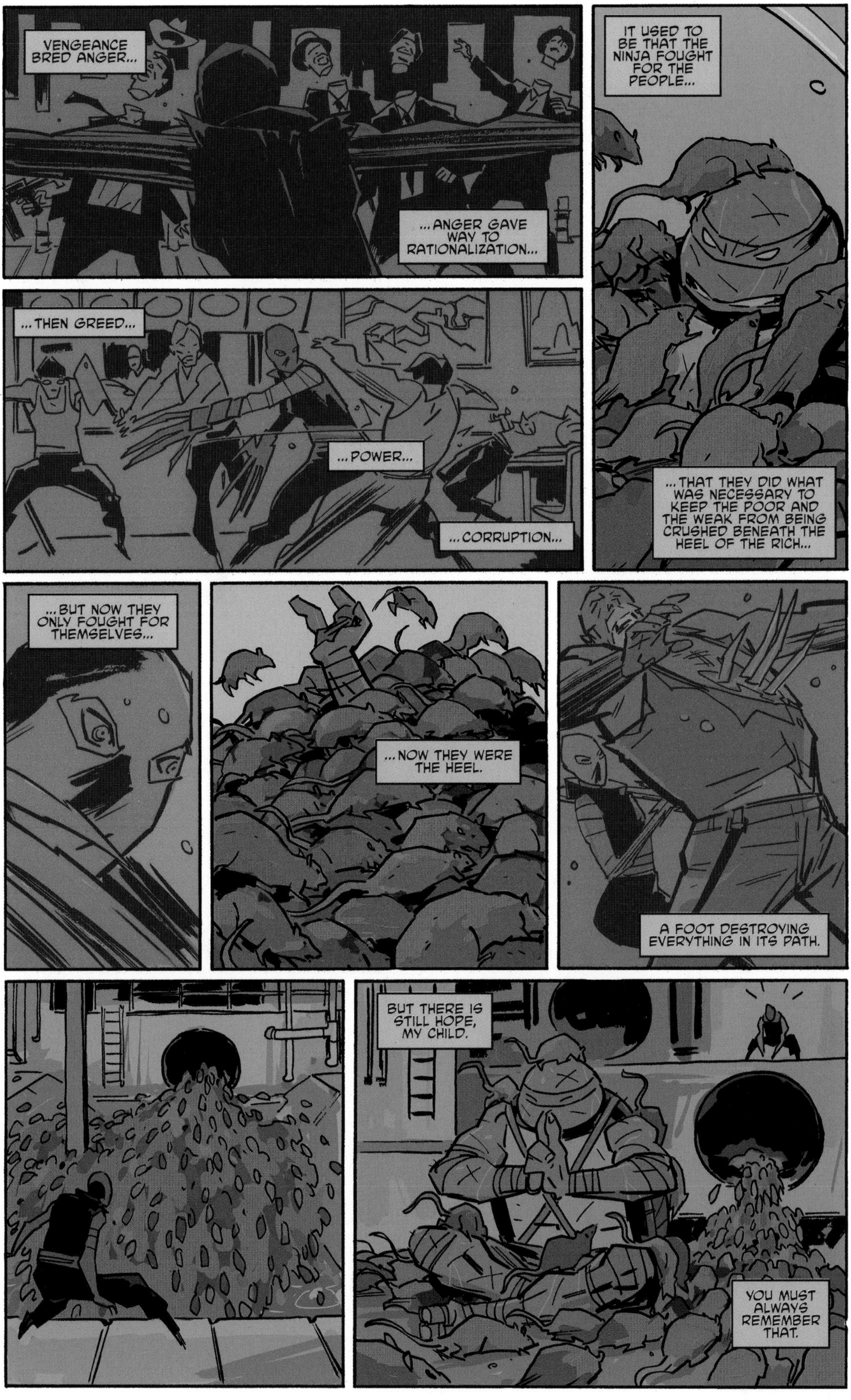
VENGEANCE BRED ANGER...
...ANGER GAVE WAY TO RATIONALIZATION...
IT USED TO BE THAT THE NINJA FOUGHT FOR THE PEOPLE...
...THEN GREED...
...POWER...
...CORRUPTION...
...THAT THEY DID WHAT WAS NECESSARY TO KEEP THE POOR AND THE WEAK FROM BEING CRUSHED BENEATH THE HEEL OF THE RICH...
...BUT NOW THEY ONLY FOUGHT FOR THEMSELVES...
...NOW THEY WERE THE HEEL.
A FOOT DESTROYING EVERYTHING IN ITS PATH.
BUT THERE IS STILL HOPE, MY CHILD.
YOU MUST ALWAYS REMEMBER THAT.

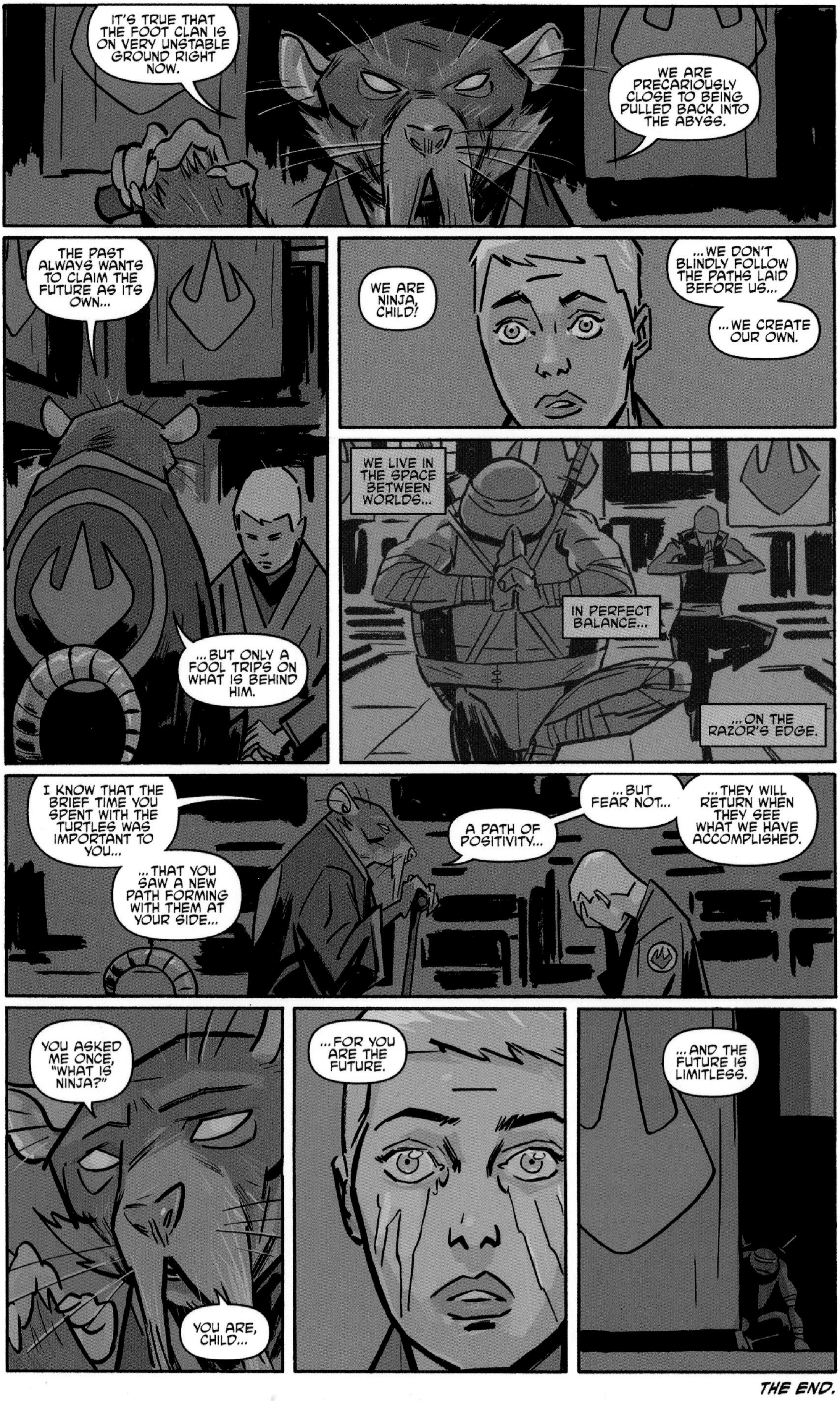
IT'S TRUE THAT THE FOOT CLAN IS ON VERY UNSTABLE GROUND RIGHT NOW.
WE ARE PRECARIOUSLY CLOSE TO BEING PULLED BACK INTO THE ABYSS.
THE PAST ALWAYS WANTS TO CLAIM THE FUTURE AS ITS OWN...
...BUT ONLY A FOOL TRIPS ON WHAT IS BEHIND HIM.
WE ARE NINJA, CHILD!
...WE DON'T BLINDLY FOLLOW THE PATHS LAID BEFORE US...
...WE CREATE OUR OWN.
WE LIVE IN THE SPACE BETWEEN WORLDS...
IN PERFECT BALANCE...
...ON THE RAZOR'S EDGE.
I KNOW THAT THE BRIEF TIME YOU SPENT WITH THE TURTLES WAS IMPORTANT TO YOU...
...THAT YOU SAW A NEW PATH FORMING WITH THEM AT YOUR SIDE...
A PATH OF POSITIVITY...
...BUT FEAR NOT...
...THEY WILL RETURN WHEN THEY SEE WHAT WE HAVE ACCOMPLISHED.
YOU ASKED ME ONCE, "WHAT IS NINJA?"
YOU ARE, CHILD...
...FOR YOU ARE THE FUTURE.
...AND THE FUTURE IS LIMITLESS.

THE END.

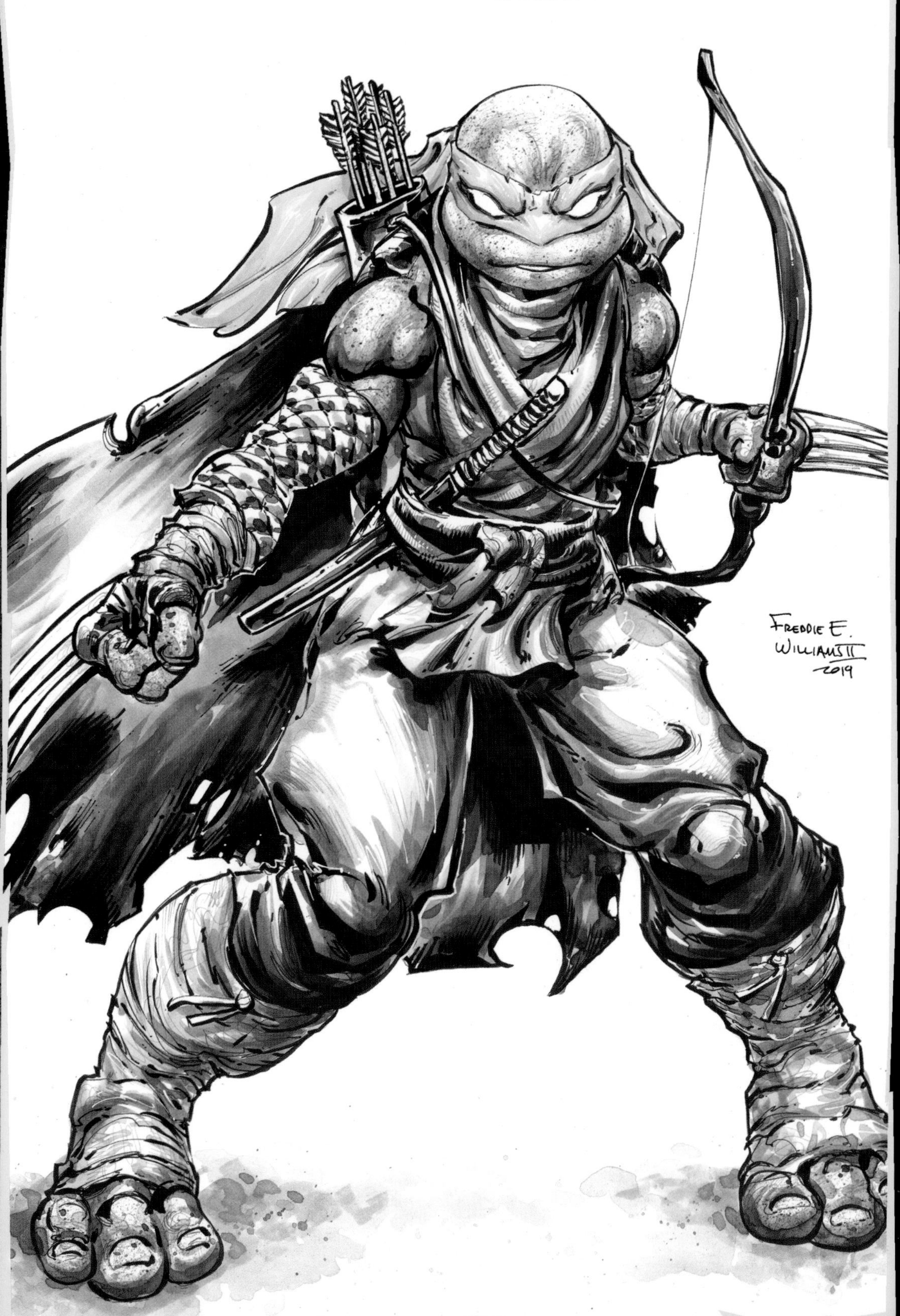
FREDDIE E. WILLIAMS II 2019
Art by Freddie Williams II

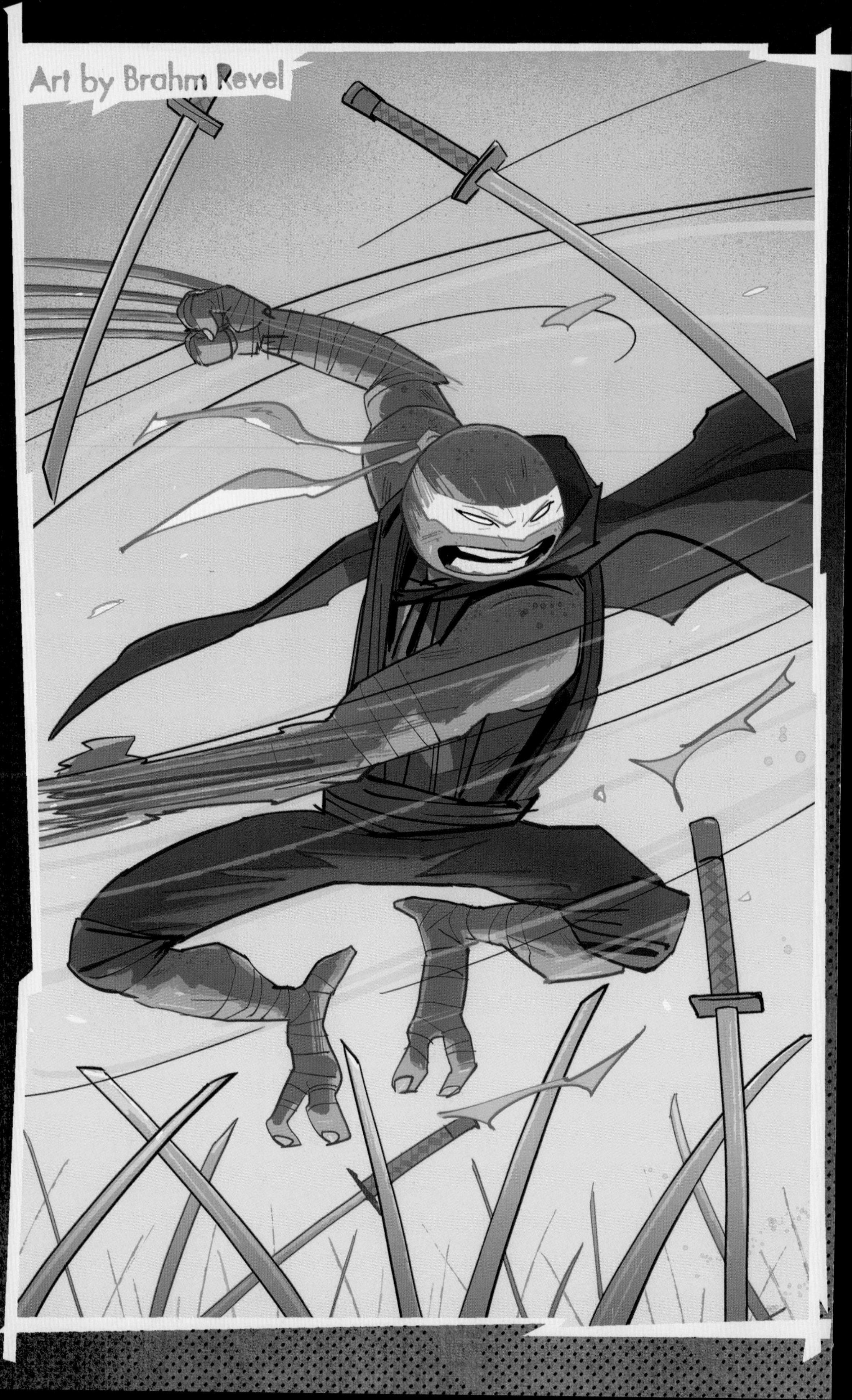
Art by Brahm Revel

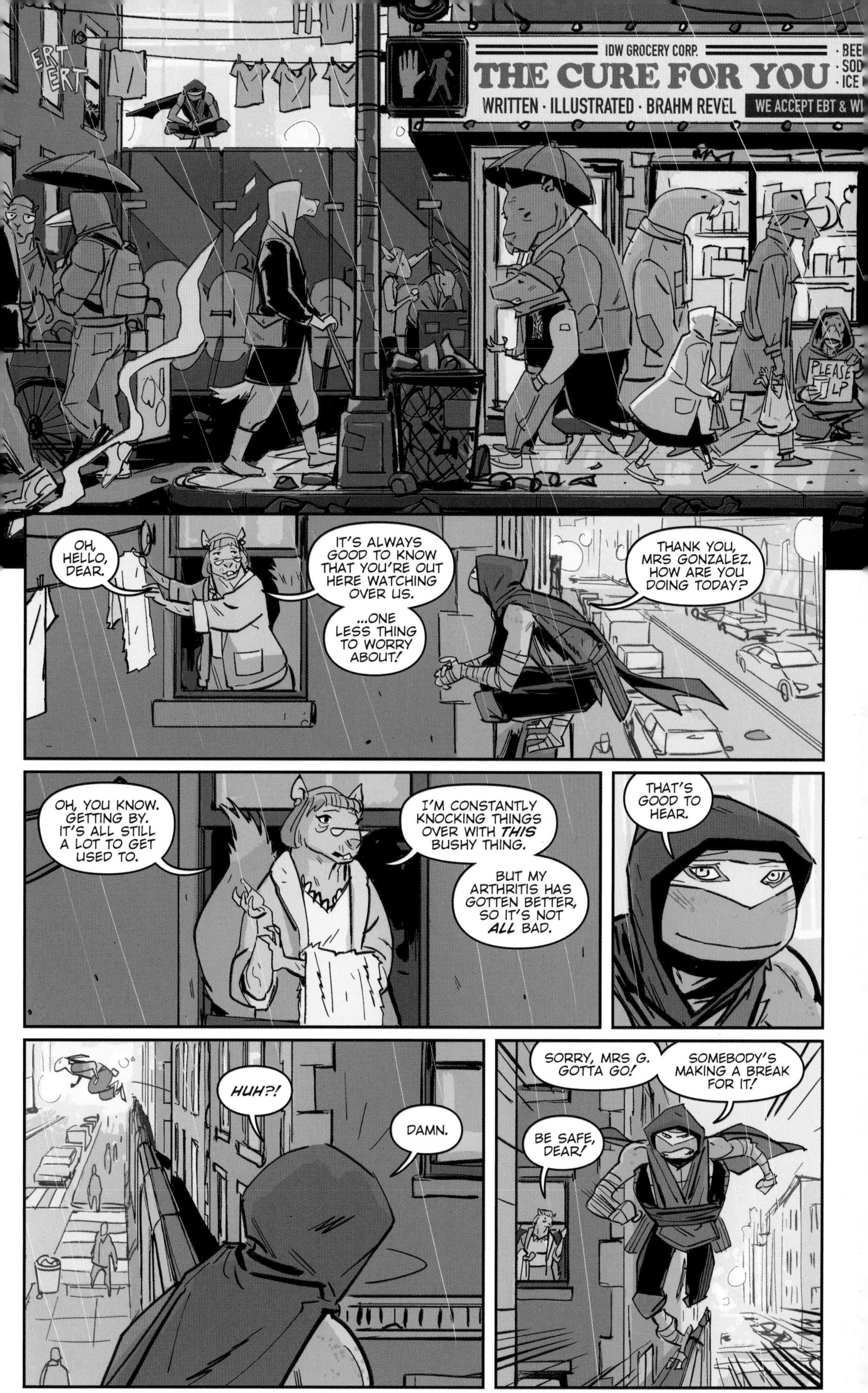
IDW GROCERY CORP.
THE CURE FOR YOU
WRITTEN · ILLUSTRATED · BRAHM REVEL
WE ACCEPT EBT & WI
ERT ERT
PLEASE HELP
OH, HELLO, DEAR.
IT'S ALWAYS GOOD TO KNOW THAT YOU'RE OUT HERE WATCHING OVER US.
...ONE LESS THING TO WORRY ABOUT!
THANK YOU, MRS GONZALEZ. HOW ARE YOU DOING TODAY?
OH, YOU KNOW. GETTING BY. IT'S ALL STILL A LOT TO GET USED TO.
I'M CONSTANTLY KNOCKING THINGS OVER WITH *THIS* BUSHY THING.
BUT MY ARTHRITIS HAS GOTTEN BETTER, SO IT'S NOT *ALL* BAD.
THAT'S GOOD TO HEAR.
HUH?!
DAMN.
SORRY, MRS G. GOTTA GO!
SOMEBODY'S MAKING A BREAK FOR IT!
BE SAFE, DEAR!

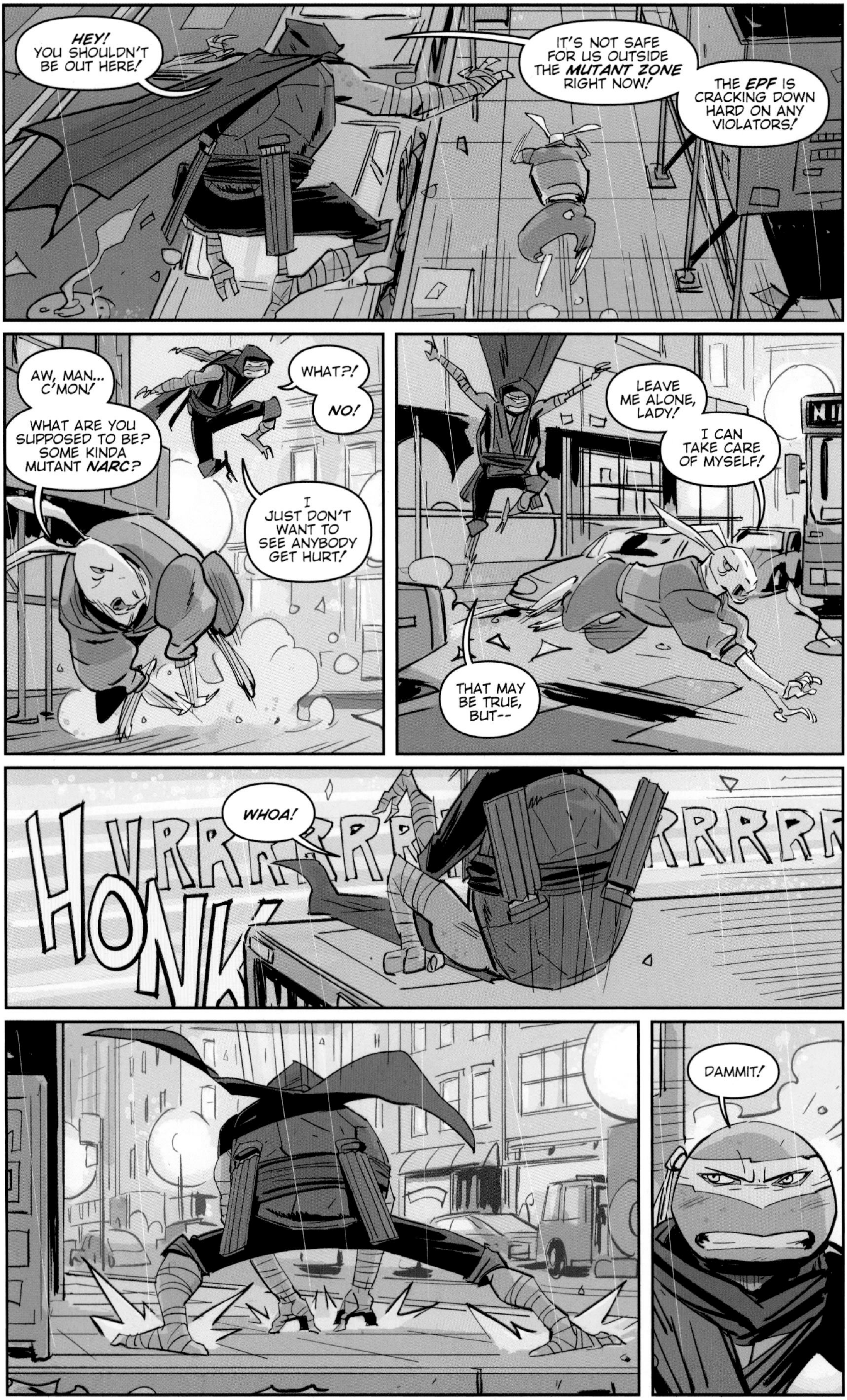
HEY! YOU SHOULDN'T BE OUT HERE!
IT'S NOT SAFE FOR US OUTSIDE THE MUTANT ZONE RIGHT NOW!
THE EPF IS CRACKING DOWN HARD ON ANY VIOLATORS!
AW, MAN... C'MON!
WHAT ARE YOU SUPPOSED TO BE? SOME KINDA MUTANT NARC?
WHAT?!
NO!
I JUST DON'T WANT TO SEE ANYBODY GET HURT!
LEAVE ME ALONE, LADY!
I CAN TAKE CARE OF MYSELF!
THAT MAY BE TRUE, BUT--
WHOA!
HVRRRRRRRRRRRR
HONK
DAMMIT!

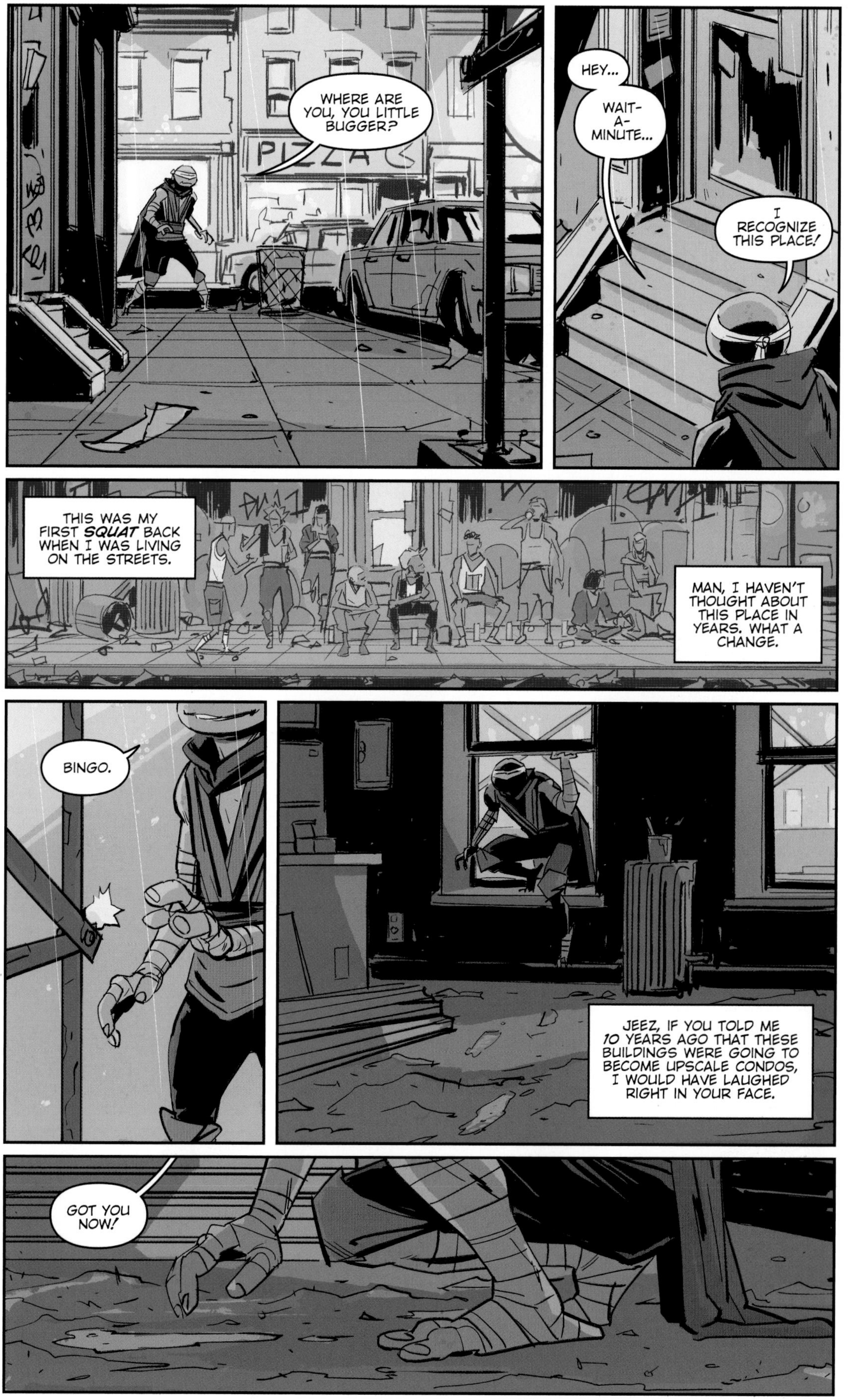

WHERE ARE YOU, YOU LITTLE BUGGER?
PIZZA
HEY...
WAIT-A-MINUTE...
I RECOGNIZE THIS PLACE!
THIS WAS MY FIRST SQUAT BACK WHEN I WAS LIVING ON THE STREETS.
MAN, I HAVEN'T THOUGHT ABOUT THIS PLACE IN YEARS. WHAT A CHANGE.
BINGO.
JEEZ, IF YOU TOLD ME 10 YEARS AGO THAT THESE BUILDINGS WERE GOING TO BECOME UPSCALE CONDOS, I WOULD HAVE LAUGHED RIGHT IN YOUR FACE.
GOT YOU NOW!

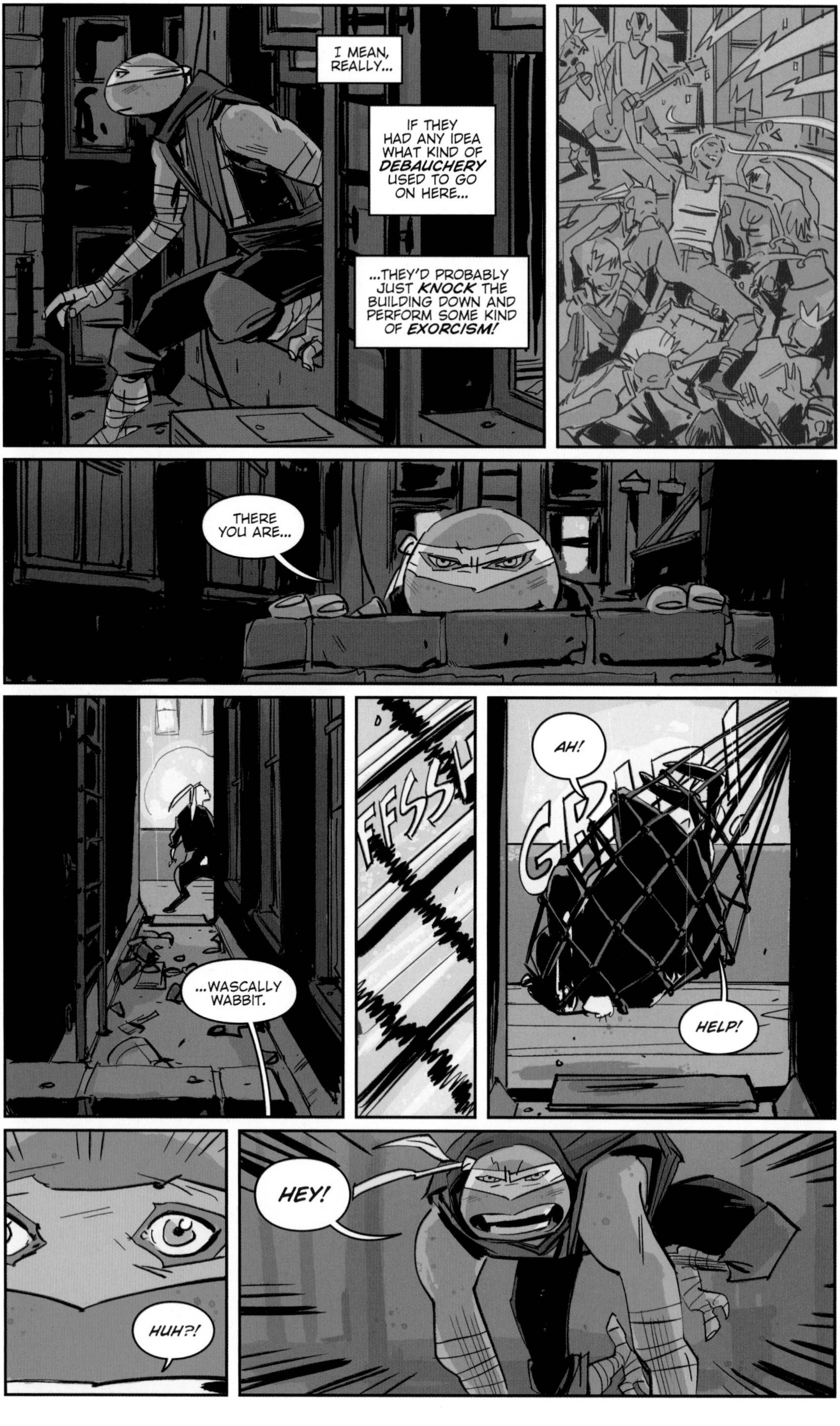
I MEAN, REALLY...
IF THEY HAD ANY IDEA WHAT KIND OF DEBAUCHERY USED TO GO ON HERE...
...THEY'D PROBABLY JUST KNOCK THE BUILDING DOWN AND PERFORM SOME KIND OF EXORCISM!
THERE YOU ARE...
...WASCALLY WABBIT.
FFSSH
AH!
HELP!
HEY!
HUH?!

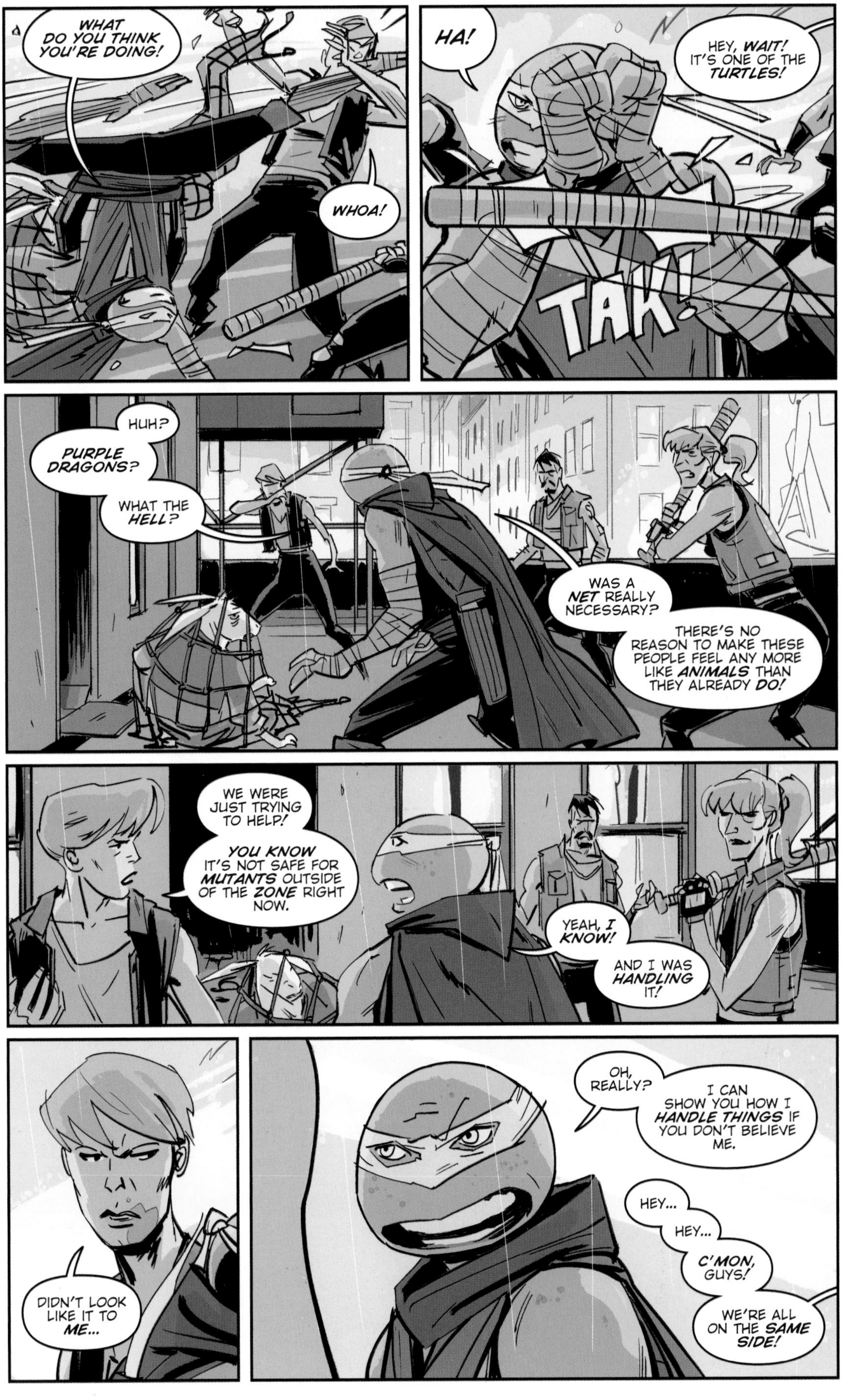
WHAT DO YOU THINK YOU'RE DOING!
WHOA!
HA!
HEY, WAIT! IT'S ONE OF THE TURTLES!
TAK!
HUH?
PURPLE DRAGONS?
WHAT THE HELL?
WAS A NET REALLY NECESSARY?
THERE'S NO REASON TO MAKE THESE PEOPLE FEEL ANY MORE LIKE ANIMALS THAN THEY ALREADY DO!
WE WERE JUST TRYING TO HELP!
YOU KNOW IT'S NOT SAFE FOR MUTANTS OUTSIDE OF THE ZONE RIGHT NOW.
YEAH, I KNOW!
AND I WAS HANDLING IT!
DIDN'T LOOK LIKE IT TO ME...
OH, REALLY?
I CAN SHOW YOU HOW I HANDLE THINGS IF YOU DON'T BELIEVE ME.
HEY...
HEY...
C'MON, GUYS!
WE'RE ALL ON THE SAME SIDE!

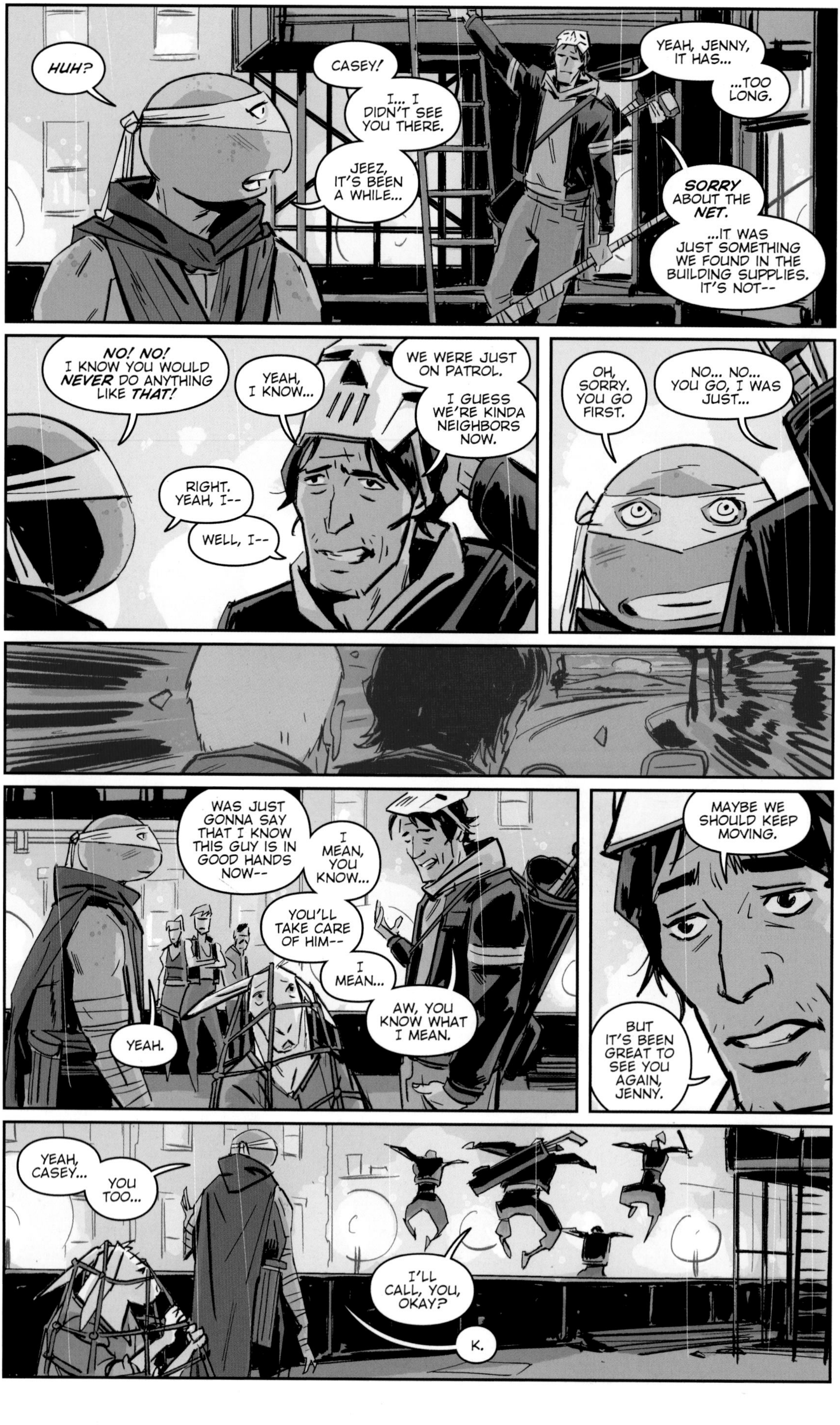
HUH?
CASEY!
I... I DIDN'T SEE YOU THERE.
JEEZ, IT'S BEEN A WHILE...
YEAH, JENNY, IT HAS...
...TOO LONG.
SORRY ABOUT THE NET.
...IT WAS JUST SOMETHING WE FOUND IN THE BUILDING SUPPLIES. IT'S NOT--
NO! NO! I KNOW YOU WOULD NEVER DO ANYTHING LIKE THAT!
YEAH, I KNOW...
WE WERE JUST ON PATROL.
I GUESS WE'RE KINDA NEIGHBORS NOW.
RIGHT. YEAH, I--
WELL, I--
OH, SORRY. YOU GO FIRST.
NO... NO... YOU GO, I WAS JUST...
WAS JUST GONNA SAY THAT I KNOW THIS GUY IS IN GOOD HANDS NOW--
I MEAN, YOU KNOW...
YOU'LL TAKE CARE OF HIM--
I MEAN...
AW, YOU KNOW WHAT I MEAN.
YEAH.
MAYBE WE SHOULD KEEP MOVING.
BUT IT'S BEEN GREAT TO SEE YOU AGAIN, JENNY.
YEAH, CASEY...
YOU TOO...
I'LL CALL, YOU, OKAY?
K.

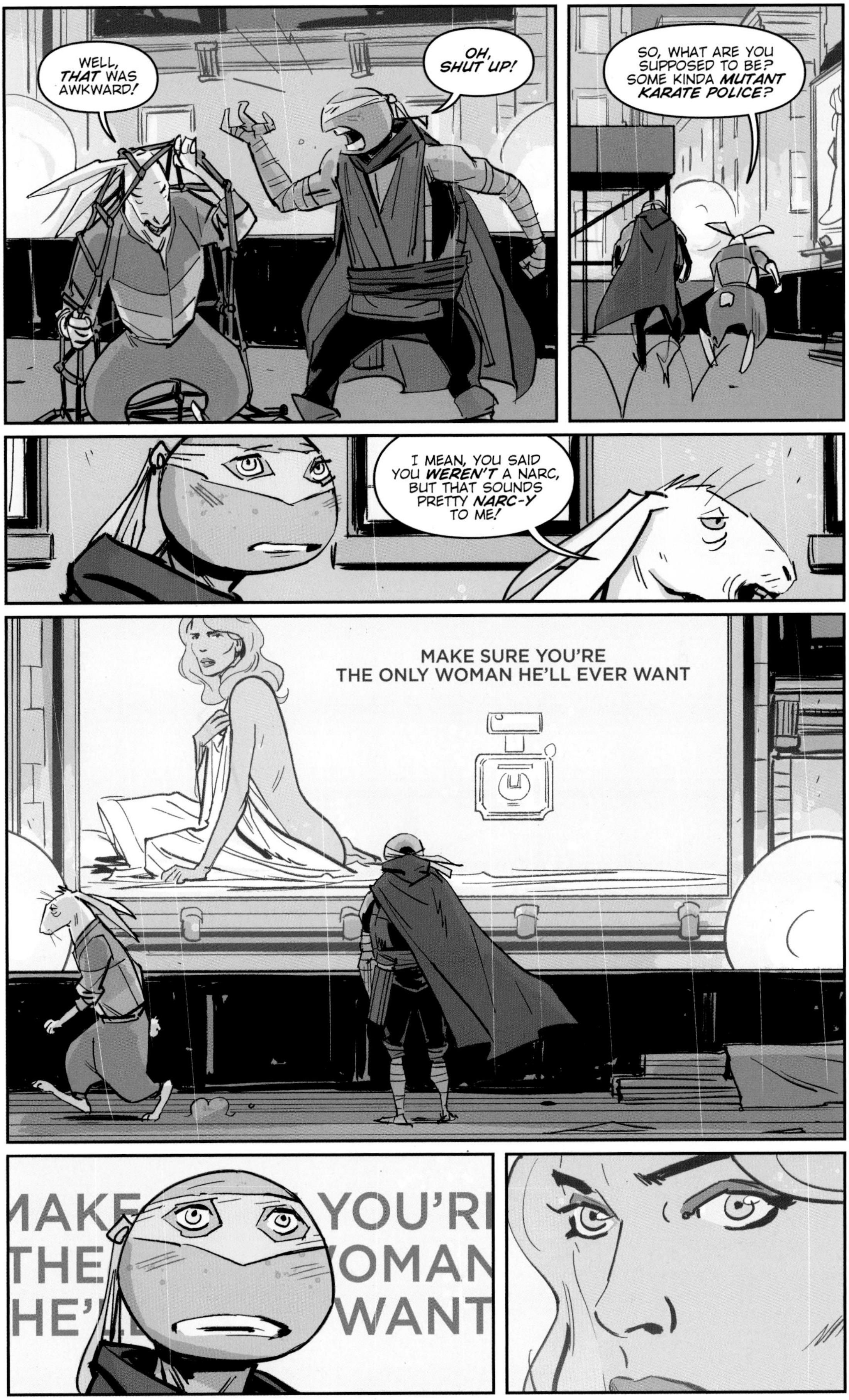
WELL, THAT WAS AWKWARD!
OH, SHUT UP!
SO, WHAT ARE YOU SUPPOSED TO BE? SOME KINDA MUTANT KARATE POLICE?
I MEAN, YOU SAID YOU WEREN'T A NARC, BUT THAT SOUNDS PRETTY NARC-Y TO ME!
MAKE SURE YOU'RE THE ONLY WOMAN HE'LL EVER WANT

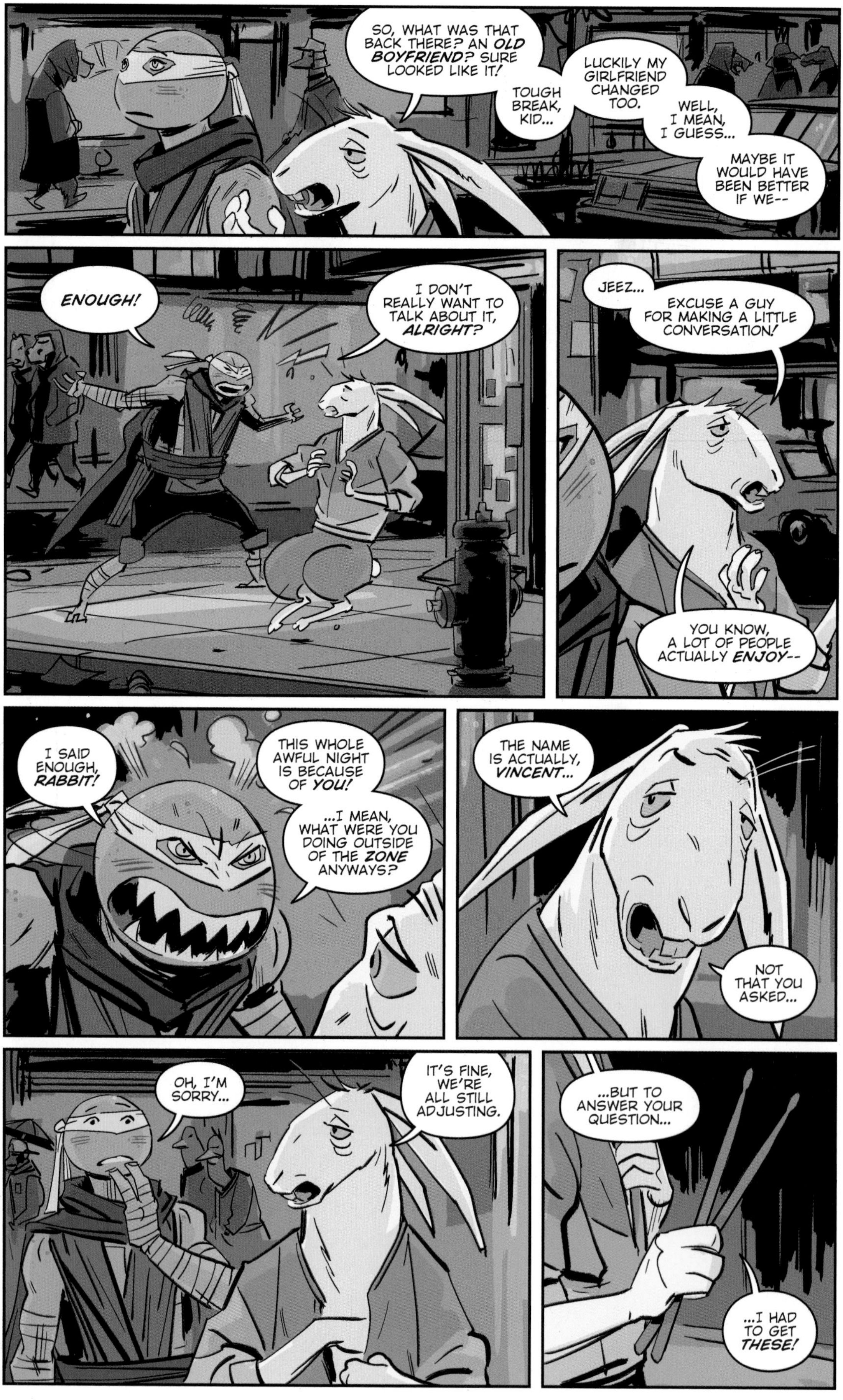

SO, WHAT WAS THAT BACK THERE? AN *OLD BOYFRIEND?* SURE LOOKED LIKE IT!
TOUGH BREAK, KID...
LUCKILY MY GIRLFRIEND CHANGED TOO.
WELL, I MEAN, I GUESS...
MAYBE IT WOULD HAVE BEEN BETTER IF WE--
ENOUGH!
I DON'T REALLY WANT TO TALK ABOUT IT, *ALRIGHT?*
JEEZ...
EXCUSE A GUY FOR MAKING A LITTLE CONVERSATION!
YOU KNOW, A LOT OF PEOPLE ACTUALLY *ENJOY*--
I SAID ENOUGH, *RABBIT!*
THIS WHOLE AWFUL NIGHT IS BECAUSE OF *YOU!*
...I MEAN, WHAT WERE YOU DOING OUTSIDE OF THE *ZONE* ANYWAYS?
THE NAME IS ACTUALLY, *VINCENT...*
NOT THAT YOU ASKED...
OH, I'M SORRY...
IT'S FINE, WE'RE ALL STILL ADJUSTING.
...BUT TO ANSWER YOUR QUESTION...
...I HAD TO GET *THESE!*

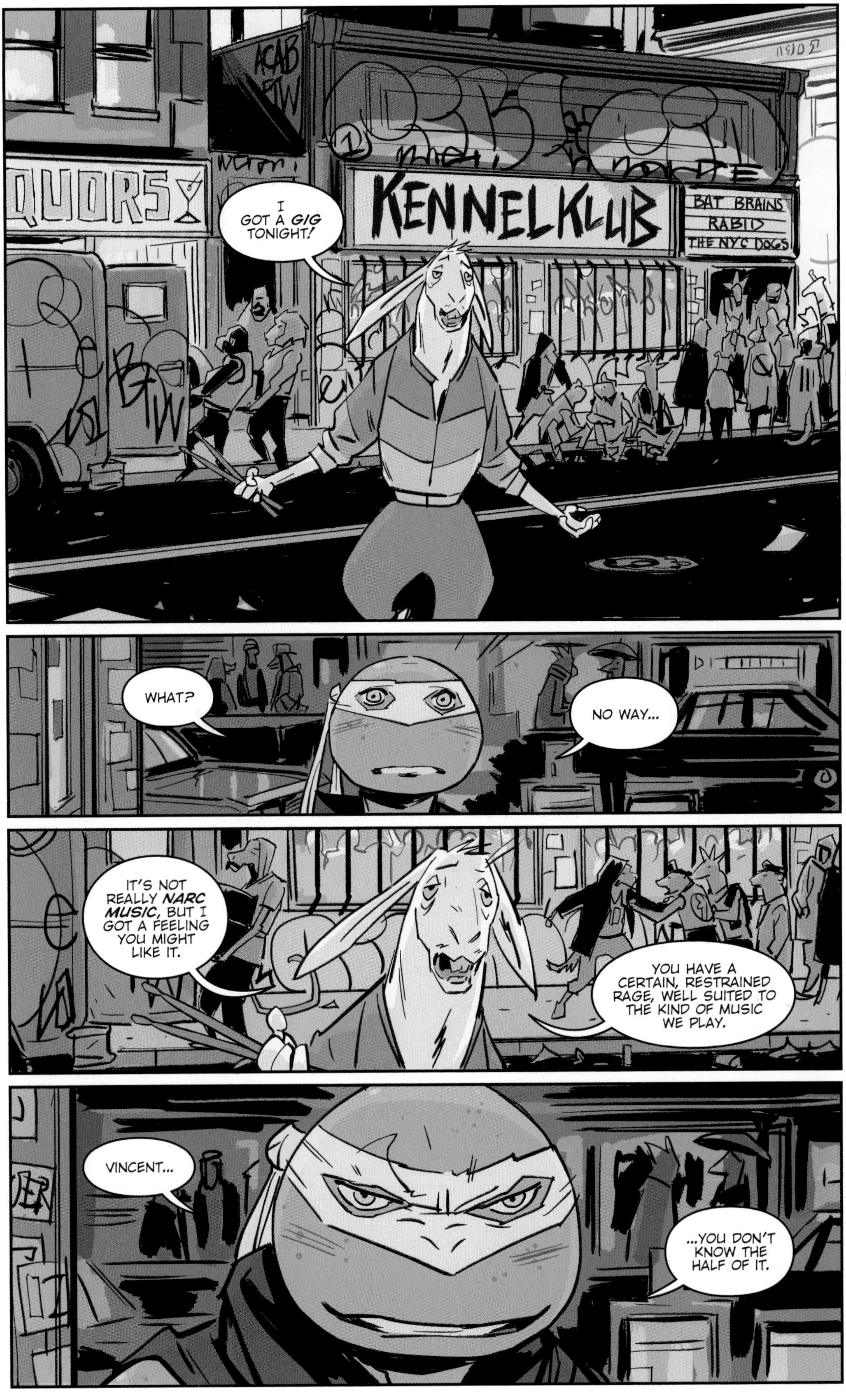
ACAB FTW
QUORS
KENNEL KLUB
BAT BRAINS
RABID
THE NYC DOGS
I GOT A *GIG* TONIGHT!
WHAT?
NO WAY...
IT'S NOT REALLY ***NARC MUSIC***, BUT I GOT A FEELING YOU MIGHT LIKE IT.
YOU HAVE A CERTAIN, RESTRAINED RAGE, WELL SUITED TO THE KIND OF MUSIC WE PLAY.
VINCENT...
...YOU DON'T KNOW THE HALF OF IT.

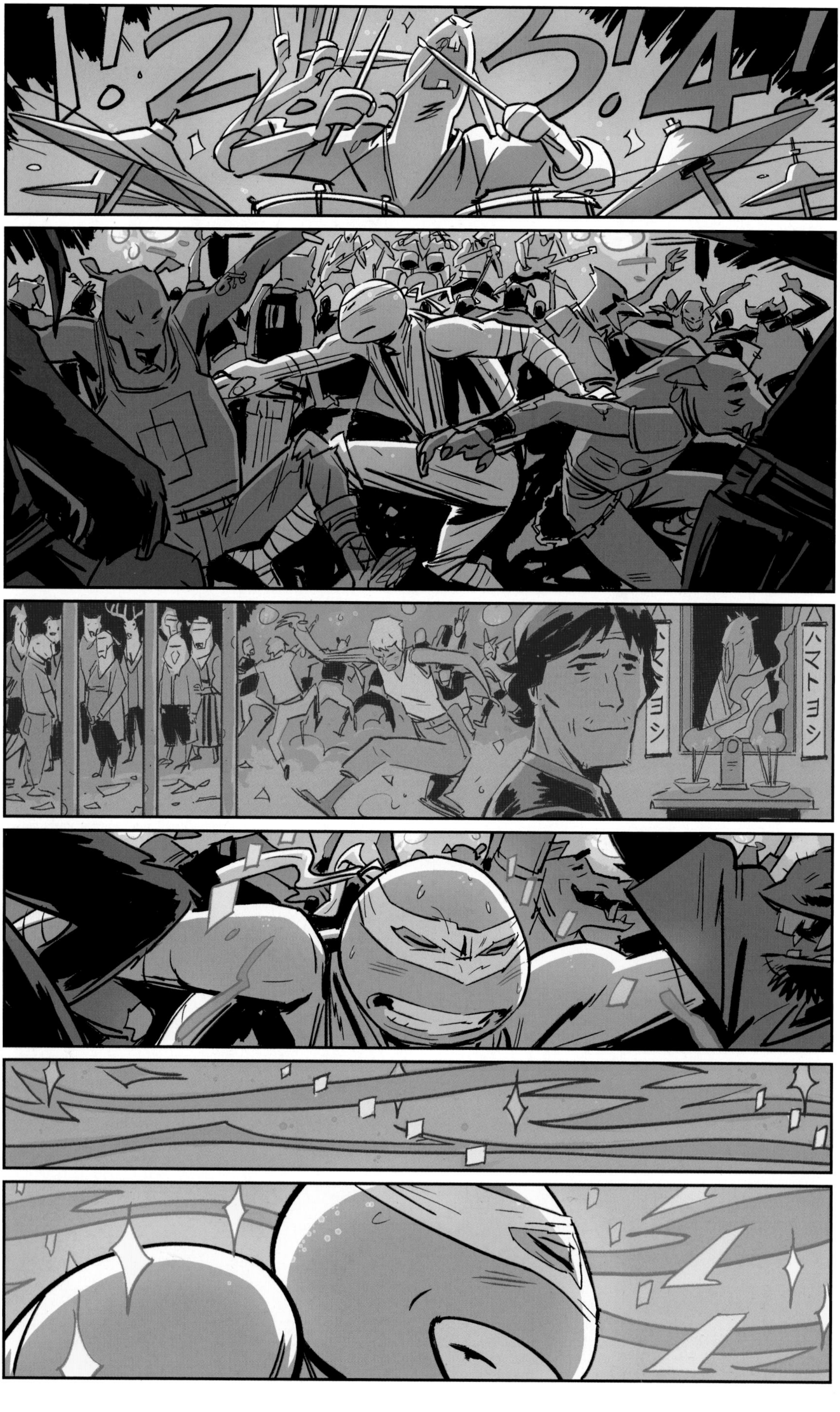
1! 2! 3! 4!
ハマトヨシ
ハマトヨシ

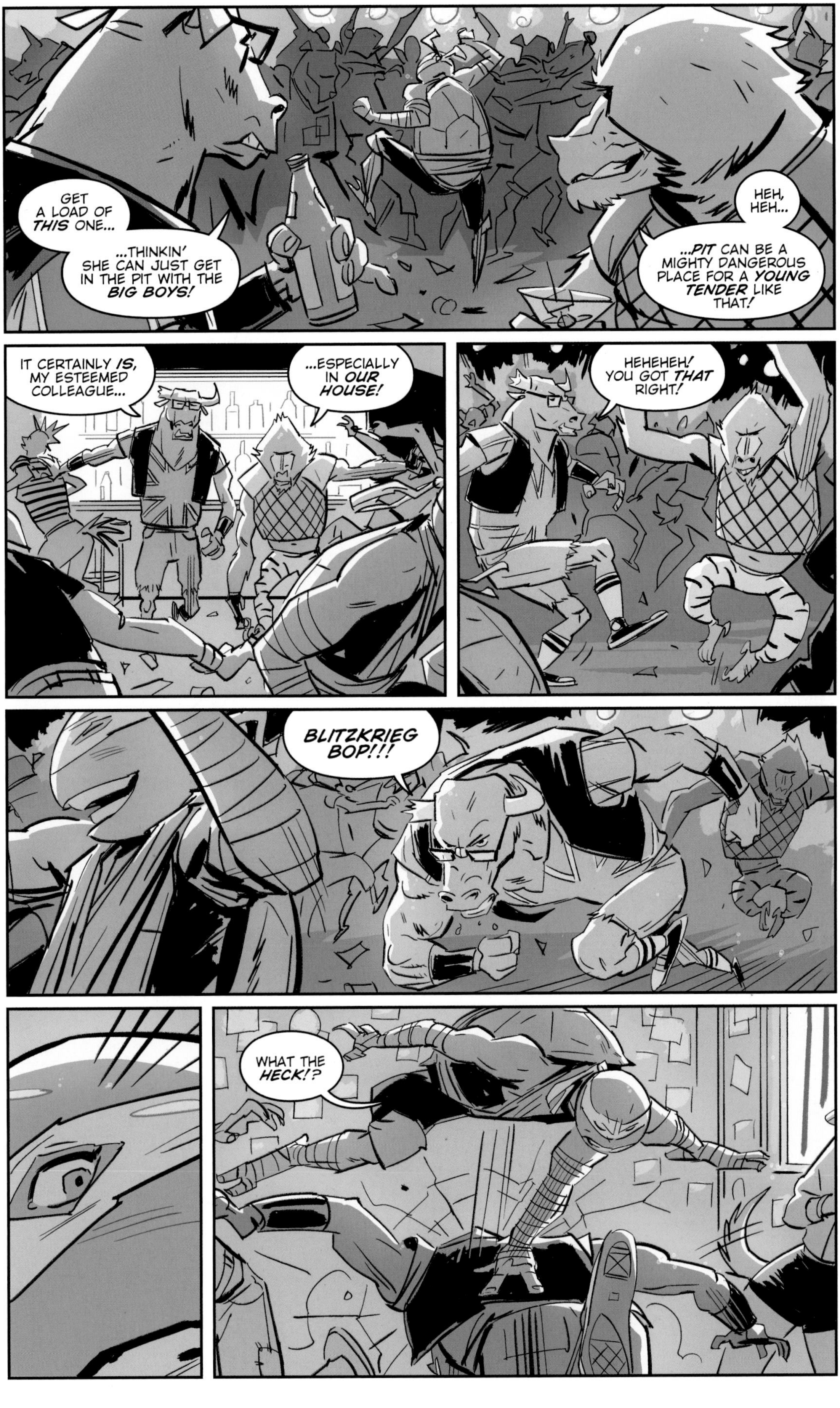
GET A LOAD OF THIS ONE...
...THINKIN' SHE CAN JUST GET IN THE PIT WITH THE BIG BOYS!
HEH, HEH...
...PIT CAN BE A MIGHTY DANGEROUS PLACE FOR A YOUNG TENDER LIKE THAT!
IT CERTAINLY IS, MY ESTEEMED COLLEAGUE...
...ESPECIALLY IN OUR HOUSE!
HEHEHEH! YOU GOT THAT RIGHT!
BLITZKRIEG BOP!!!
WHAT THE HECK!?

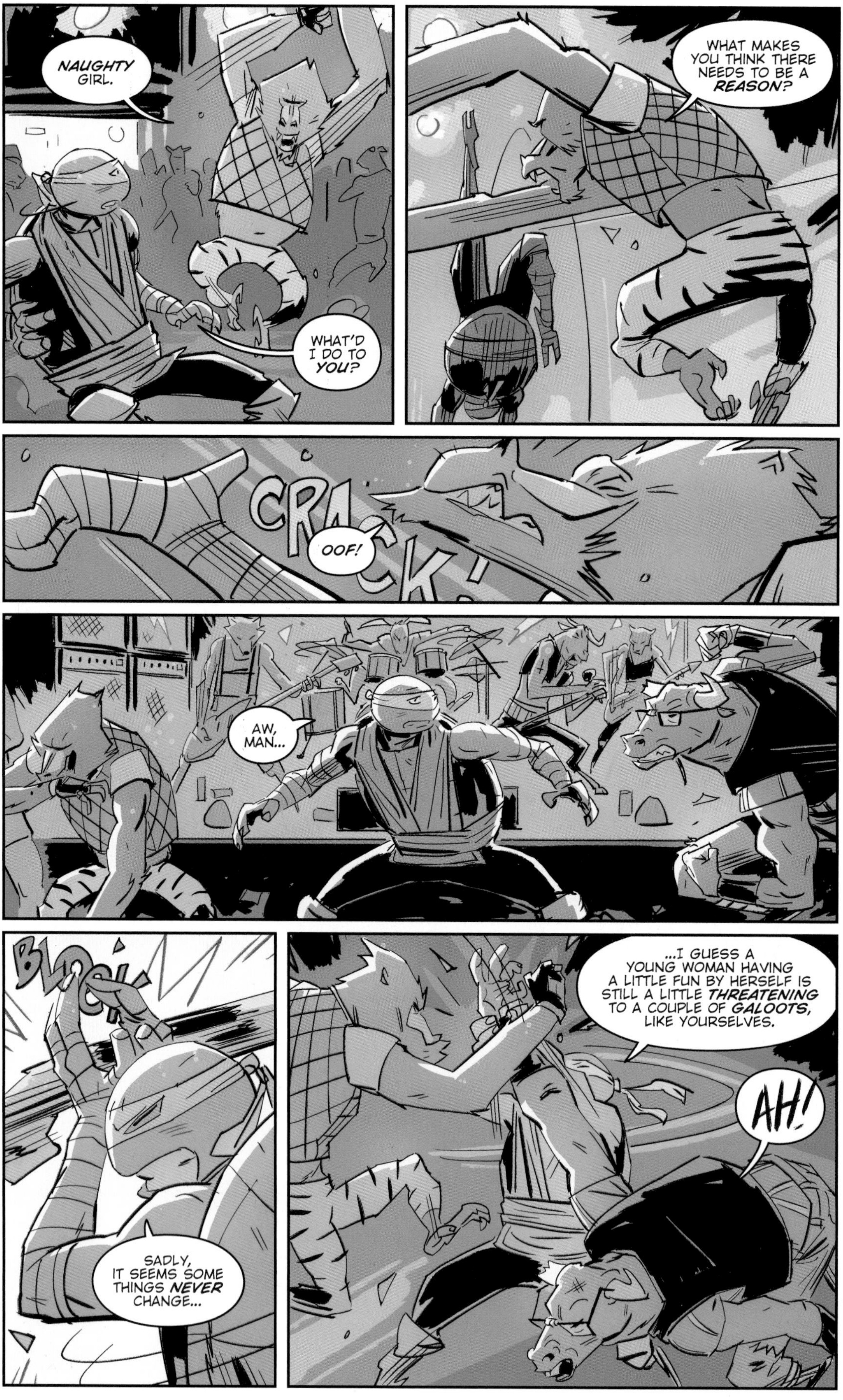
NAUGHTY GIRL.
WHAT'D I DO TO YOU?
WHAT MAKES YOU THINK THERE NEEDS TO BE A REASON?
CRACK!
OOF!
AW, MAN...
BLOCK!
SADLY, IT SEEMS SOME THINGS NEVER CHANGE...
...I GUESS A YOUNG WOMAN HAVING A LITTLE FUN BY HERSELF IS STILL A LITTLE THREATENING TO A COUPLE OF GALOOTS, LIKE YOURSELVES.
AH!

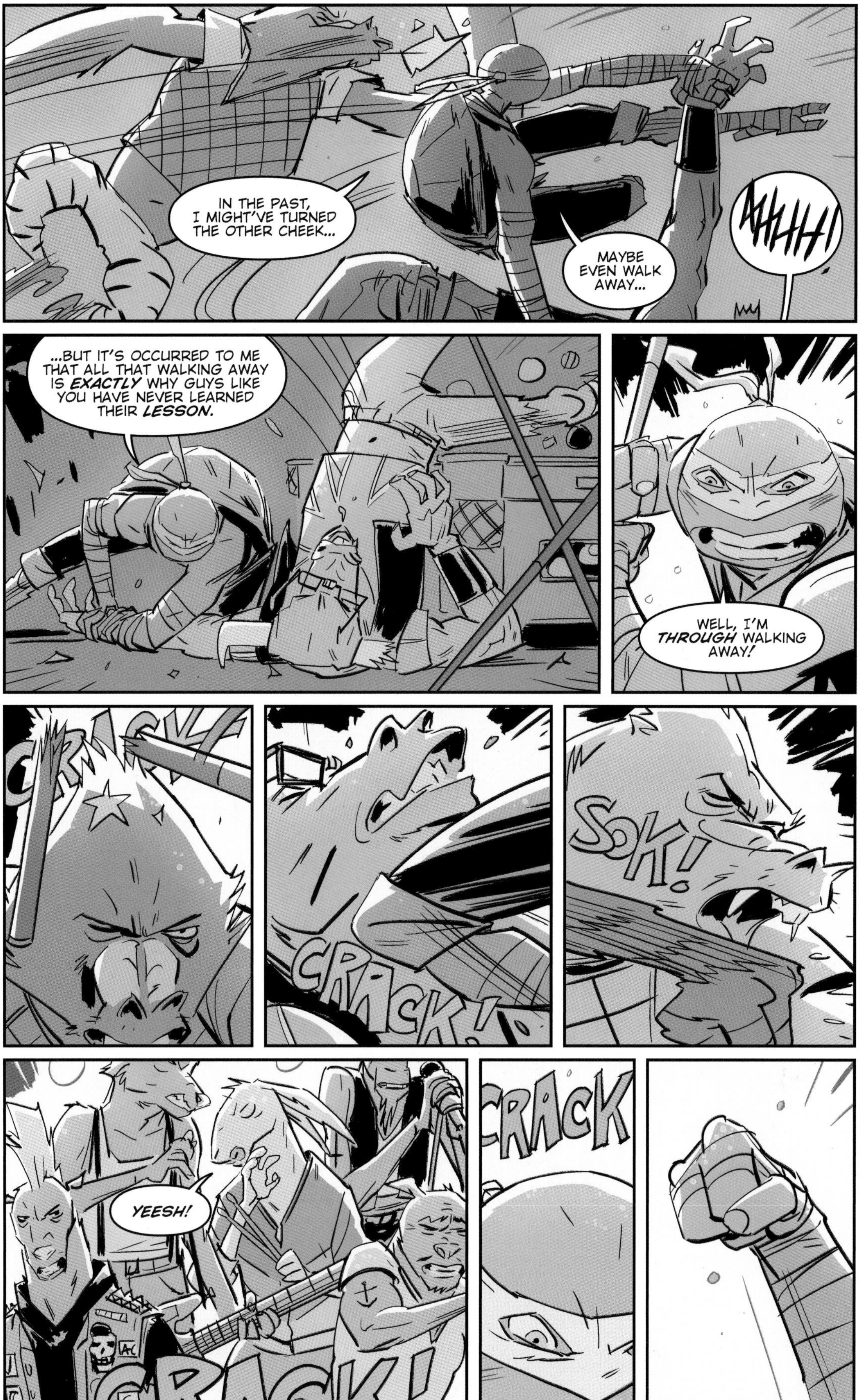

IN THE PAST, I MIGHT'VE TURNED THE OTHER CHEEK...
MAYBE EVEN WALK AWAY...
AHHH!
...BUT IT'S OCCURRED TO ME THAT ALL THAT WALKING AWAY IS EXACTLY WHY GUYS LIKE YOU HAVE NEVER LEARNED THEIR LESSON.
WELL, I'M THROUGH WALKING AWAY!
CRACK!
CRACK!
SOK!
YEESH!
CRACK!
CRACK

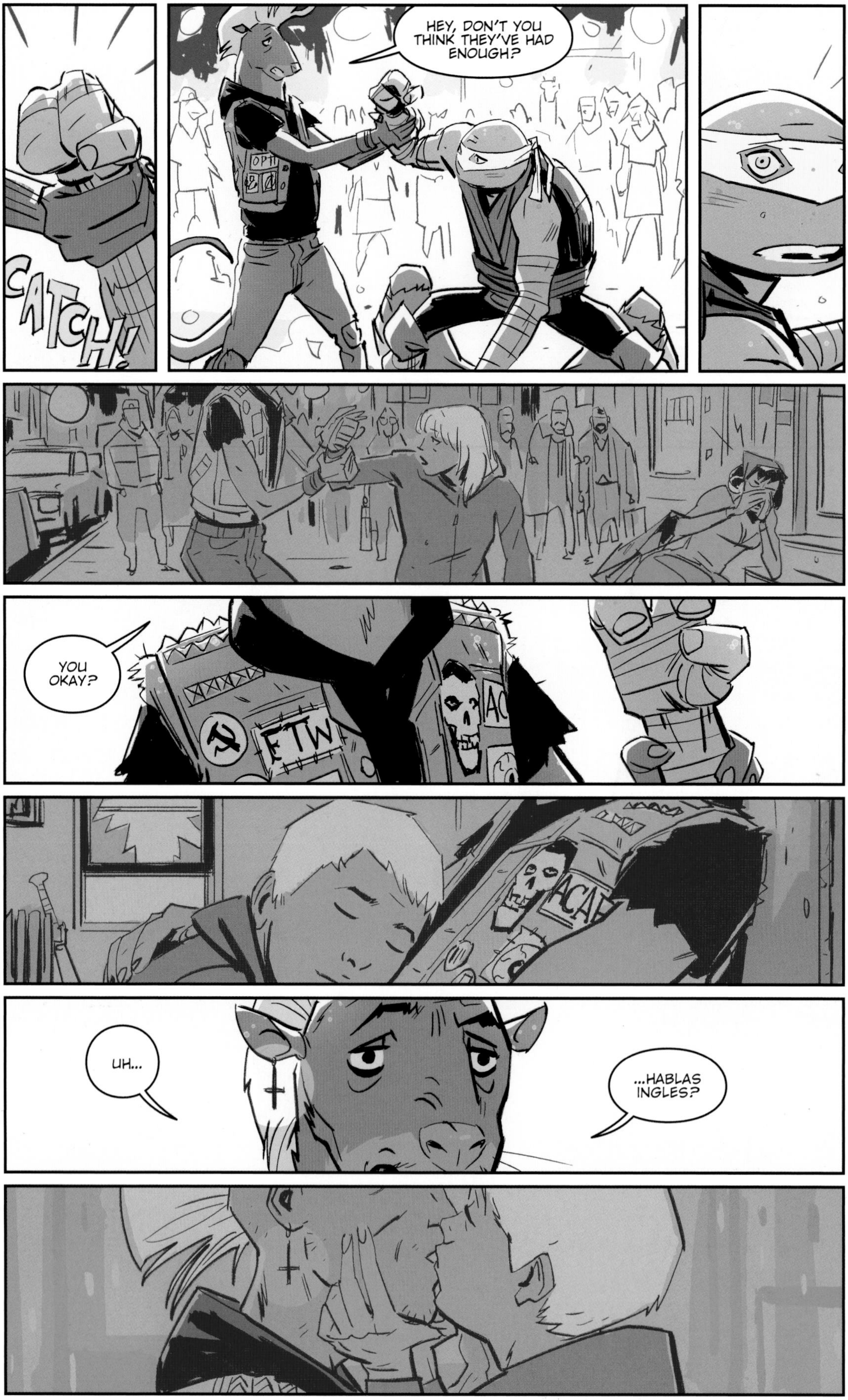

CATCH!
HEY, DON'T YOU THINK THEY'VE HAD ENOUGH?
OPH
YOU OKAY?
FTW
AC
ACAB
UH...
...HABLAS INGLES?

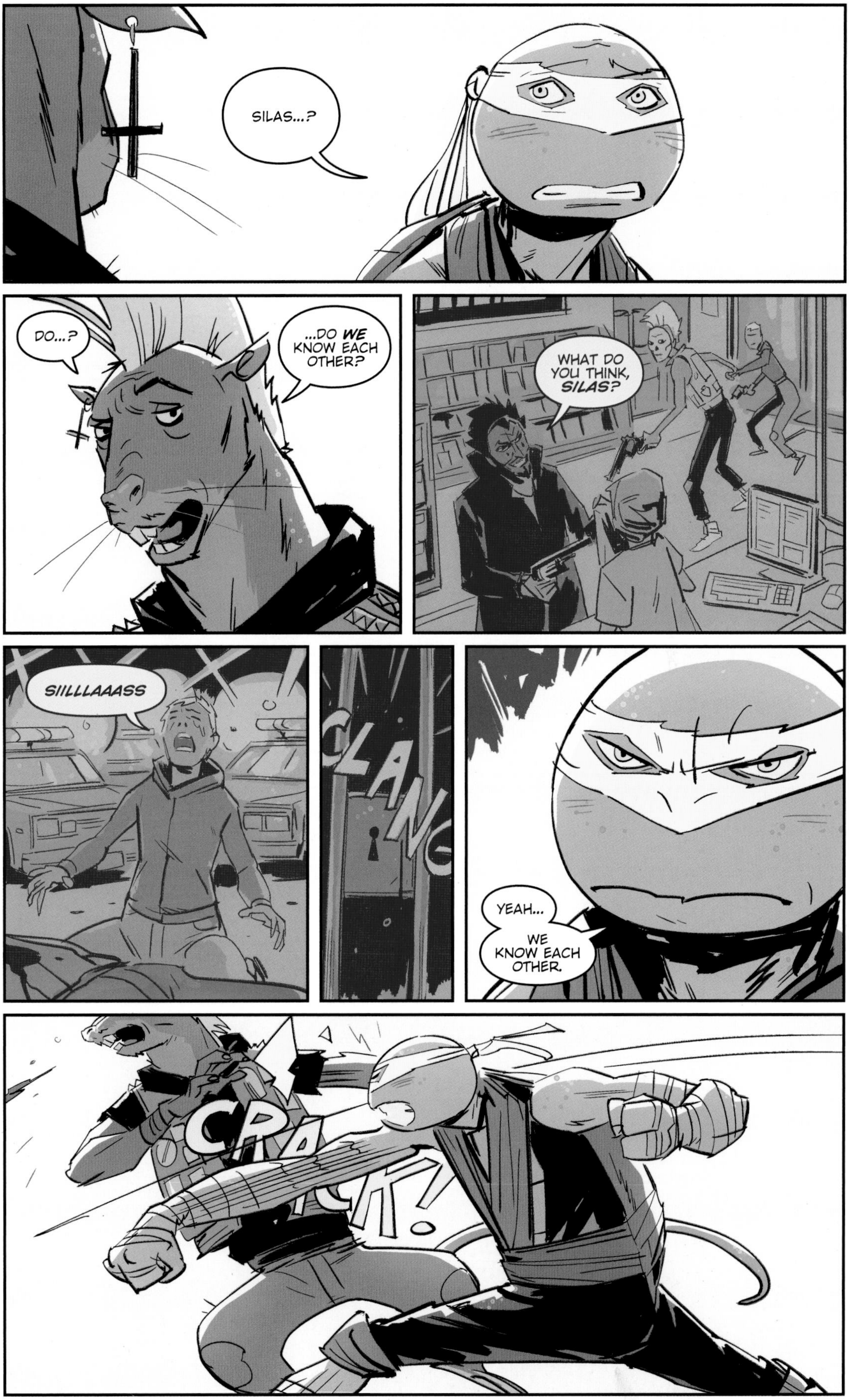
SILAS...?
DO...?
...DO WE KNOW EACH OTHER?
WHAT DO YOU THINK, SILAS?
SIILLLAAASS
CLANG
YEAH...
WE KNOW EACH OTHER.
CRACK!

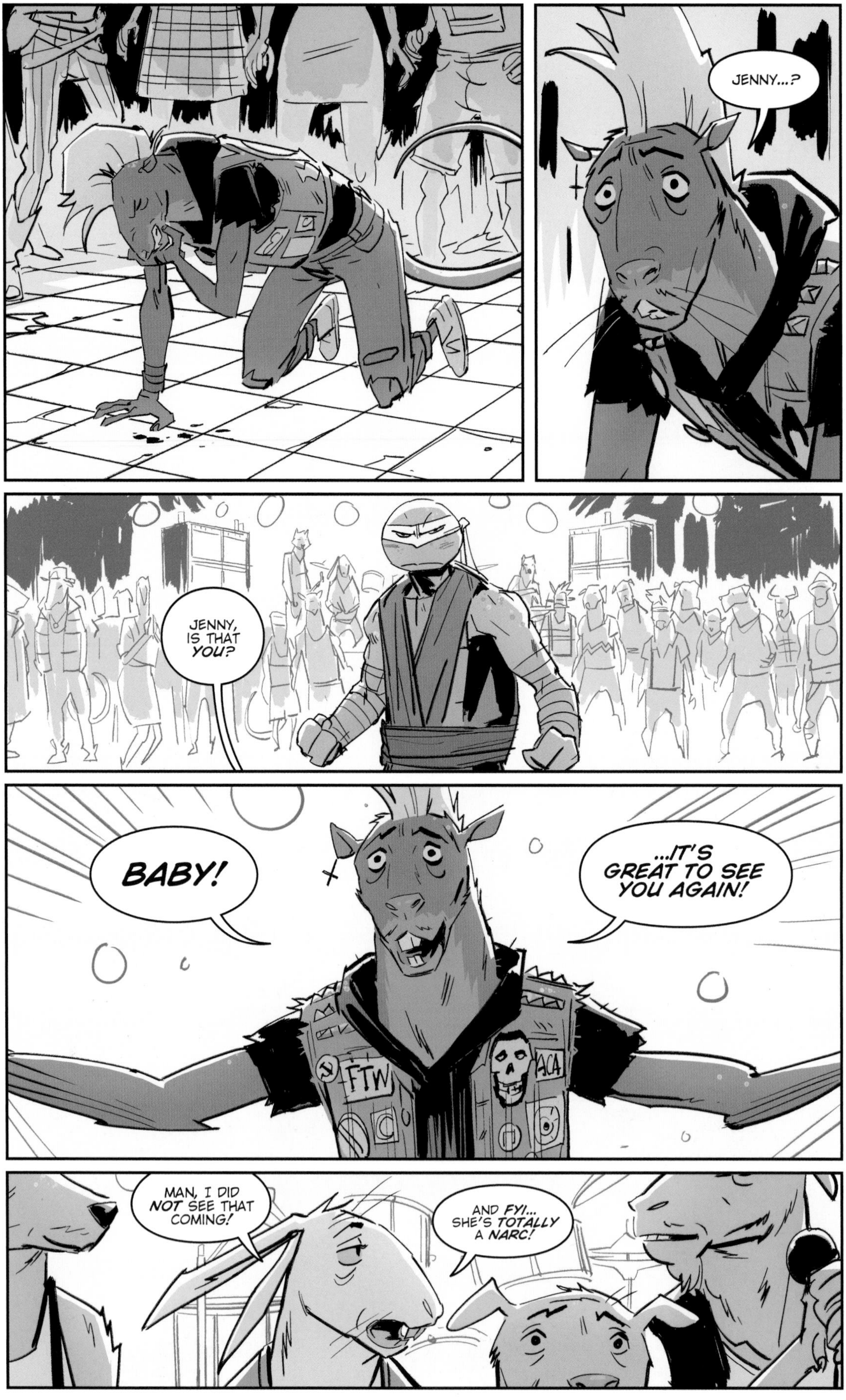
JENNY...?
JENNY, IS THAT YOU?
BABY!
...IT'S GREAT TO SEE YOU AGAIN!
FTW
ACA
MAN, I DID NOT SEE THAT COMING!
AND FYI... SHE'S TOTALLY A NARC!

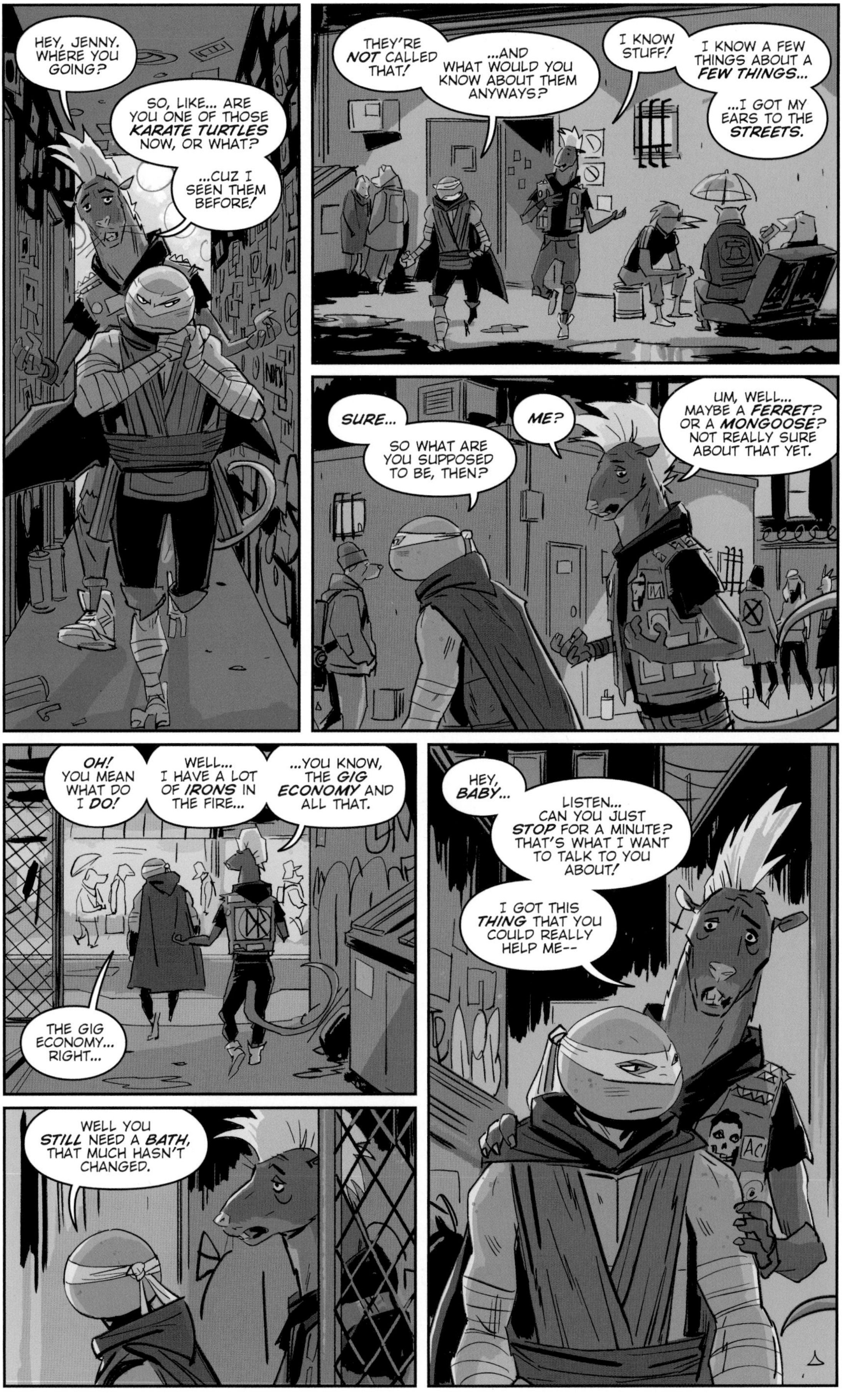

HEY, JENNY. WHERE YOU GOING?
SO, LIKE... ARE YOU ONE OF THOSE KARATE TURTLES NOW, OR WHAT?
...CUZ I SEEN THEM BEFORE!
THEY'RE NOT CALLED THAT!
...AND WHAT WOULD YOU KNOW ABOUT THEM ANYWAYS?
I KNOW STUFF!
I KNOW A FEW THINGS ABOUT A FEW THINGS...
...I GOT MY EARS TO THE STREETS.
SURE...
SO WHAT ARE YOU SUPPOSED TO BE, THEN?
ME?
UM, WELL... MAYBE A FERRET? OR A MONGOOSE? NOT REALLY SURE ABOUT THAT YET.
OH! YOU MEAN WHAT DO I DO!
WELL... I HAVE A LOT OF IRONS IN THE FIRE...
...YOU KNOW, THE GIG ECONOMY AND ALL THAT.
THE GIG ECONOMY... RIGHT...
WELL YOU STILL NEED A BATH, THAT MUCH HASN'T CHANGED.
HEY, BABY...
LISTEN... CAN YOU JUST STOP FOR A MINUTE? THAT'S WHAT I WANT TO TALK TO YOU ABOUT!
I GOT THIS THING THAT YOU COULD REALLY HELP ME--

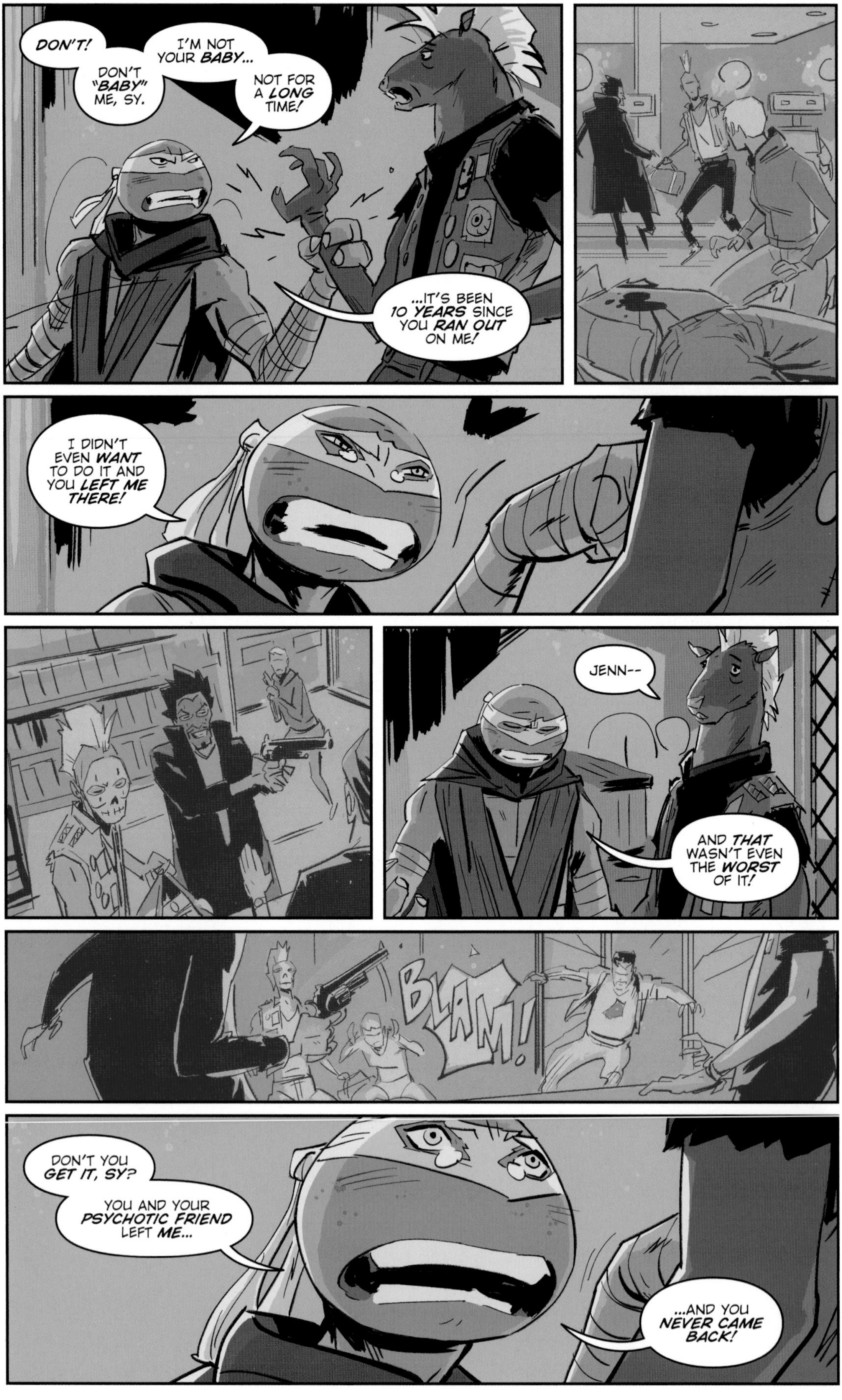

DON'T!
DON'T "BABY" ME, SY.
I'M NOT YOUR BABY...
NOT FOR A LONG TIME!
...IT'S BEEN 10 YEARS SINCE YOU RAN OUT ON ME!
I DIDN'T EVEN WANT TO DO IT AND YOU LEFT ME THERE!
JENN--
AND THAT WASN'T EVEN THE WORST OF IT!
BLAM!
DON'T YOU GET IT, SY?
YOU AND YOUR PSYCHOTIC FRIEND LEFT ME...
...AND YOU NEVER CAME BACK!

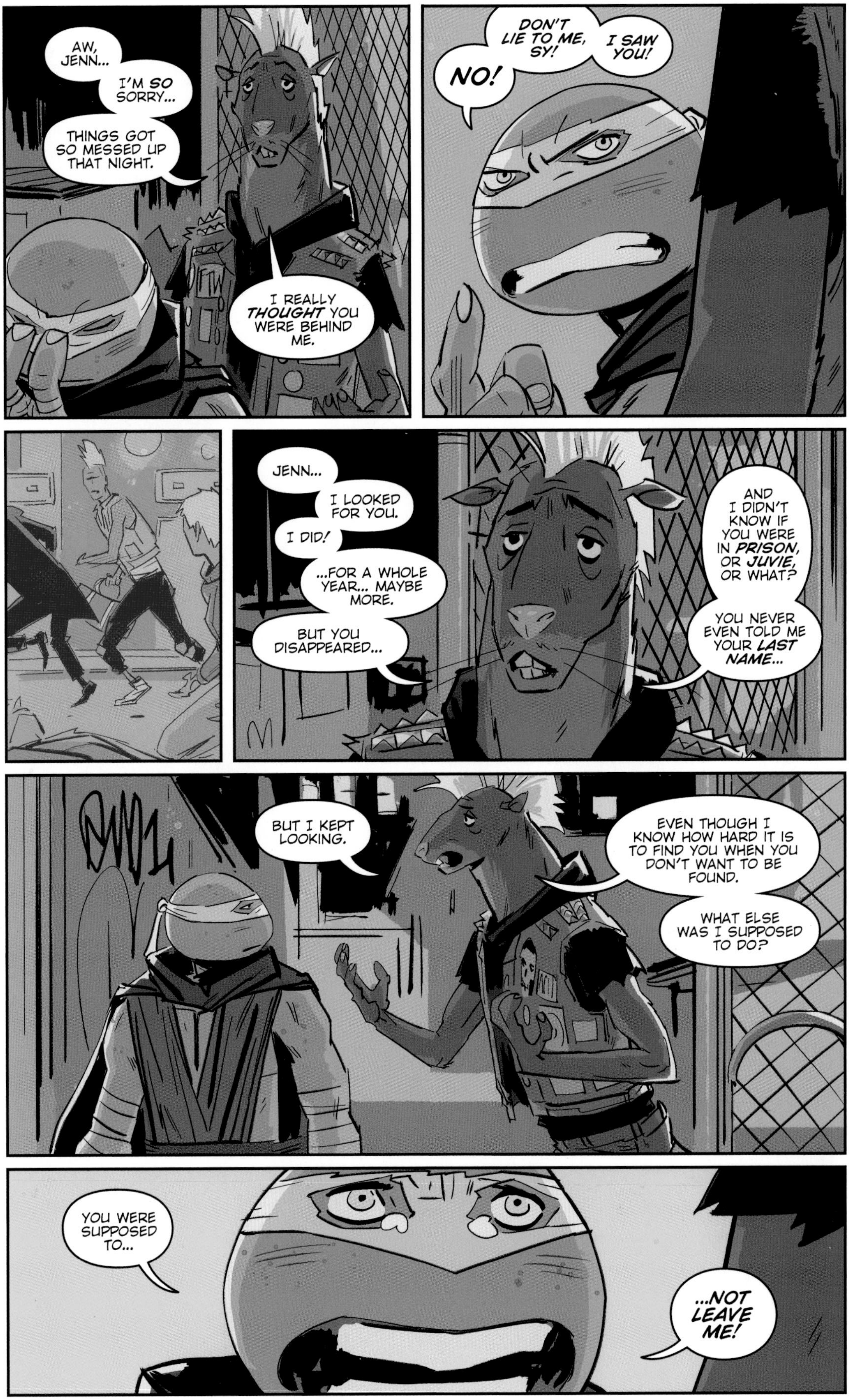

AW, JENN...
I'M **SO** SORRY...
THINGS GOT SO MESSED UP THAT NIGHT.
I REALLY **THOUGHT** YOU WERE BEHIND ME.
NO!
DON'T LIE TO ME, SY!
I SAW YOU!
JENN...
I LOOKED FOR YOU.
I DID!
...FOR A WHOLE YEAR... MAYBE MORE.
BUT YOU DISAPPEARED...
AND I DIDN'T KNOW IF YOU WERE IN **PRISON**, OR **JUVIE**, OR WHAT?
YOU NEVER EVEN TOLD ME YOUR **LAST NAME**...
BUT I KEPT LOOKING.
EVEN THOUGH I KNOW HOW HARD IT IS TO FIND YOU WHEN YOU DON'T WANT TO BE FOUND.
WHAT ELSE WAS I SUPPOSED TO DO?
YOU WERE SUPPOSED TO...
...NOT LEAVE ME!

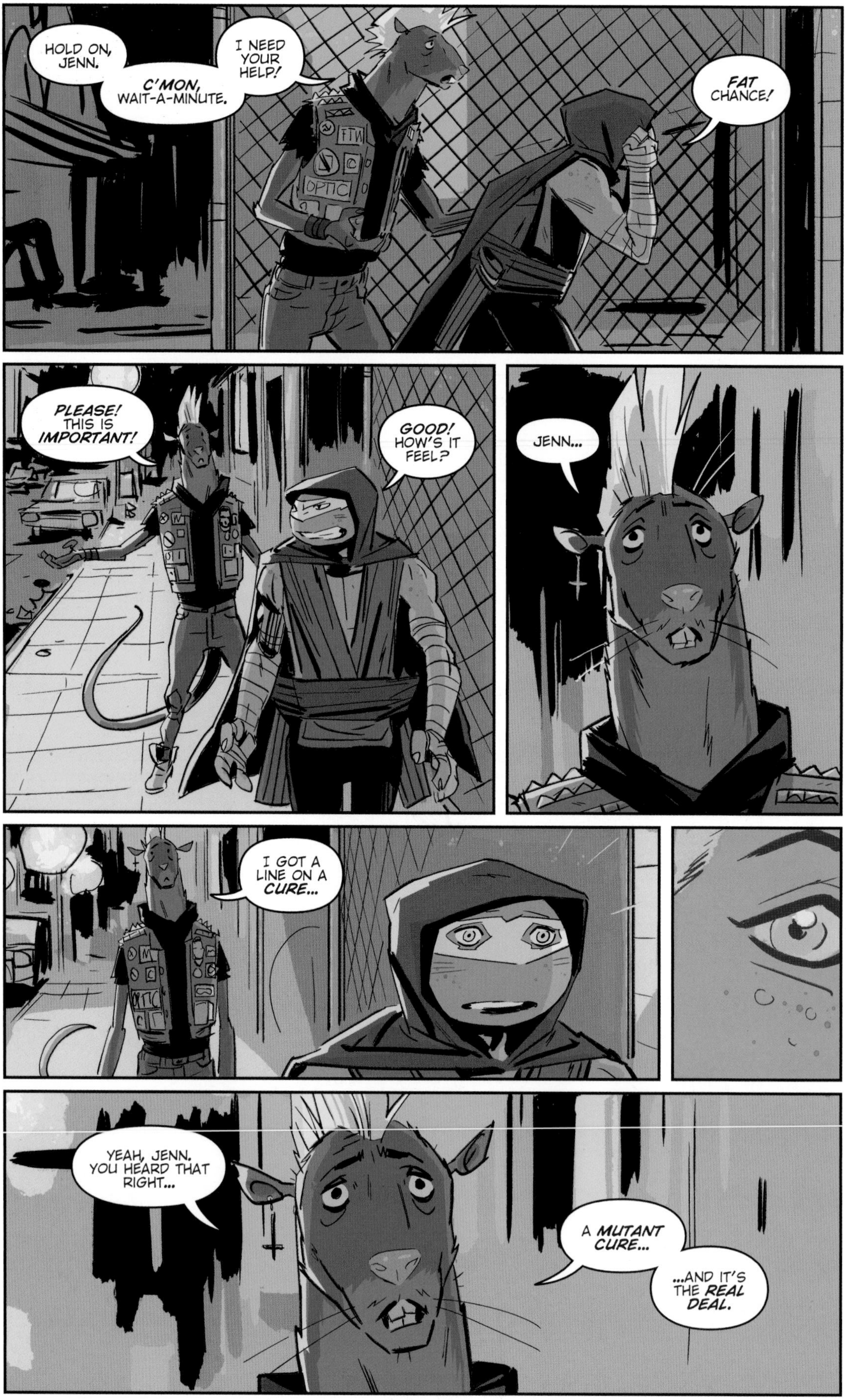
HOLD ON, JENN.
C'MON, WAIT-A-MINUTE.
I NEED YOUR HELP!
FAT CHANCE!
PLEASE! THIS IS IMPORTANT!
GOOD! HOW'S IT FEEL?
JENN...
I GOT A LINE ON A CURE...
YEAH, JENN. YOU HEARD THAT RIGHT...
A MUTANT CURE...
...AND IT'S THE REAL DEAL.

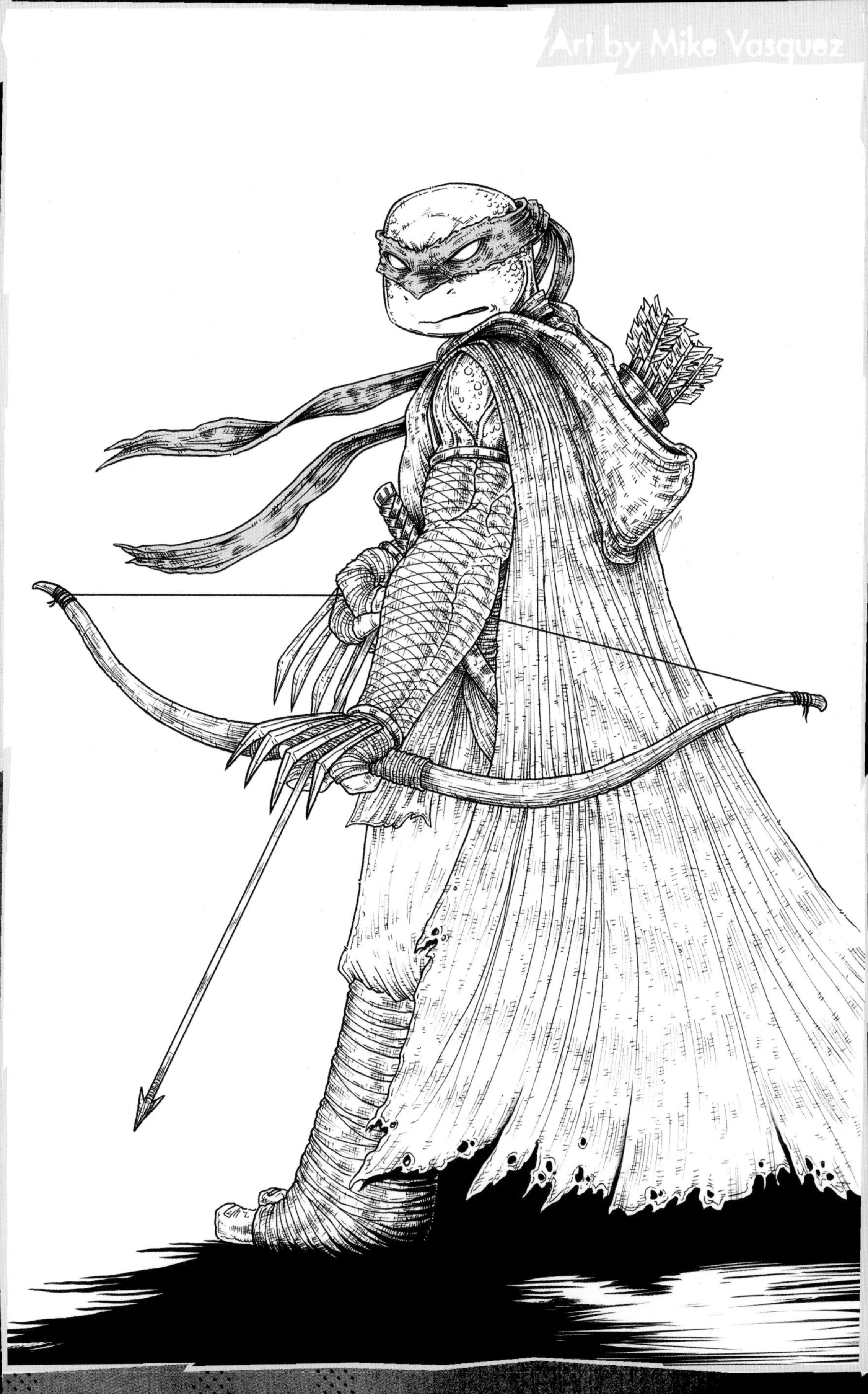
Art by Mike Vasquez

Art by Brahm Revel

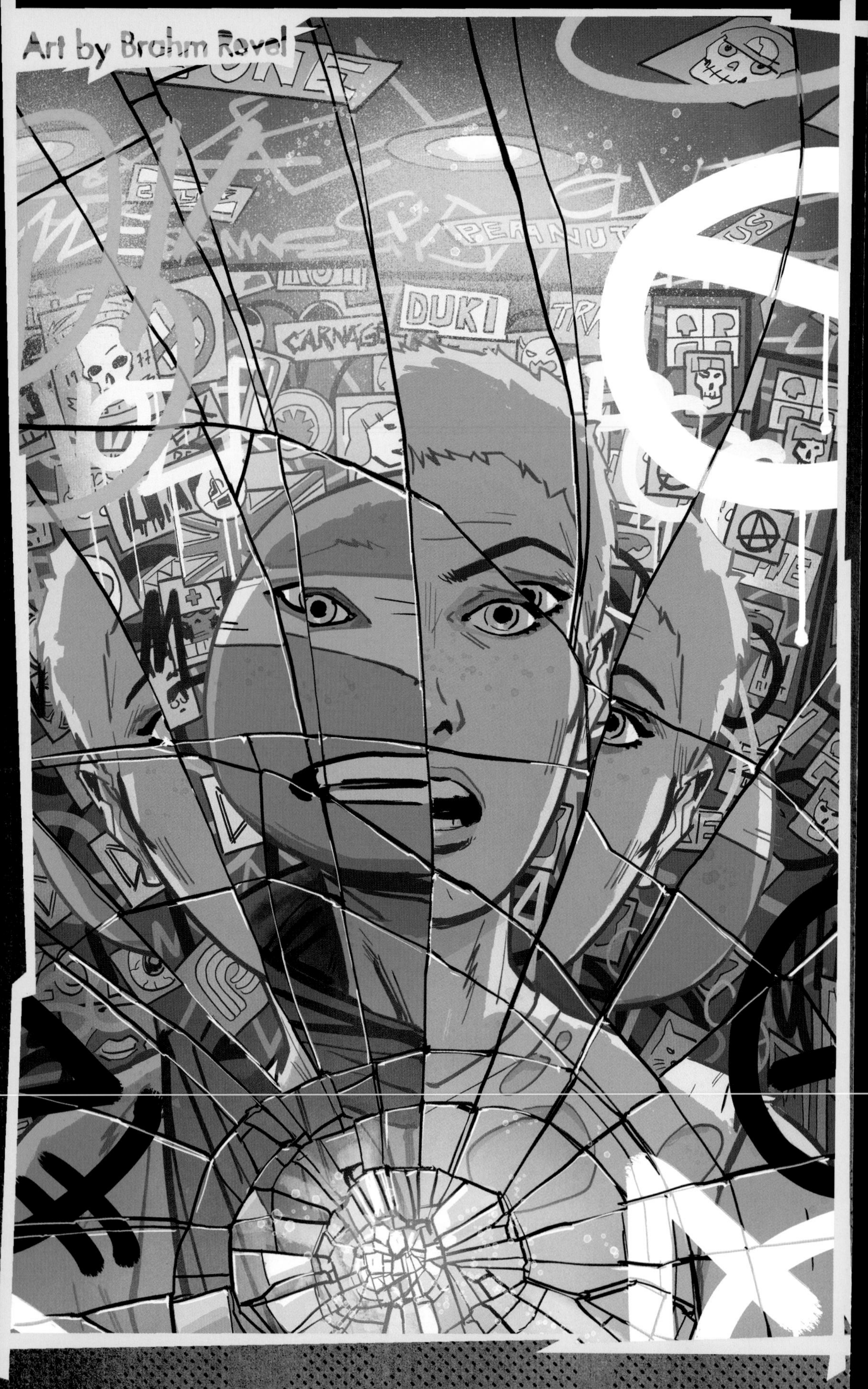

DUKI
CARNAGE

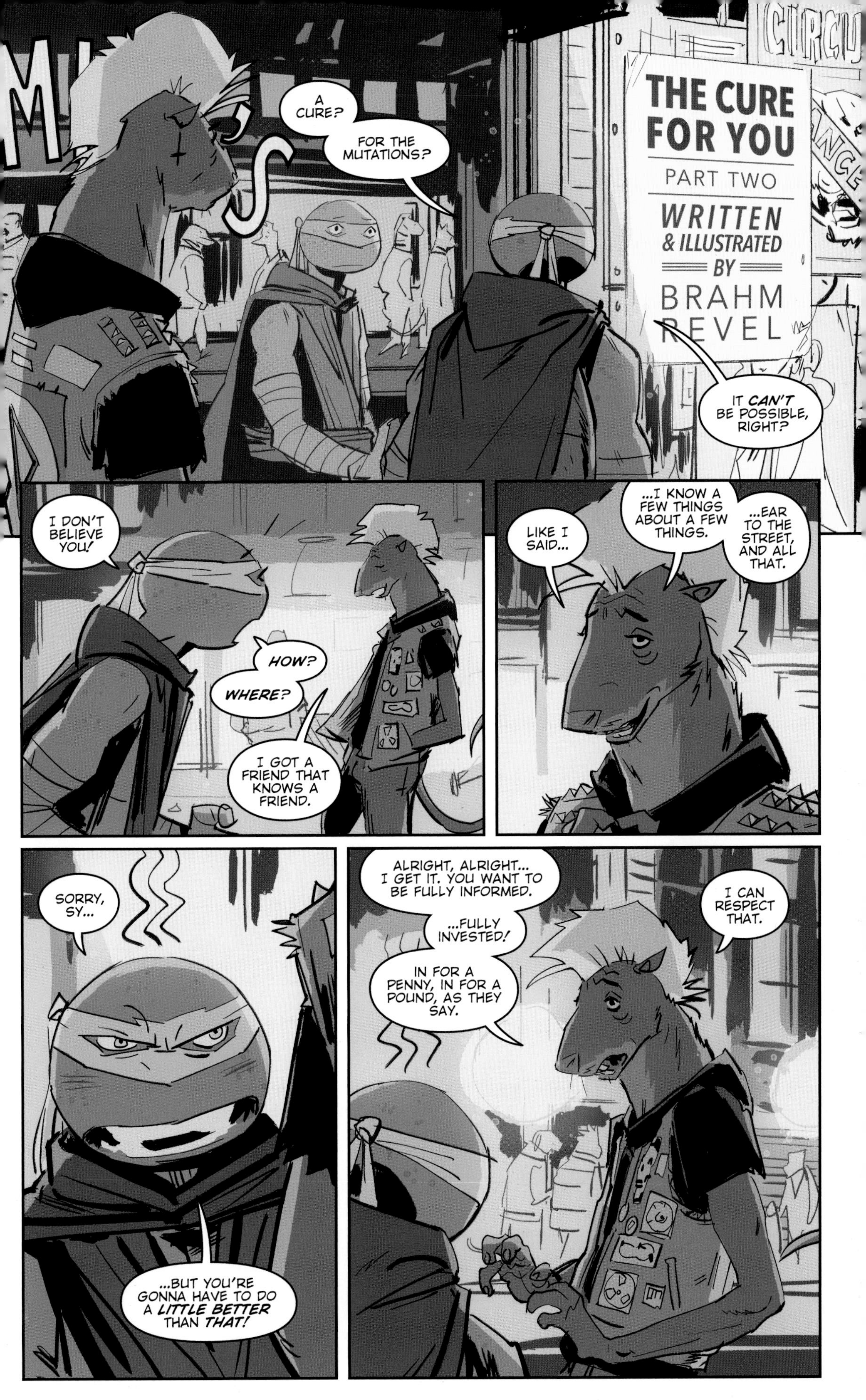
A CURE?
FOR THE MUTATIONS?
THE CURE FOR YOU
PART TWO
WRITTEN & ILLUSTRATED BY
BRAHM REVEL
IT CAN'T BE POSSIBLE, RIGHT?
I DON'T BELIEVE YOU!
HOW?
WHERE?
I GOT A FRIEND THAT KNOWS A FRIEND.
LIKE I SAID...
...I KNOW A FEW THINGS ABOUT A FEW THINGS.
...EAR TO THE STREET, AND ALL THAT.
SORRY, SY...
...BUT YOU'RE GONNA HAVE TO DO A LITTLE BETTER THAN THAT!
ALRIGHT, ALRIGHT... I GET IT. YOU WANT TO BE FULLY INFORMED.
...FULLY INVESTED!
IN FOR A PENNY, IN FOR A POUND, AS THEY SAY.
I CAN RESPECT THAT.

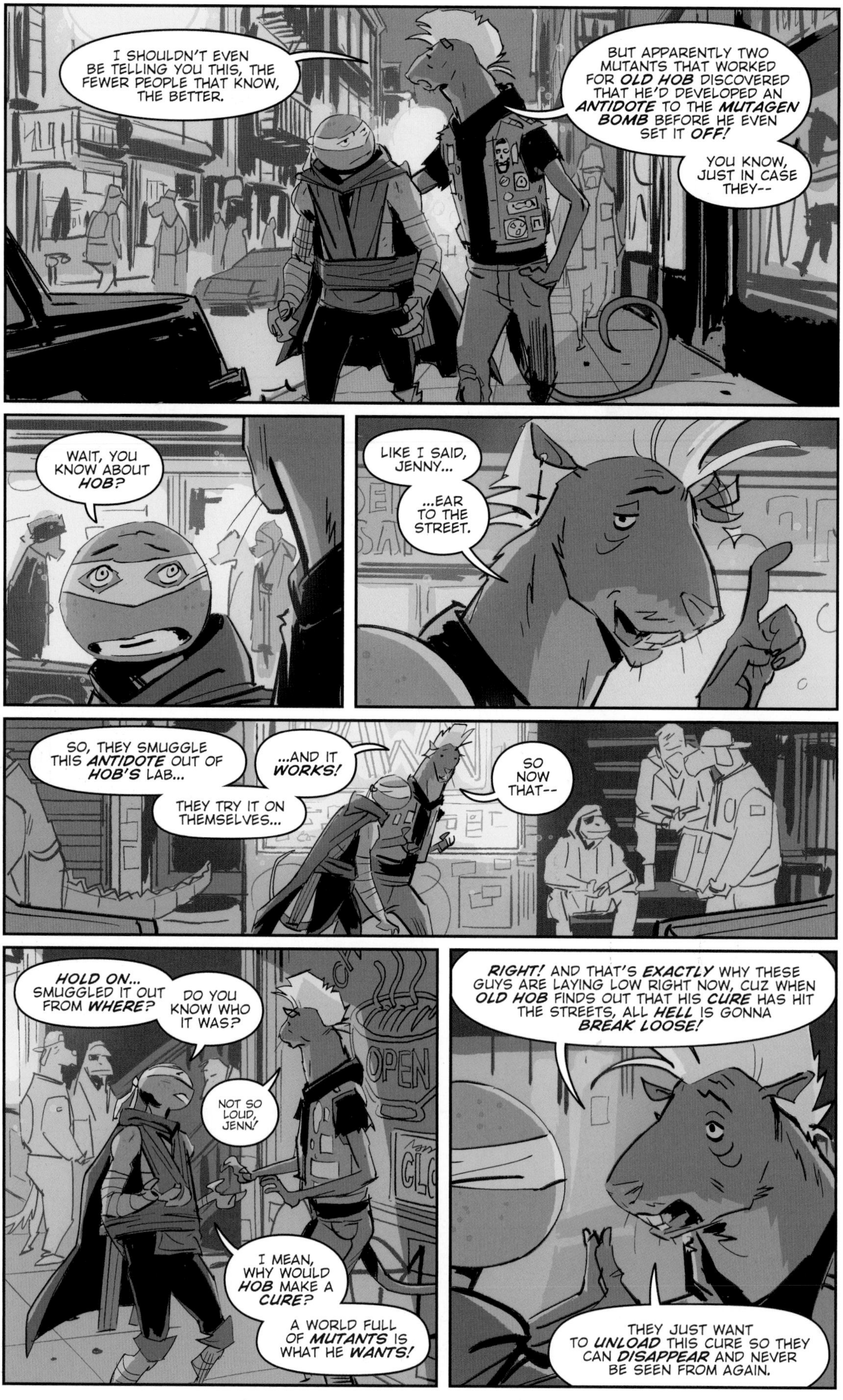

I SHOULDN'T EVEN BE TELLING YOU THIS, THE FEWER PEOPLE THAT KNOW, THE BETTER.
BUT APPARENTLY TWO MUTANTS THAT WORKED FOR OLD HOB DISCOVERED THAT HE'D DEVELOPED AN ANTIDOTE TO THE MUTAGEN BOMB BEFORE HE EVEN SET IT OFF!
YOU KNOW, JUST IN CASE THEY--
WAIT, YOU KNOW ABOUT HOB?
LIKE I SAID, JENNY...
...EAR TO THE STREET.
SO, THEY SMUGGLE THIS ANTIDOTE OUT OF HOB'S LAB...
THEY TRY IT ON THEMSELVES...
...AND IT WORKS!
SO NOW THAT--
HOLD ON... SMUGGLED IT OUT FROM WHERE?
DO YOU KNOW WHO IT WAS?
NOT SO LOUD, JENN!
I MEAN, WHY WOULD HOB MAKE A CURE?
A WORLD FULL OF MUTANTS IS WHAT HE WANTS!
RIGHT! AND THAT'S EXACTLY WHY THESE GUYS ARE LAYING LOW RIGHT NOW, CUZ WHEN OLD HOB FINDS OUT THAT HIS CURE HAS HIT THE STREETS, ALL HELL IS GONNA BREAK LOOSE!
THEY JUST WANT TO UNLOAD THIS CURE SO THEY CAN DISAPPEAR AND NEVER BE SEEN FROM AGAIN.

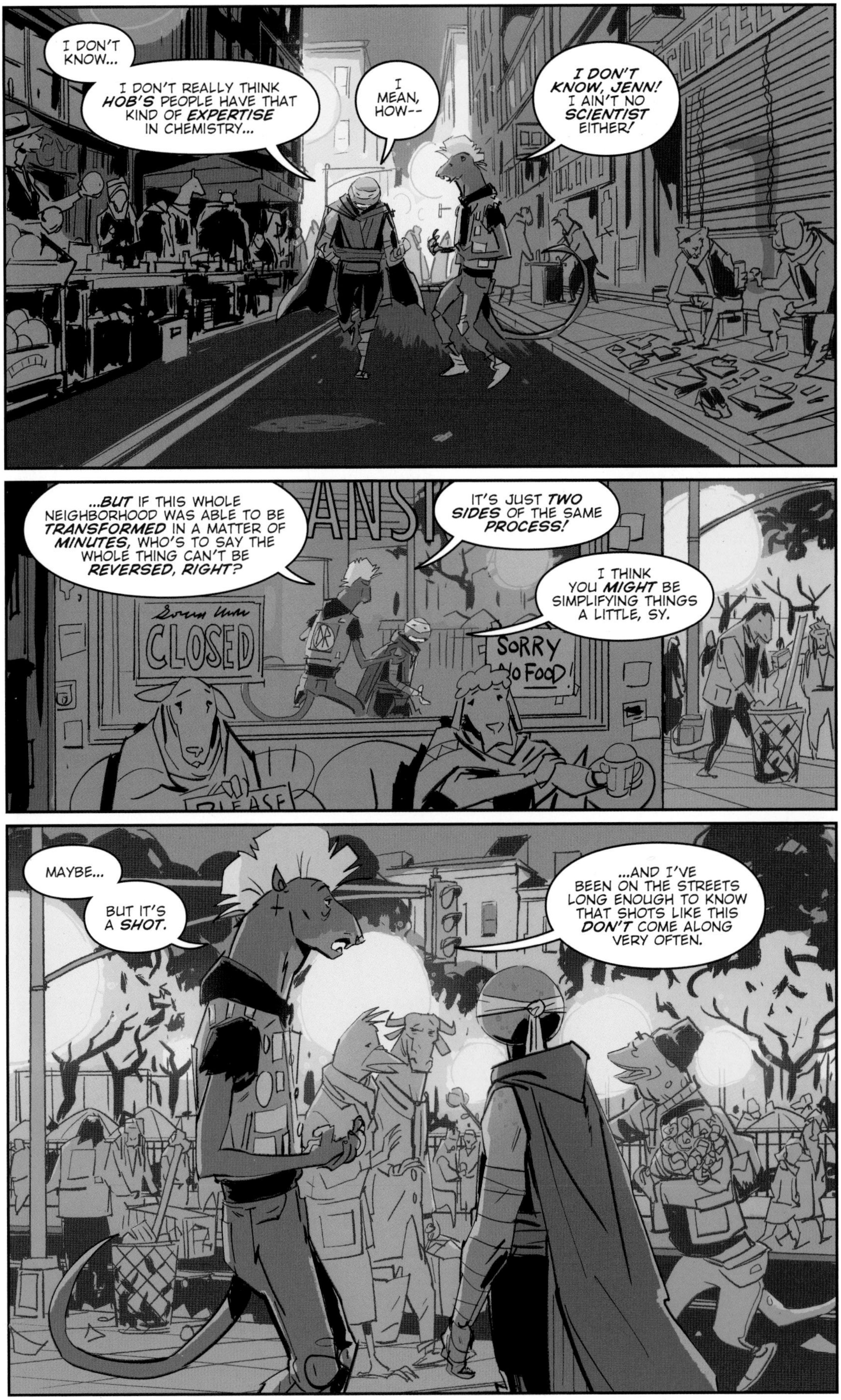
I DON'T KNOW...
I DON'T REALLY THINK HOB'S PEOPLE HAVE THAT KIND OF EXPERTISE IN CHEMISTRY...
I MEAN, HOW--
I DON'T KNOW, JENN! I AIN'T NO SCIENTIST EITHER!
...BUT IF THIS WHOLE NEIGHBORHOOD WAS ABLE TO BE TRANSFORMED IN A MATTER OF MINUTES, WHO'S TO SAY THE WHOLE THING CAN'T BE REVERSED, RIGHT?
IT'S JUST TWO SIDES OF THE SAME PROCESS!
I THINK YOU MIGHT BE SIMPLIFYING THINGS A LITTLE, SY.
CLOSED
SORRY NO FOOD!
MAYBE...
BUT IT'S A SHOT.
...AND I'VE BEEN ON THE STREETS LONG ENOUGH TO KNOW THAT SHOTS LIKE THIS DON'T COME ALONG VERY OFTEN.

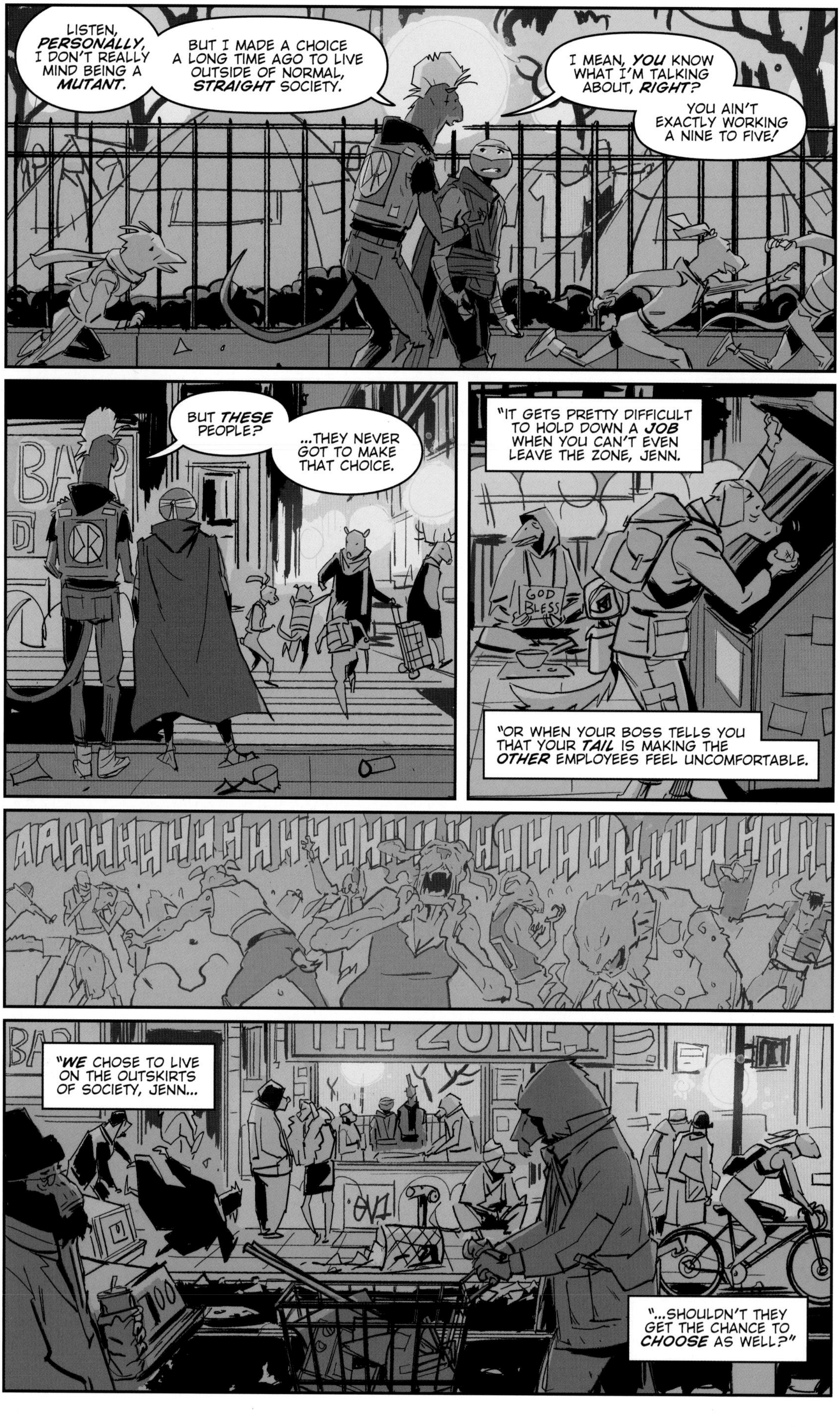
LISTEN, **PERSONALLY,** I DON'T REALLY MIND BEING A **MUTANT.**
BUT I MADE A CHOICE A LONG TIME AGO TO LIVE OUTSIDE OF NORMAL, **STRAIGHT** SOCIETY.
I MEAN, **YOU** KNOW WHAT I'M TALKING ABOUT, **RIGHT?**
YOU AIN'T EXACTLY WORKING A NINE TO FIVE!
BAR
BUT **THESE** PEOPLE?
...THEY NEVER GOT TO MAKE THAT CHOICE.
"IT GETS PRETTY DIFFICULT TO HOLD DOWN A **JOB** WHEN YOU CAN'T EVEN LEAVE THE ZONE, JENN.
GOD BLESS
"OR WHEN YOUR BOSS TELLS YOU THAT YOUR **TAIL** IS MAKING THE **OTHER** EMPLOYEES FEEL UNCOMFORTABLE.
AAHHHHHHHHHHHHHHHHHHHHHHHHHHH
BAR
THE ZONE
"**WE** CHOSE TO LIVE ON THE OUTSKIRTS OF SOCIETY, JENN...
100
"...SHOULDN'T THEY GET THE CHANCE TO **CHOOSE** AS WELL?"

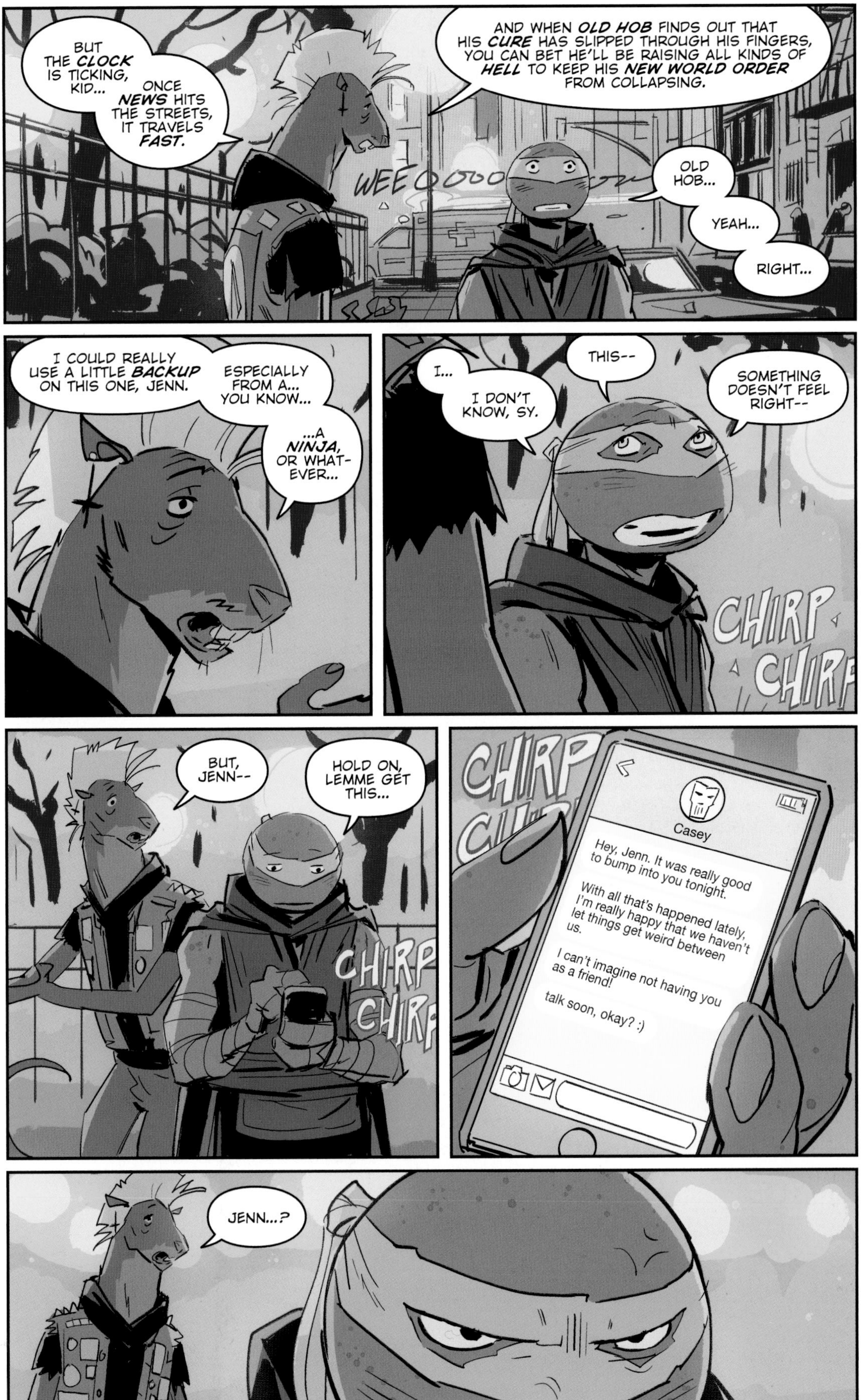
BUT THE CLOCK IS TICKING, KID...
ONCE NEWS HITS THE STREETS, IT TRAVELS FAST.
AND WHEN OLD HOB FINDS OUT THAT HIS CURE HAS SLIPPED THROUGH HIS FINGERS, YOU CAN BET HE'LL BE RAISING ALL KINDS OF HELL TO KEEP HIS NEW WORLD ORDER FROM COLLAPSING.
WEEOOOO
OLD HOB...
YEAH...
RIGHT...
I COULD REALLY USE A LITTLE BACKUP ON THIS ONE, JENN.
ESPECIALLY FROM A... YOU KNOW...
...A NINJA, OR WHAT-EVER...
I...
I DON'T KNOW, SY.
THIS--
SOMETHING DOESN'T FEEL RIGHT--
CHIRP
CHIRP
BUT, JENN--
HOLD ON, LEMME GET THIS...
CHIRP
CHIRP
CHIRP
Casey
Hey, Jenn. It was really good to bump into you tonight.
With all that's happened lately, I'm really happy that we haven't let things get weird between us.
I can't imagine not having you as a friend!
talk soon, okay? :)
JENN...?

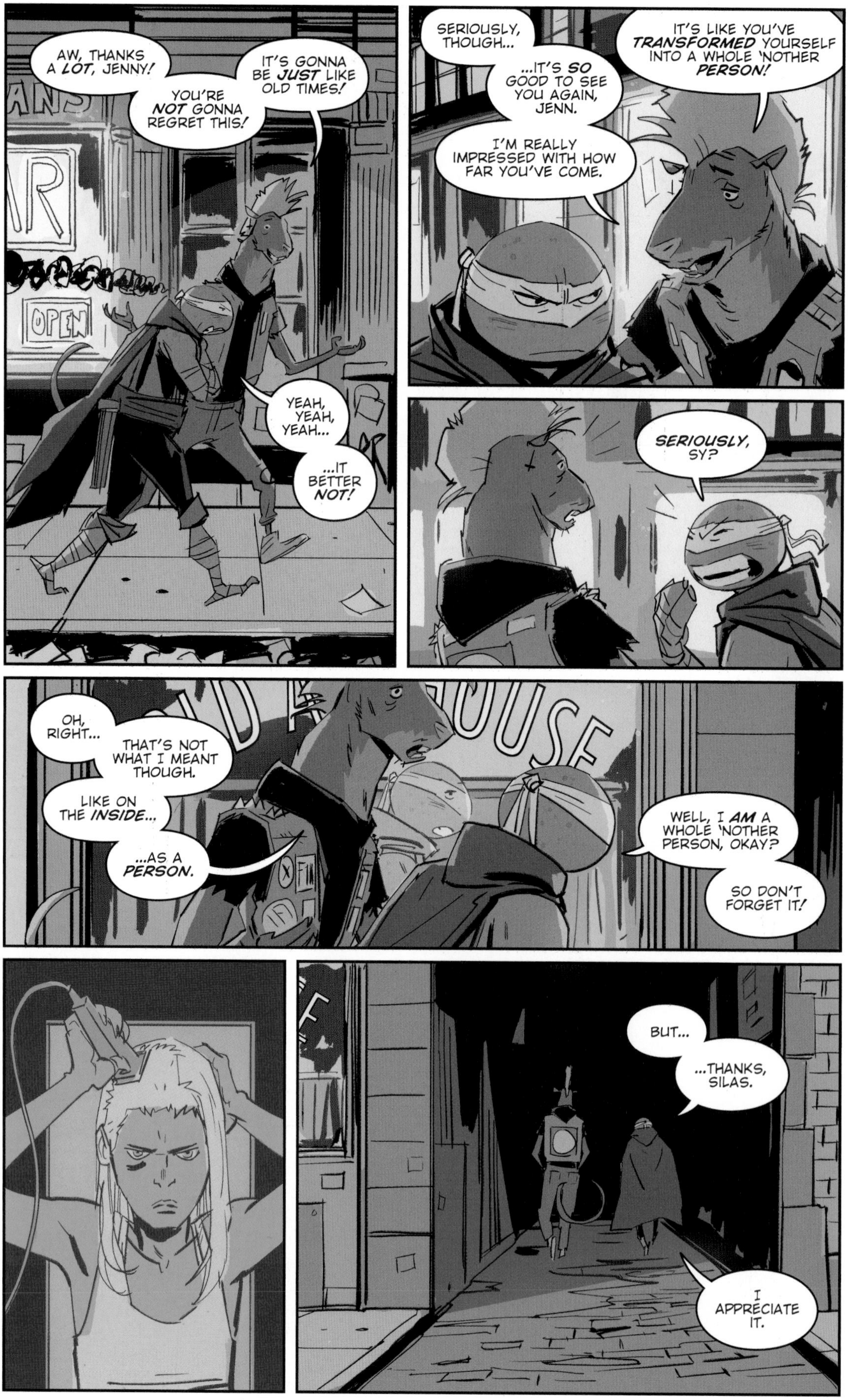
AW, THANKS A LOT, JENNY!
YOU'RE NOT GONNA REGRET THIS!
IT'S GONNA BE JUST LIKE OLD TIMES!
YEAH, YEAH, YEAH...
...IT BETTER NOT!
SERIOUSLY, THOUGH...
...IT'S SO GOOD TO SEE YOU AGAIN, JENN.
I'M REALLY IMPRESSED WITH HOW FAR YOU'VE COME.
IT'S LIKE YOU'VE TRANSFORMED YOURSELF INTO A WHOLE 'NOTHER PERSON!
SERIOUSLY, SY?
OH, RIGHT...
THAT'S NOT WHAT I MEANT THOUGH.
LIKE ON THE INSIDE...
...AS A PERSON.
WELL, I AM A WHOLE 'NOTHER PERSON, OKAY?
SO DON'T FORGET IT!
BUT...
...THANKS, SILAS.
I APPRECIATE IT.

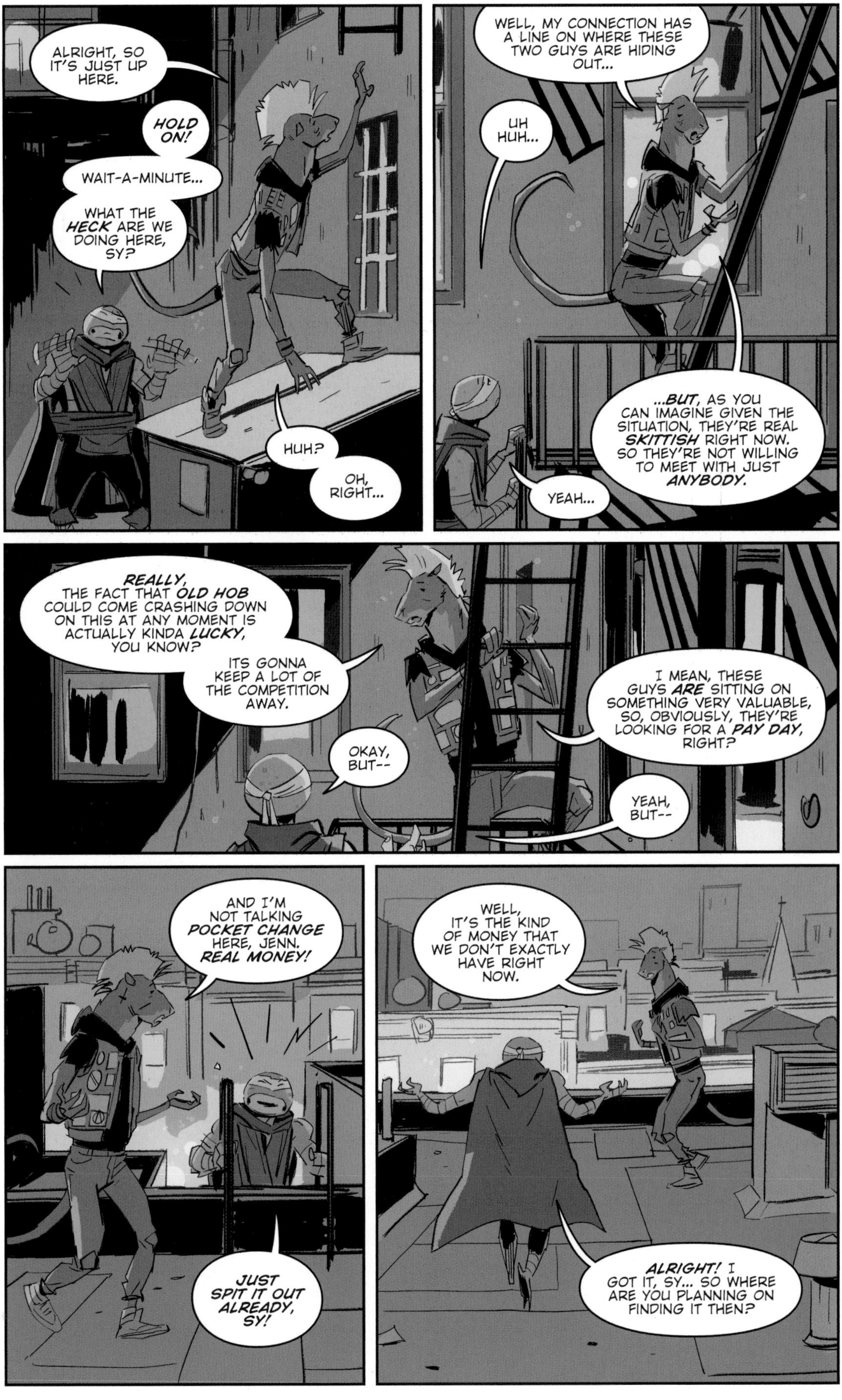
ALRIGHT, SO IT'S JUST UP HERE.
HOLD ON!
WAIT-A-MINUTE...
WHAT THE HECK ARE WE DOING HERE, SY?
HUH?
OH, RIGHT...
WELL, MY CONNECTION HAS A LINE ON WHERE THESE TWO GUYS ARE HIDING OUT...
UH HUH...
...BUT, AS YOU CAN IMAGINE GIVEN THE SITUATION, THEY'RE REAL SKITTISH RIGHT NOW. SO THEY'RE NOT WILLING TO MEET WITH JUST ANYBODY.
YEAH...
REALLY, THE FACT THAT OLD HOB COULD COME CRASHING DOWN ON THIS AT ANY MOMENT IS ACTUALLY KINDA LUCKY, YOU KNOW?
ITS GONNA KEEP A LOT OF THE COMPETITION AWAY.
OKAY, BUT--
I MEAN, THESE GUYS ARE SITTING ON SOMETHING VERY VALUABLE, SO, OBVIOUSLY, THEY'RE LOOKING FOR A PAY DAY, RIGHT?
YEAH, BUT--
AND I'M NOT TALKING POCKET CHANGE HERE, JENN. REAL MONEY!
JUST SPIT IT OUT ALREADY, SY!
WELL, IT'S THE KIND OF MONEY THAT WE DON'T EXACTLY HAVE RIGHT NOW.
ALRIGHT! I GOT IT, SY... SO WHERE ARE YOU PLANNING ON FINDING IT THEN?

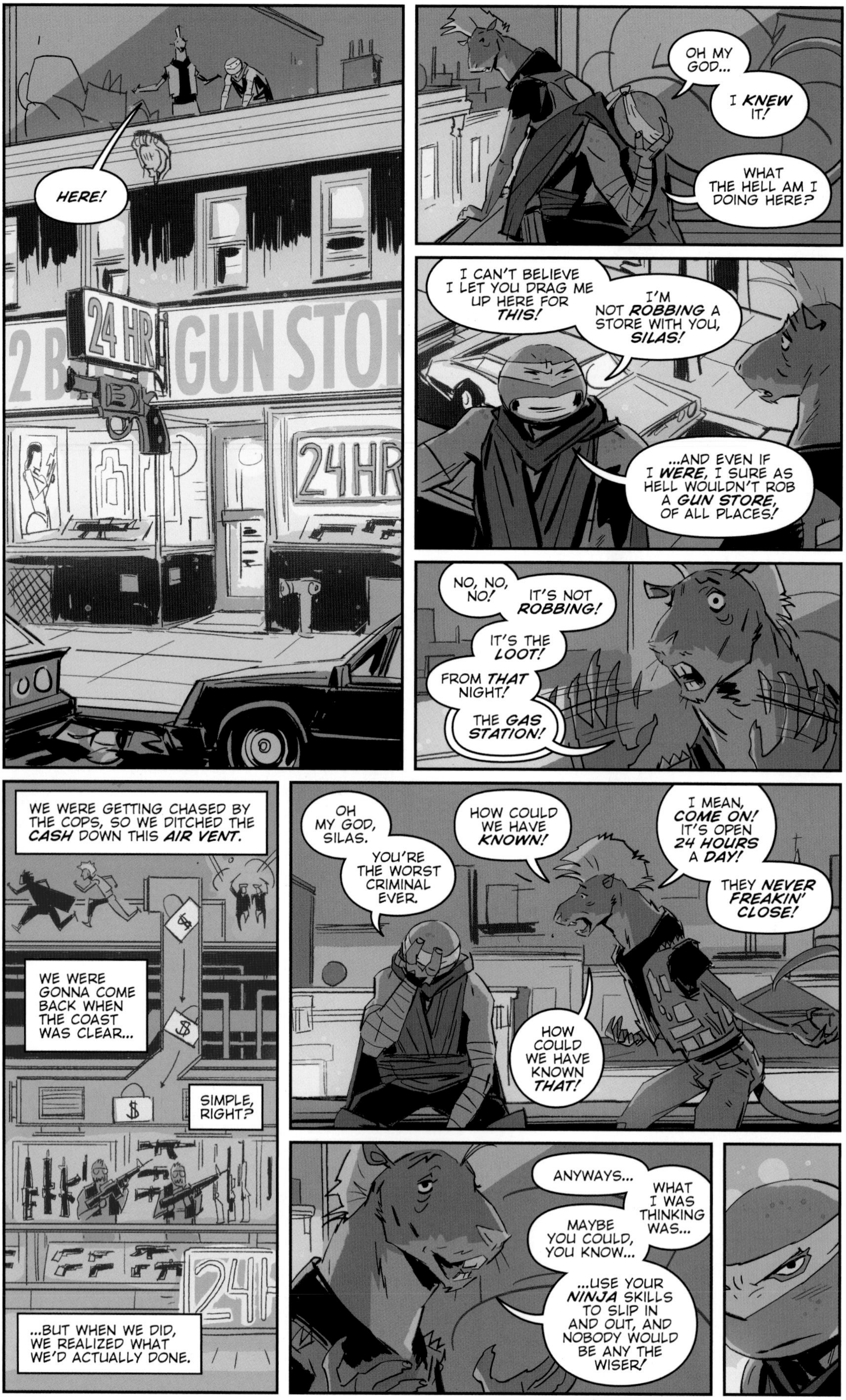
HERE!
24 HR
2 B GUN STOR
24HR
OH MY GOD...
I KNEW IT!
WHAT THE HELL AM I DOING HERE?
I CAN'T BELIEVE I LET YOU DRAG ME UP HERE FOR THIS!
I'M NOT ROBBING A STORE WITH YOU, SILAS!
...AND EVEN IF I WERE, I SURE AS HELL WOULDN'T ROB A GUN STORE, OF ALL PLACES!
NO, NO, NO!
IT'S NOT ROBBING!
IT'S THE LOOT!
FROM THAT NIGHT!
THE GAS STATION!
WE WERE GETTING CHASED BY THE COPS, SO WE DITCHED THE CASH DOWN THIS AIR VENT.
WE WERE GONNA COME BACK WHEN THE COAST WAS CLEAR...
SIMPLE, RIGHT?
...BUT WHEN WE DID, WE REALIZED WHAT WE'D ACTUALLY DONE.
OH MY GOD, SILAS.
YOU'RE THE WORST CRIMINAL EVER.
HOW COULD WE HAVE KNOWN!
I MEAN, COME ON! IT'S OPEN 24 HOURS A DAY!
THEY NEVER FREAKIN' CLOSE!
HOW COULD WE HAVE KNOWN THAT!
ANYWAYS...
WHAT I WAS THINKING WAS...
MAYBE YOU COULD, YOU KNOW...
...USE YOUR NINJA SKILLS TO SLIP IN AND OUT, AND NOBODY WOULD BE ANY THE WISER!

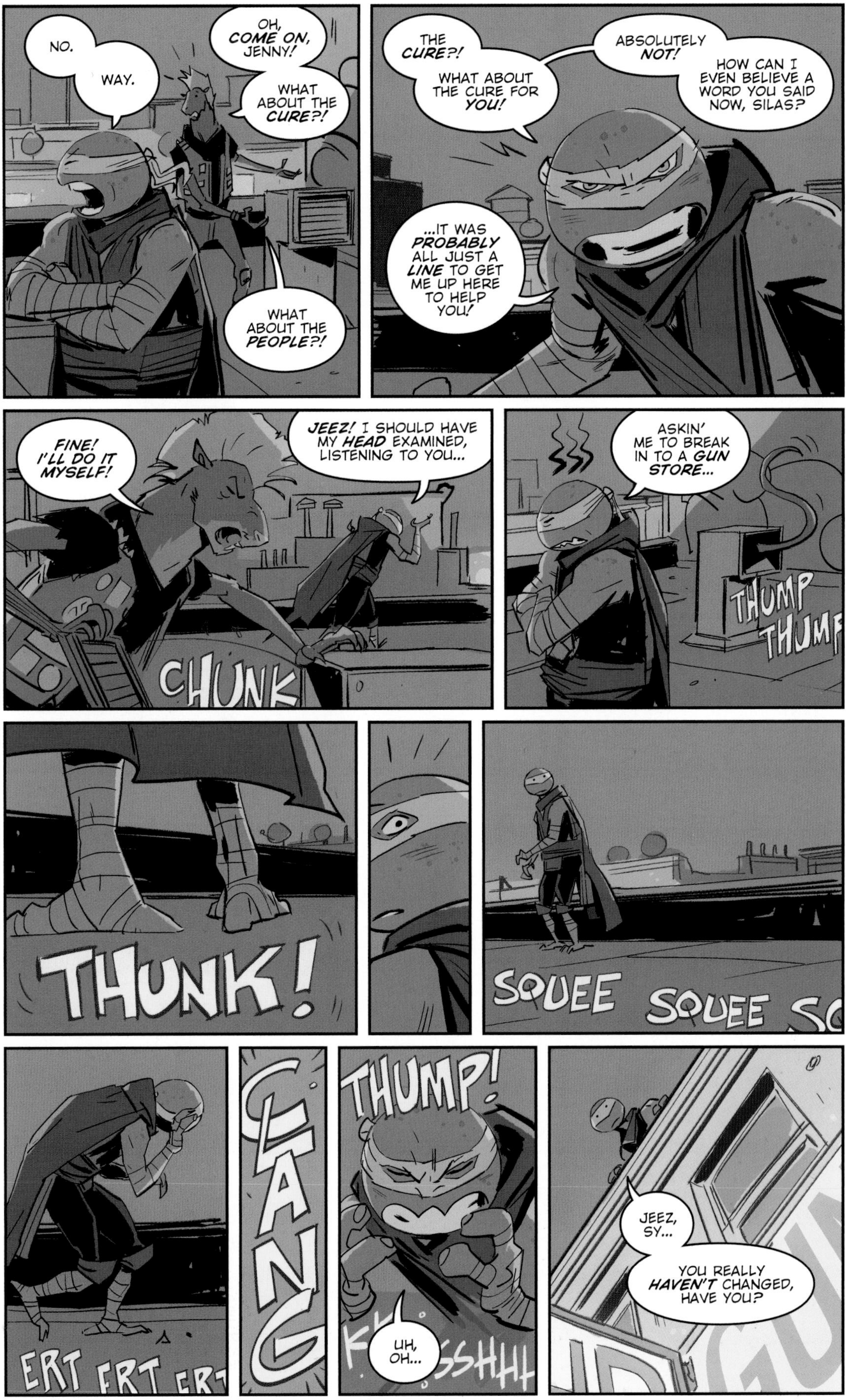

NO.
WAY.
OH, COME ON, JENNY!
WHAT ABOUT THE CURE?!
WHAT ABOUT THE PEOPLE?!
THE CURE?!
WHAT ABOUT THE CURE FOR YOU!
ABSOLUTELY NOT!
HOW CAN I EVEN BELIEVE A WORD YOU SAID NOW, SILAS?
...IT WAS PROBABLY ALL JUST A LINE TO GET ME UP HERE TO HELP YOU!
FINE! I'LL DO IT MYSELF!
JEEZ! I SHOULD HAVE MY HEAD EXAMINED, LISTENING TO YOU...
CHUNK
ASKIN' ME TO BREAK IN TO A GUN STORE...
THUMP
THUMP
THUNK!
SQUEE SQUEE
ERT ERT
CLANG
THUMP!
UH, OH...
JEEZ, SY...
YOU REALLY HAVEN'T CHANGED, HAVE YOU?

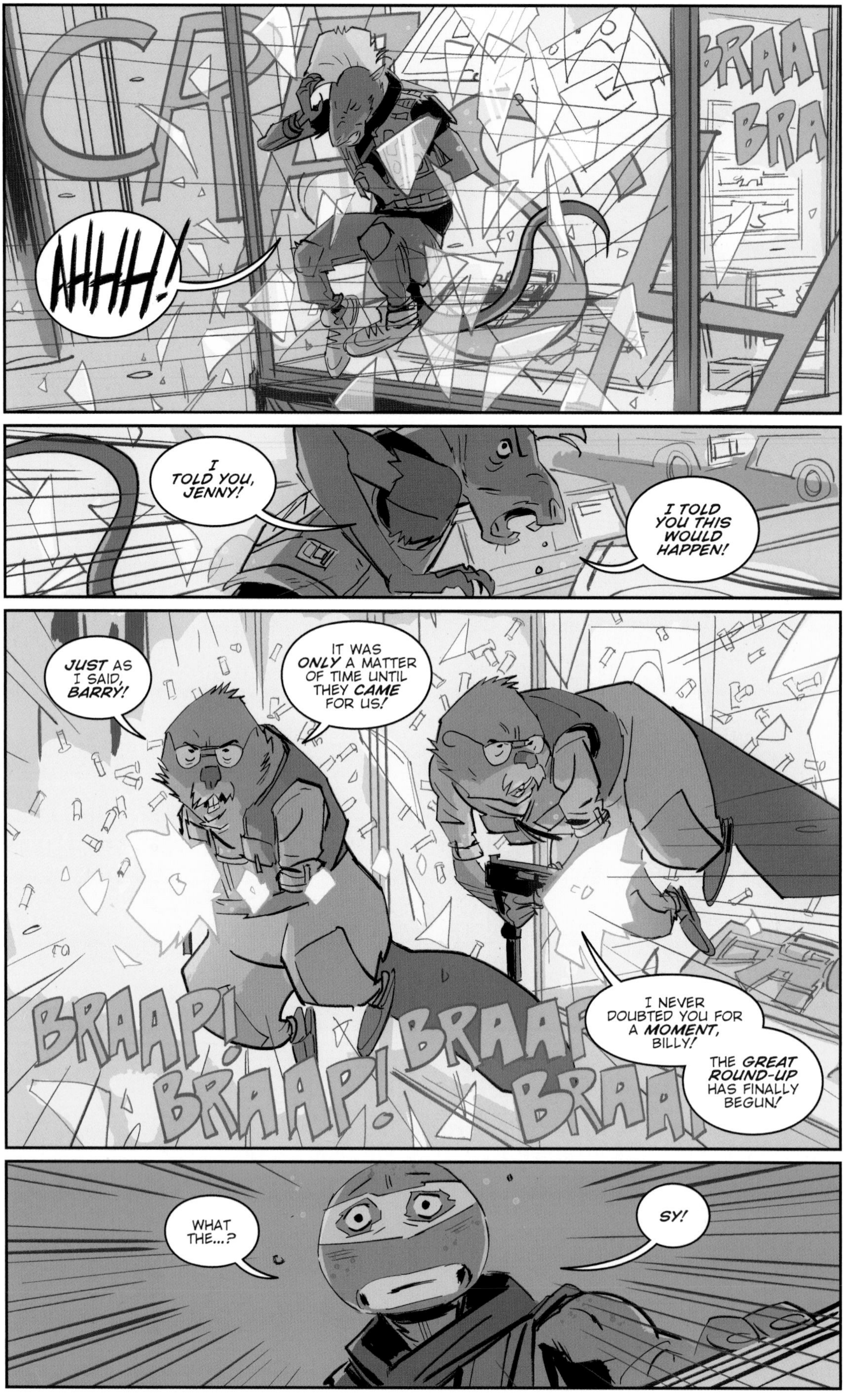

AHHH!
I TOLD YOU, JENNY!
I TOLD YOU THIS WOULD HAPPEN!
JUST AS I SAID, BARRY!
IT WAS ONLY A MATTER OF TIME UNTIL THEY CAME FOR US!
I NEVER DOUBTED YOU FOR A MOMENT, BILLY!
THE GREAT ROUND-UP HAS FINALLY BEGUN!
BRAAP! BRAAP!
WHAT THE...?
SY!

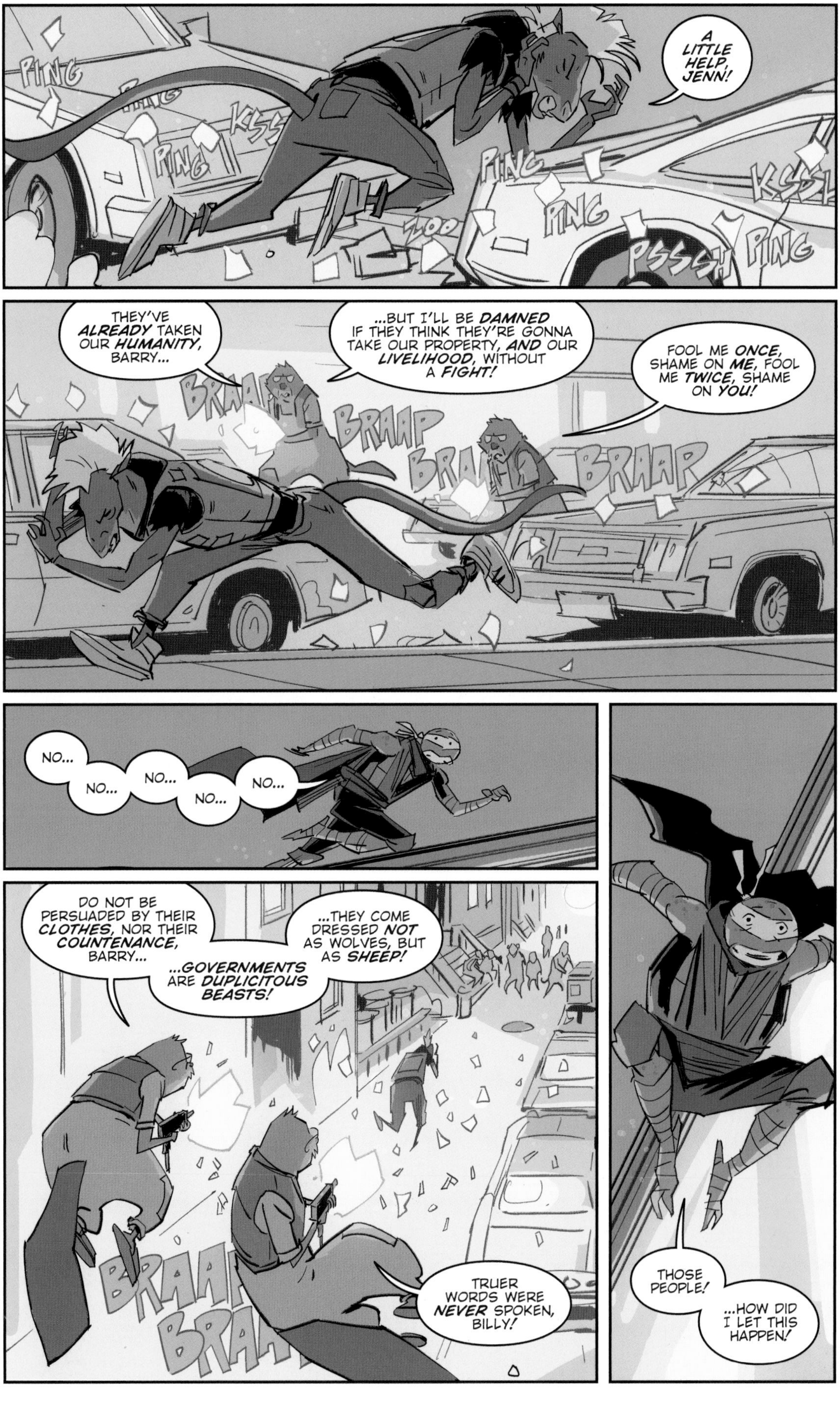
PING
PING
KSSS
PING
A LITTLE HELP, JENN!
PING
PING
ZOO
KSSSL
PSSSH
PING
THEY'VE *ALREADY* TAKEN OUR *HUMANITY*, BARRY...
...BUT I'LL BE *DAMNED* IF THEY THINK THEY'RE GONNA TAKE OUR PROPERTY, *AND* OUR *LIVELIHOOD*, WITHOUT A *FIGHT!*
FOOL ME *ONCE*, SHAME ON *ME*, FOOL ME *TWICE*, SHAME ON *YOU!*
BRAAP
BRAAP
BRAAP
BRAAP
NO...
NO...
NO...
NO...
NO...
DO NOT BE PERSUADED BY THEIR *CLOTHES*, NOR THEIR *COUNTENANCE*, BARRY...
...*GOVERNMENTS* ARE *DUPLICITOUS BEASTS!*
...THEY COME DRESSED *NOT* AS WOLVES, BUT AS *SHEEP!*
TRUER WORDS WERE *NEVER* SPOKEN, BILLY!
THOSE PEOPLE!
...HOW DID I LET THIS HAPPEN!

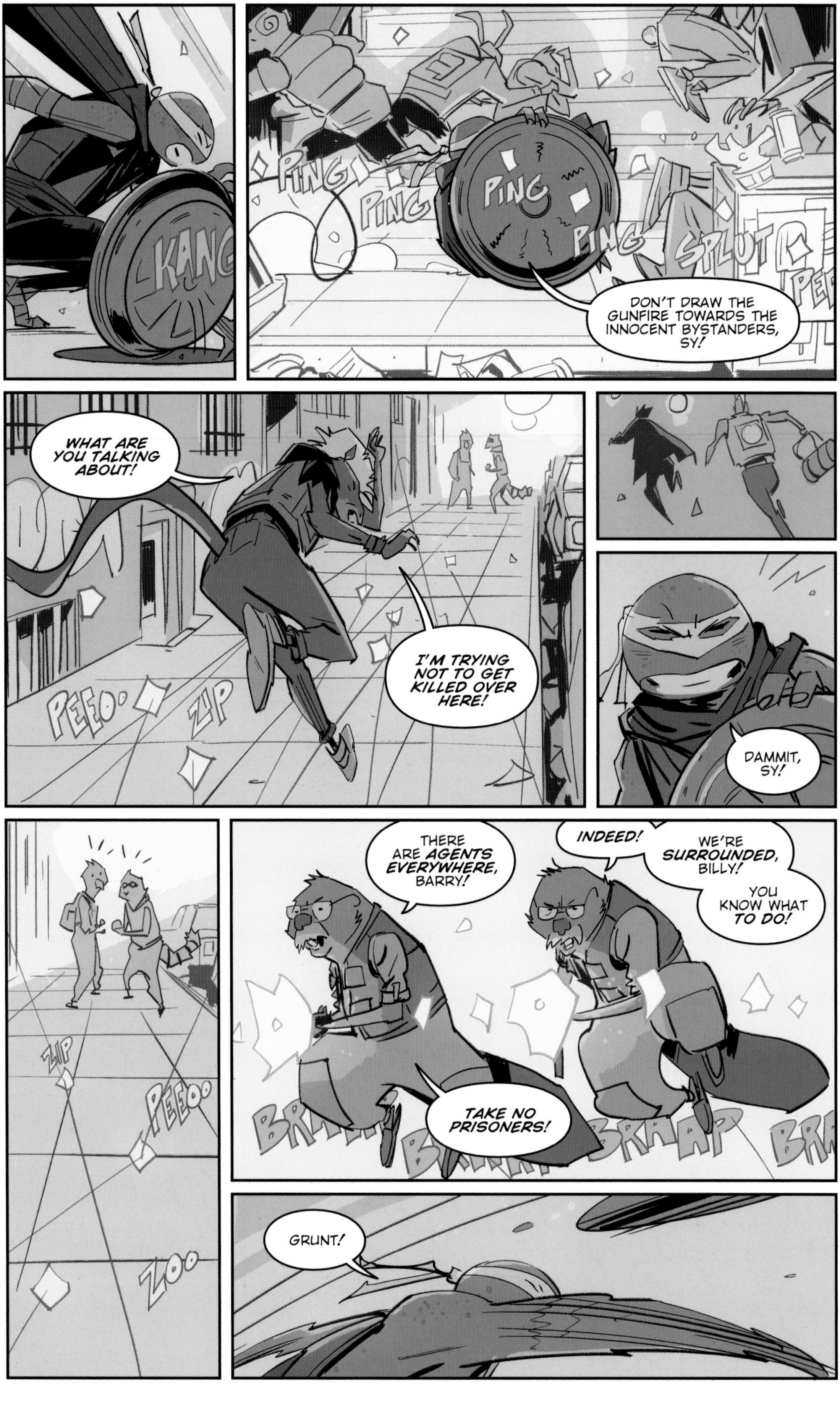
KANG
PING
PING
PING
PING
SPLUT
DON'T DRAW THE GUNFIRE TOWARDS THE INNOCENT BYSTANDERS, SY!
WHAT ARE YOU TALKING ABOUT!
I'M TRYING NOT TO GET KILLED OVER HERE!
PEEOO
ZIP
DAMMIT, SY!
ZIP
PEEOO
ZOO
THERE ARE AGENTS EVERYWHERE, BARRY!
INDEED!
WE'RE SURROUNDED, BILLY!
YOU KNOW WHAT TO DO!
TAKE NO PRISONERS!
BRAAP
GRUNT!

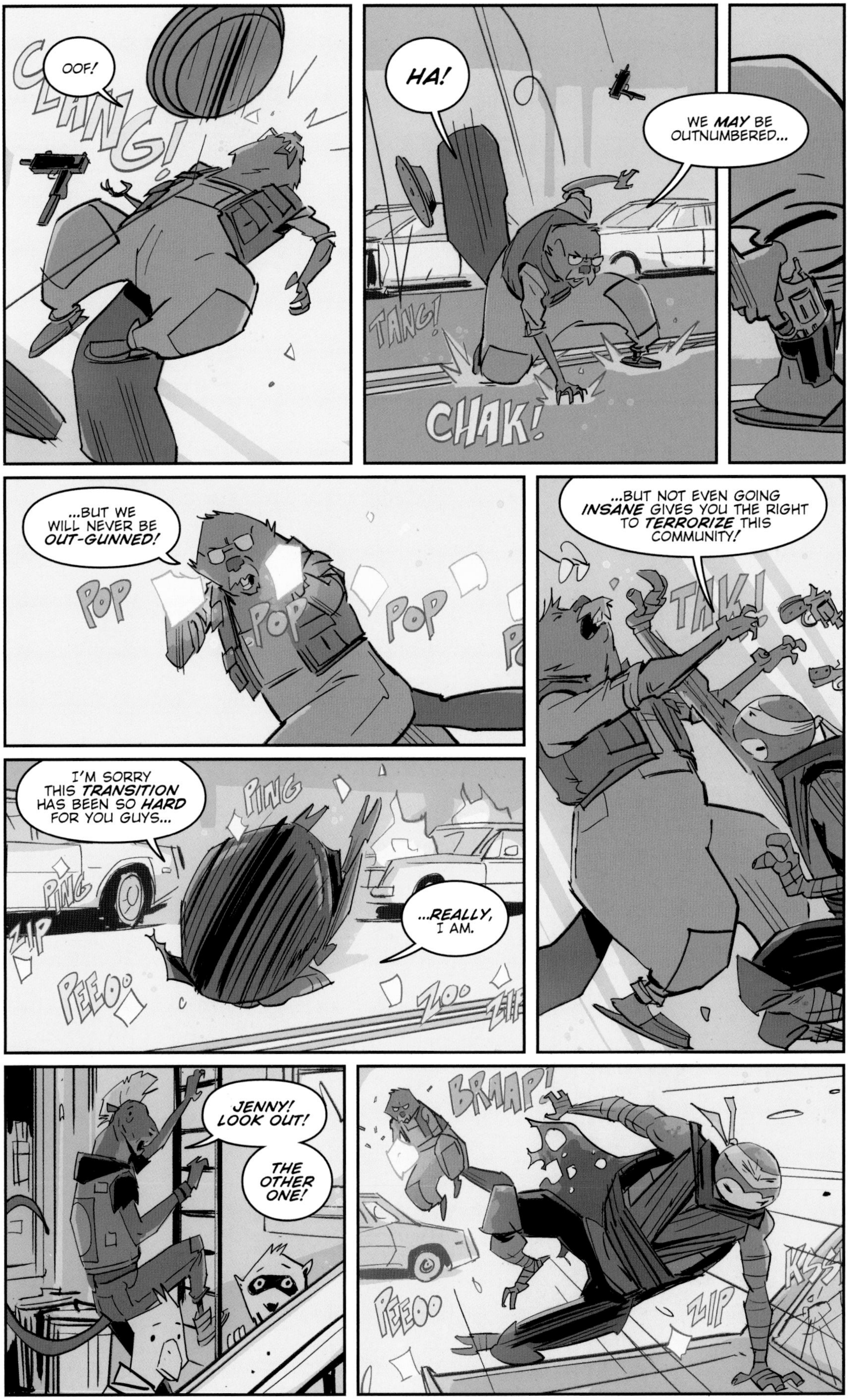

CLANG!
OOF!
HA!
TANG!
CHAK!
WE MAY BE OUTNUMBERED...
...BUT WE WILL NEVER BE OUT-GUNNED!
POP
POP
POP
...BUT NOT EVEN GOING INSANE GIVES YOU THE RIGHT TO TERRORIZE THIS COMMUNITY!
TAK!
I'M SORRY THIS TRANSITION HAS BEEN SO HARD FOR YOU GUYS...
PING
PING
...REALLY, I AM.
ZIP
PEEOO
ZOO
JENNY! LOOK OUT!
THE OTHER ONE!
BRAAP!
PEEOO
ZIP

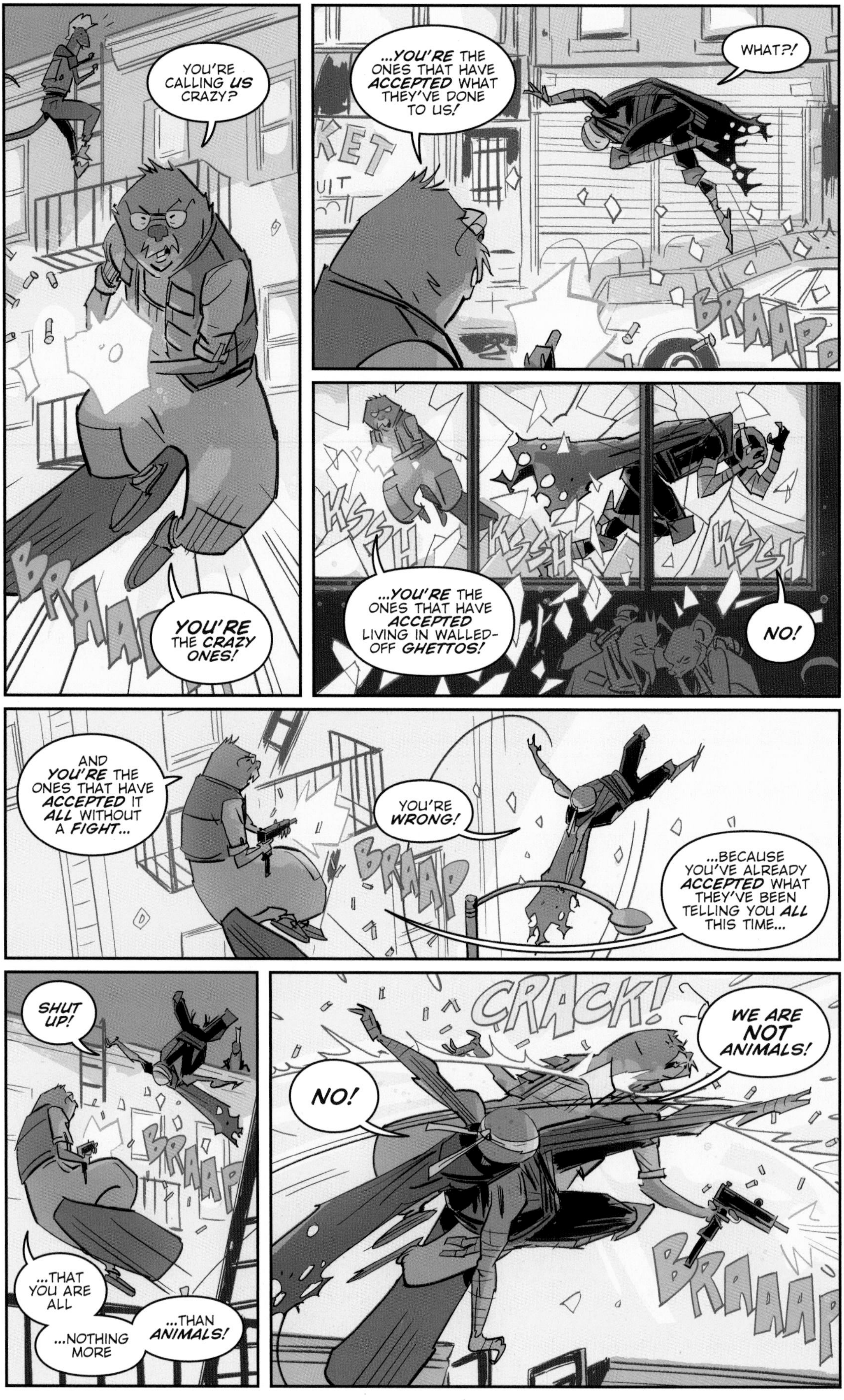
YOU'RE CALLING US CRAZY?
...YOU'RE THE ONES THAT HAVE ACCEPTED WHAT THEY'VE DONE TO US!
WHAT?!
KET
UIT
BRAAAP
BRAAAP
YOU'RE THE CRAZY ONES!
KSSH
KSSH
KSSH
...YOU'RE THE ONES THAT HAVE ACCEPTED LIVING IN WALLED-OFF GHETTOS!
NO!
AND YOU'RE THE ONES THAT HAVE ACCEPTED IT ALL WITHOUT A FIGHT...
YOU'RE WRONG!
BRAAAP
...BECAUSE YOU'VE ALREADY ACCEPTED WHAT THEY'VE BEEN TELLING YOU ALL THIS TIME...
SHUT UP!
BRAAAP
...THAT YOU ARE ALL
...NOTHING MORE
...THAN ANIMALS!
CRACK!
WE ARE NOT ANIMALS!
NO!
BRAAAP

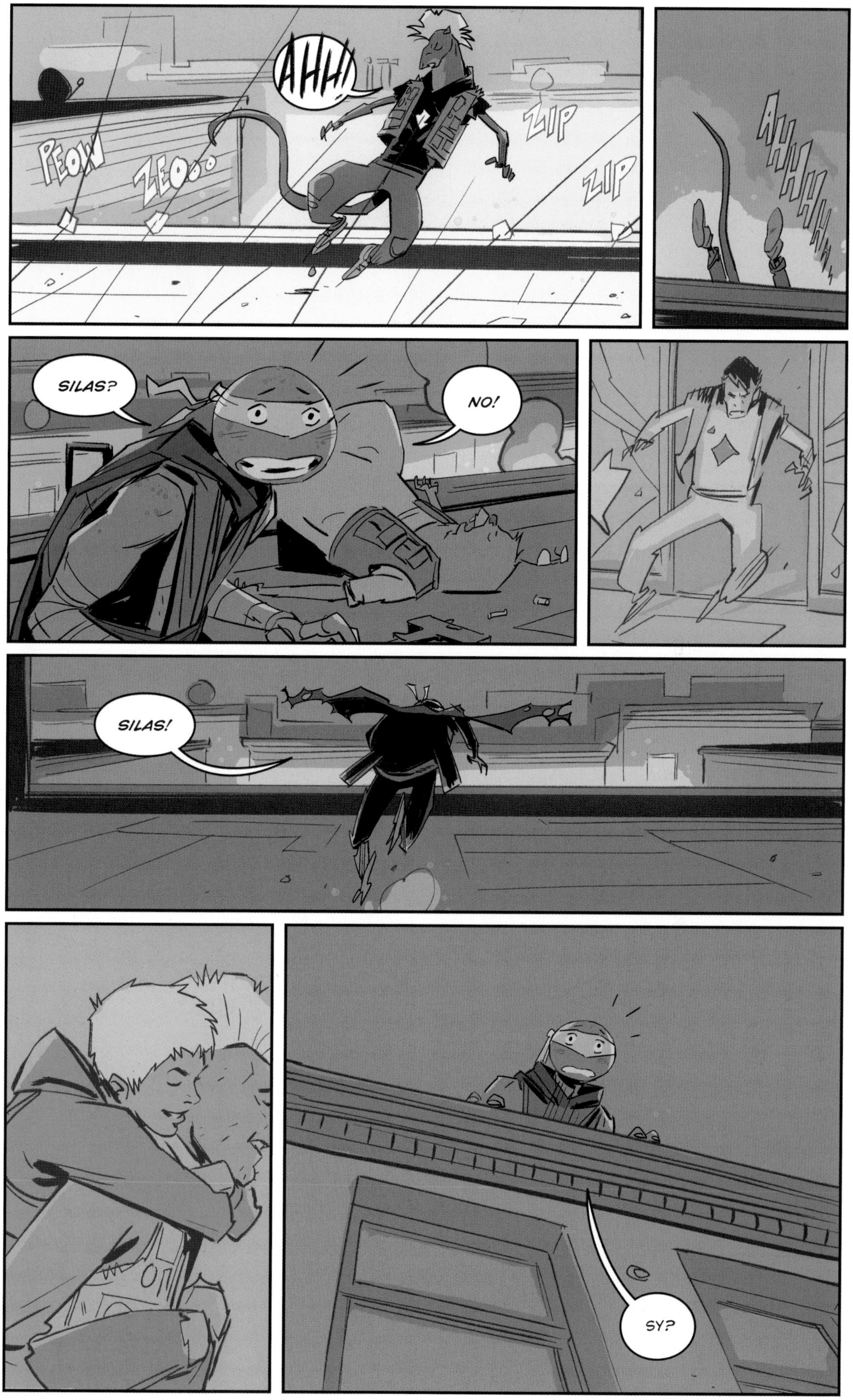

AHH!
PEOW
ZEOoo
ZIP
ZIP
AHHHHHH
SILAS?
NO!
SILAS!
SY?

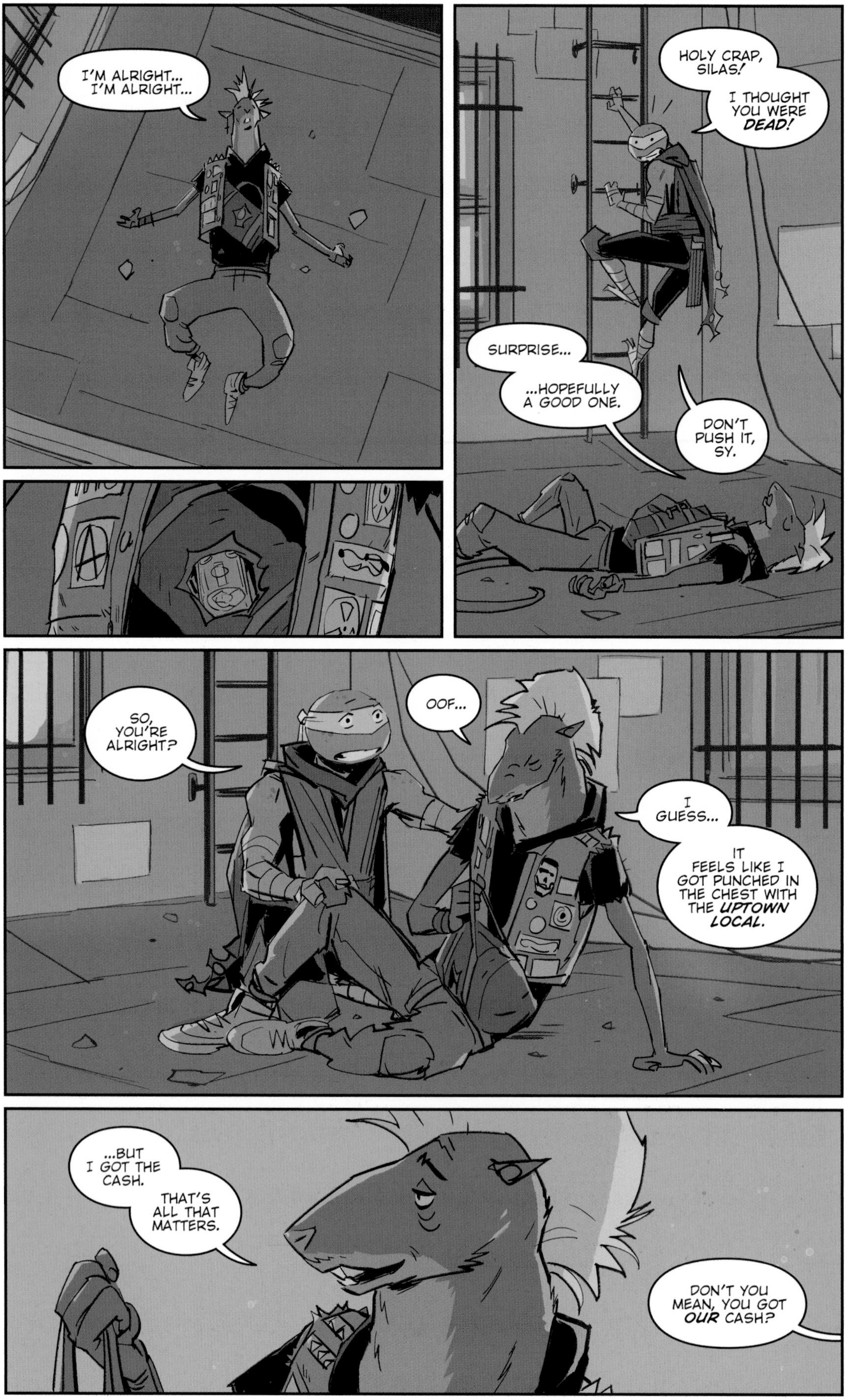
I'M ALRIGHT... I'M ALRIGHT...
HOLY CRAP, SILAS!
I THOUGHT YOU WERE DEAD!
SURPRISE...
...HOPEFULLY A GOOD ONE.
DON'T PUSH IT, SY.
SO, YOU'RE ALRIGHT?
OOF...
I GUESS...
IT FEELS LIKE I GOT PUNCHED IN THE CHEST WITH THE UPTOWN LOCAL.
...BUT I GOT THE CASH.
THAT'S ALL THAT MATTERS.
DON'T YOU MEAN, YOU GOT OUR CASH?

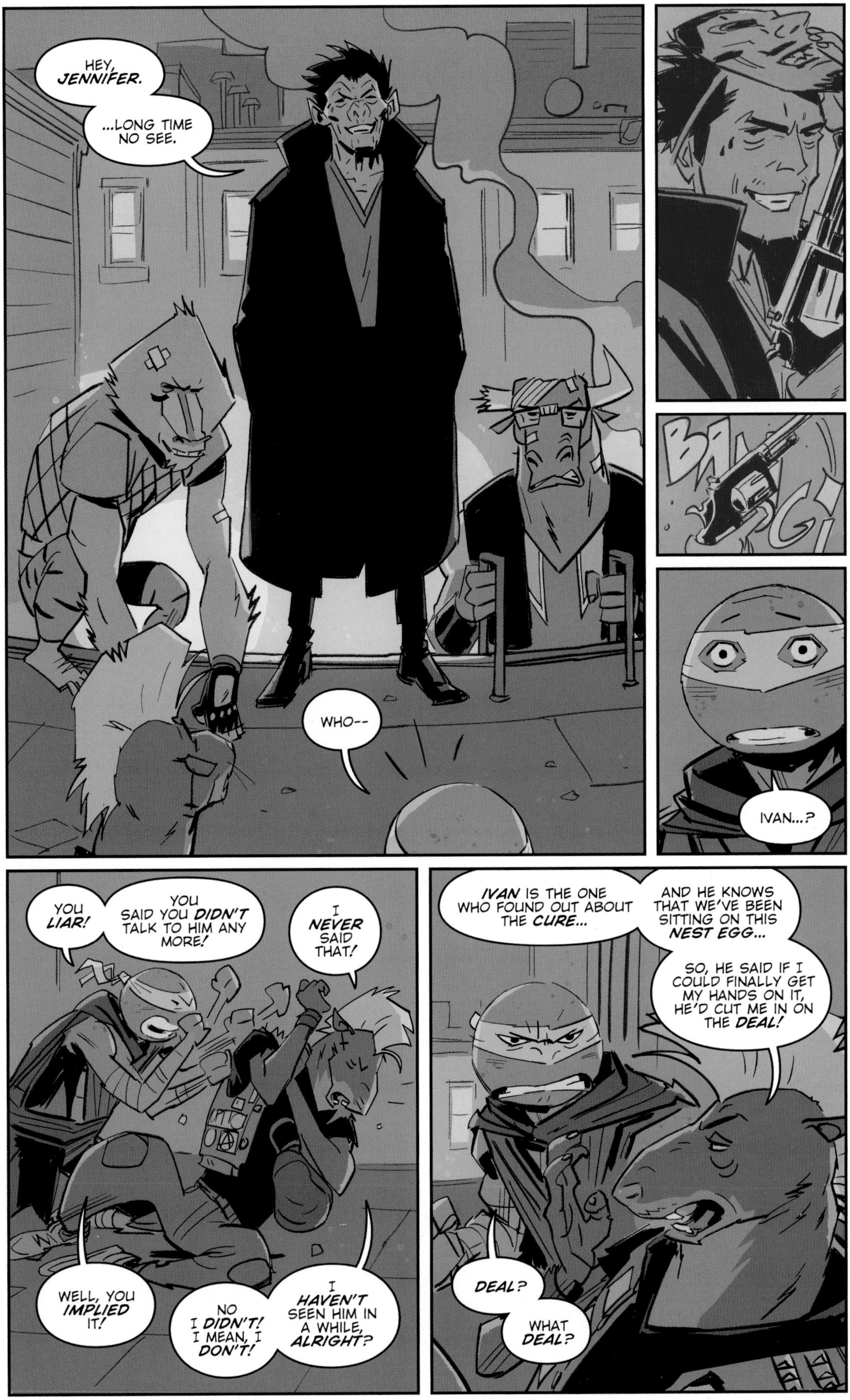
HEY, JENNIFER.
...LONG TIME NO SEE.
WHO--
IVAN...?
YOU LIAR!
YOU SAID YOU DIDN'T TALK TO HIM ANY MORE!
I NEVER SAID THAT!
WELL, YOU IMPLIED IT!
NO I DIDN'T! I MEAN, I DON'T!
I HAVEN'T SEEN HIM IN A WHILE, ALRIGHT?
IVAN IS THE ONE WHO FOUND OUT ABOUT THE CURE...
AND HE KNOWS THAT WE'VE BEEN SITTING ON THIS NEST EGG...
SO, HE SAID IF I COULD FINALLY GET MY HANDS ON IT, HE'D CUT ME IN ON THE DEAL!
DEAL?
WHAT DEAL?

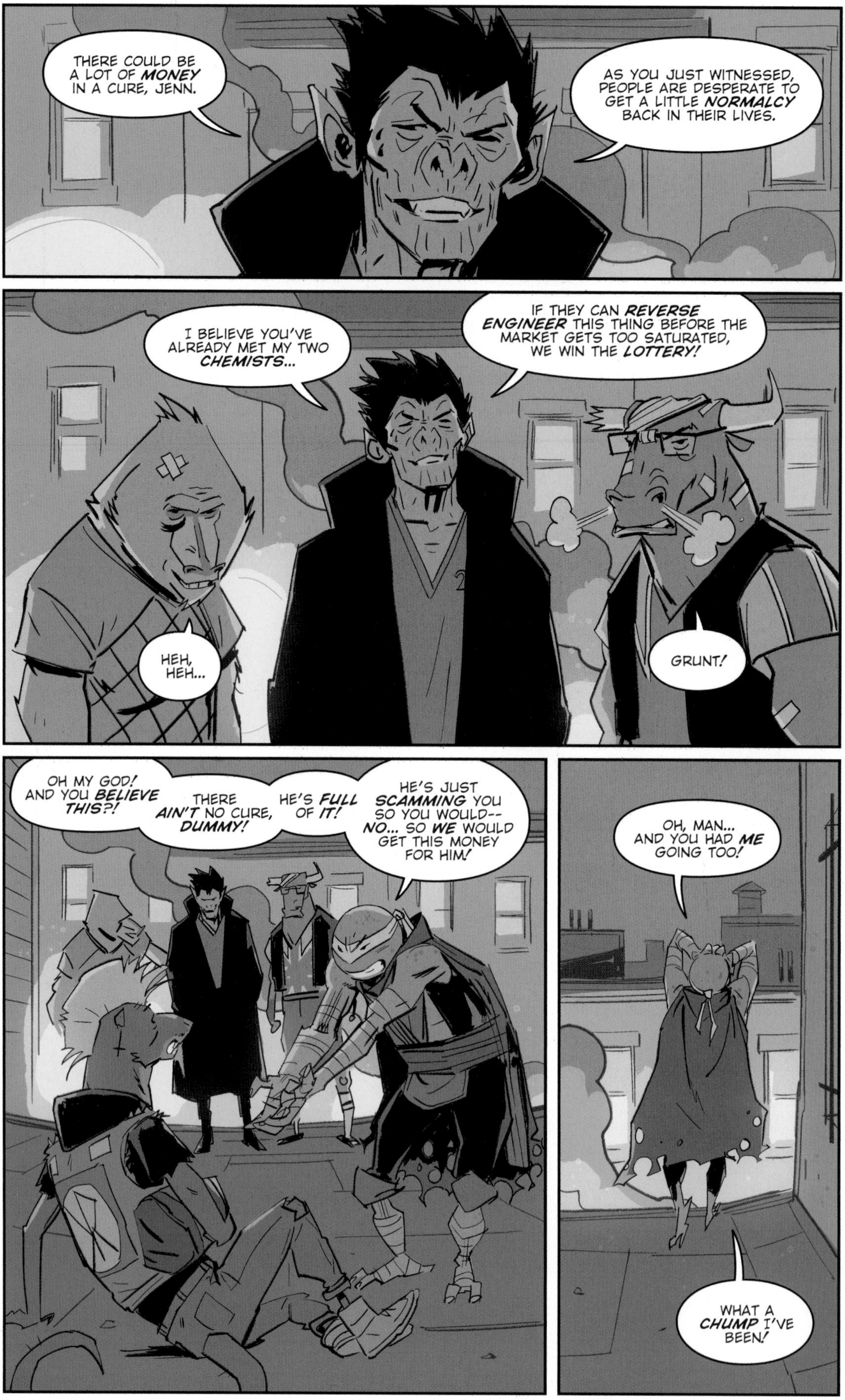

THERE COULD BE A LOT OF MONEY IN A CURE, JENN.
AS YOU JUST WITNESSED, PEOPLE ARE DESPERATE TO GET A LITTLE NORMALCY BACK IN THEIR LIVES.
I BELIEVE YOU'VE ALREADY MET MY TWO CHEMISTS...
IF THEY CAN REVERSE ENGINEER THIS THING BEFORE THE MARKET GETS TOO SATURATED, WE WIN THE LOTTERY!
HEH, HEH...
GRUNT!
OH MY GOD! AND YOU BELIEVE THIS?!
THERE AIN'T NO CURE, DUMMY!
HE'S FULL OF IT!
HE'S JUST SCAMMING YOU SO YOU WOULD-- NO... SO WE WOULD GET THIS MONEY FOR HIM!
OH, MAN... AND YOU HAD ME GOING TOO!
WHAT A CHUMP I'VE BEEN!

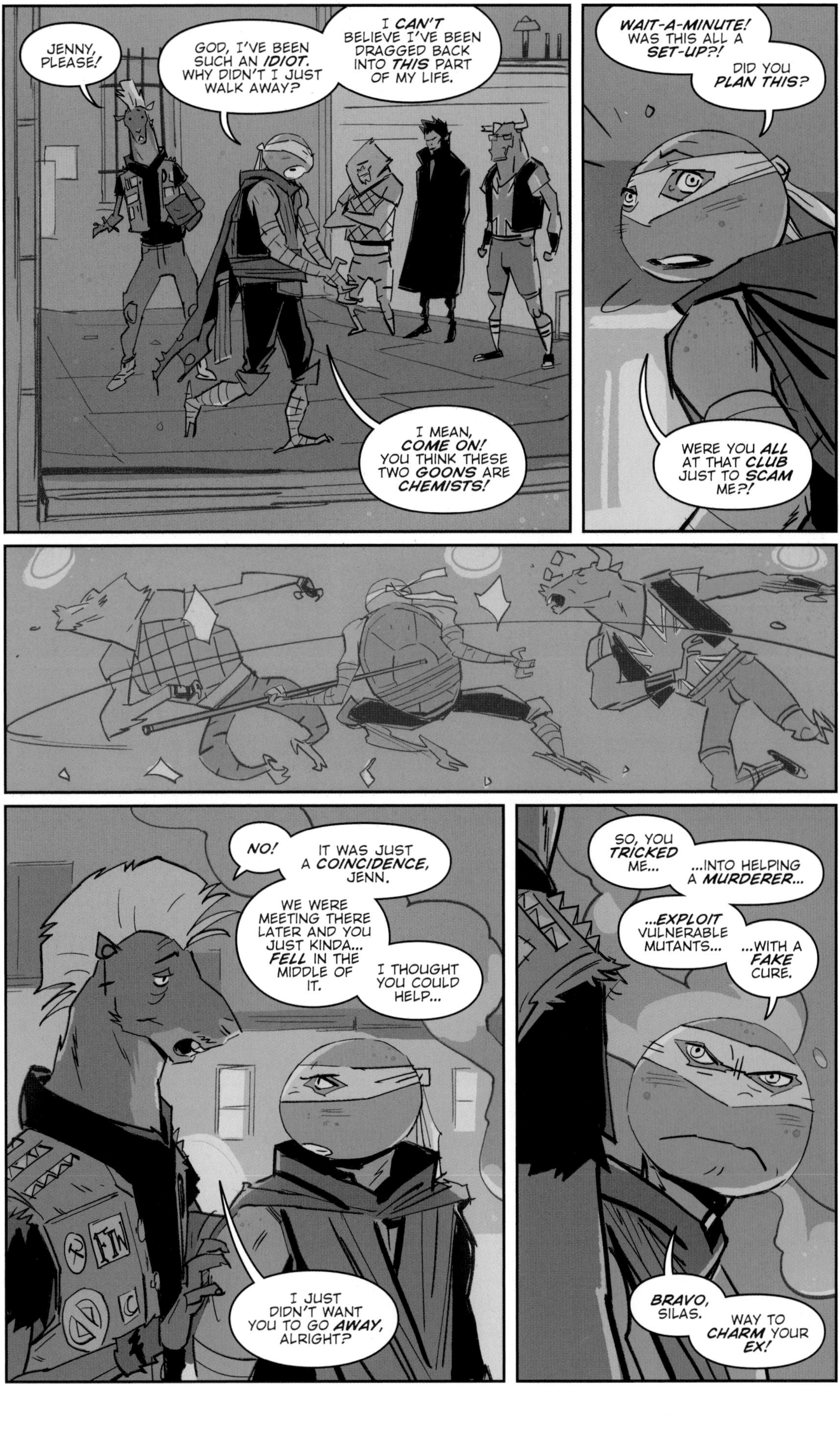

JENNY, PLEASE!
GOD, I'VE BEEN SUCH AN *IDIOT*. WHY DIDN'T I JUST WALK AWAY?
I *CAN'T* BELIEVE I'VE BEEN DRAGGED BACK INTO *THIS* PART OF MY LIFE.
I MEAN, *COME ON!* YOU THINK THESE TWO *GOONS* ARE *CHEMISTS!*
WAIT-A-MINUTE! WAS THIS ALL A *SET-UP?!*
DID YOU *PLAN THIS?*
WERE YOU *ALL* AT THAT *CLUB* JUST TO *SCAM* ME?!
NO!
IT WAS JUST A *COINCIDENCE*, JENN.
WE WERE MEETING THERE LATER AND YOU JUST KINDA... *FELL* IN THE MIDDLE OF IT.
I THOUGHT YOU COULD HELP...
I JUST DIDN'T WANT YOU TO GO *AWAY*, ALRIGHT?
SO, YOU *TRICKED* ME...
...INTO HELPING A *MURDERER*...
...*EXPLOIT* VULNERABLE MUTANTS...
...WITH A *FAKE* CURE.
BRAVO, SILAS.
WAY TO *CHARM* YOUR *EX!*

MURDERER?

HEH, HEH...

WELL, SOMETHING TELLS ME THAT YOUR HANDS *AIN'T* EXACTLY AS CLEAN AS THEY *USED* TO BE, EITHER.

...ARE THEY, *JENNIFER?*

THE NAME IS *JENNIKA.*

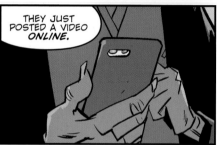
WELL, *JENNIKA,* I HATE TO BREAK IT TO YOU, BUT THE CURE IS *REAL!*

...AND I CAN *PROVE* IT!

THEY JUST POSTED A VIDEO *ONLINE.*

THERE'S NO AUDIO...

00:02

00:05

00:10

00:14

00:19

00:23

00:37

HA! I *TOLD* YOU, JENN!

IT'S *REAL!*

NO WAY...

SO WHAT DO YOU THINK, *JENNIKA?*

IN FOR A PENNY, IN FOR A POUND?

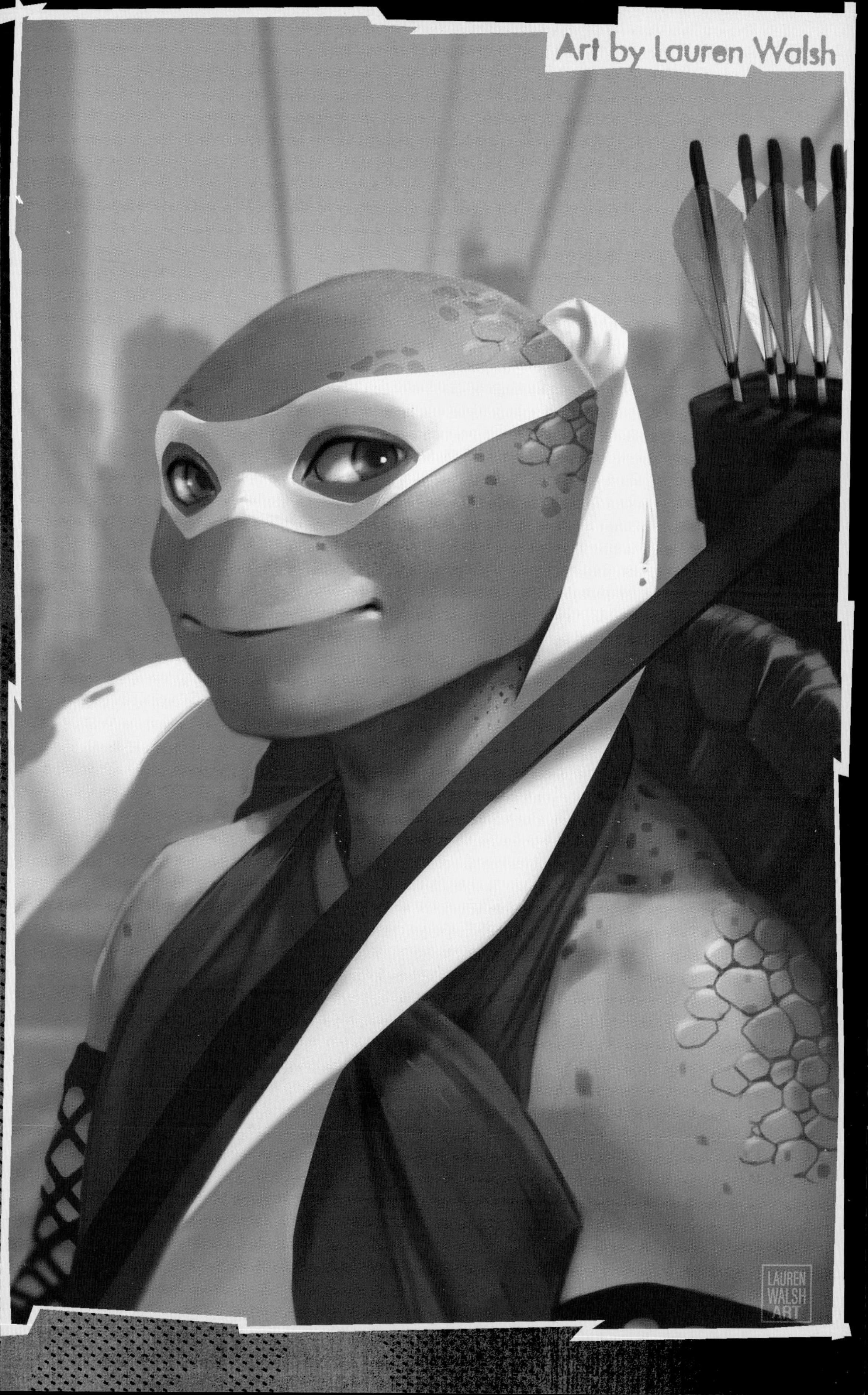
LAUREN
WALSH
ART

Art by Lauren Walsh

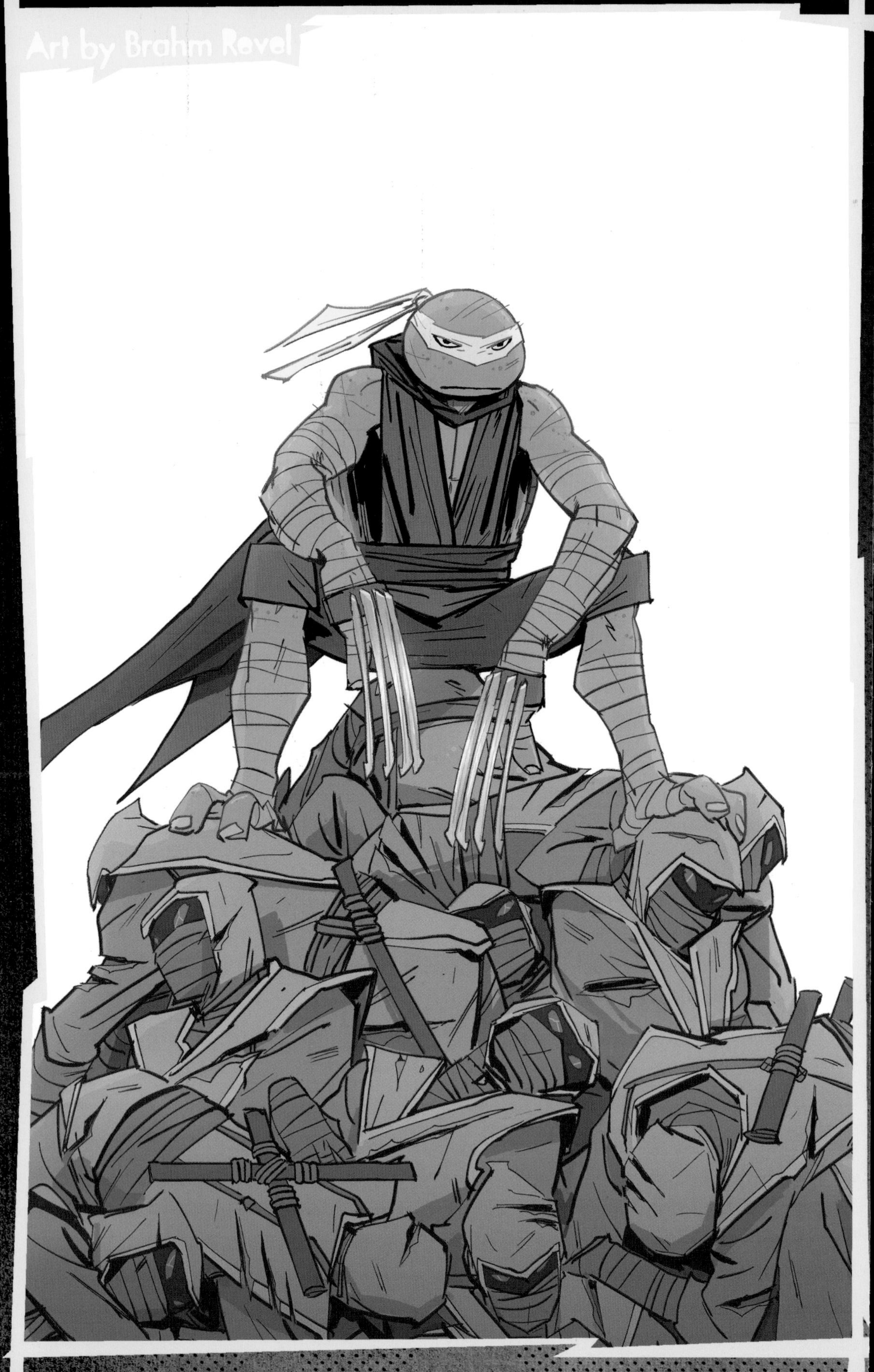
Art by Brahm Revel

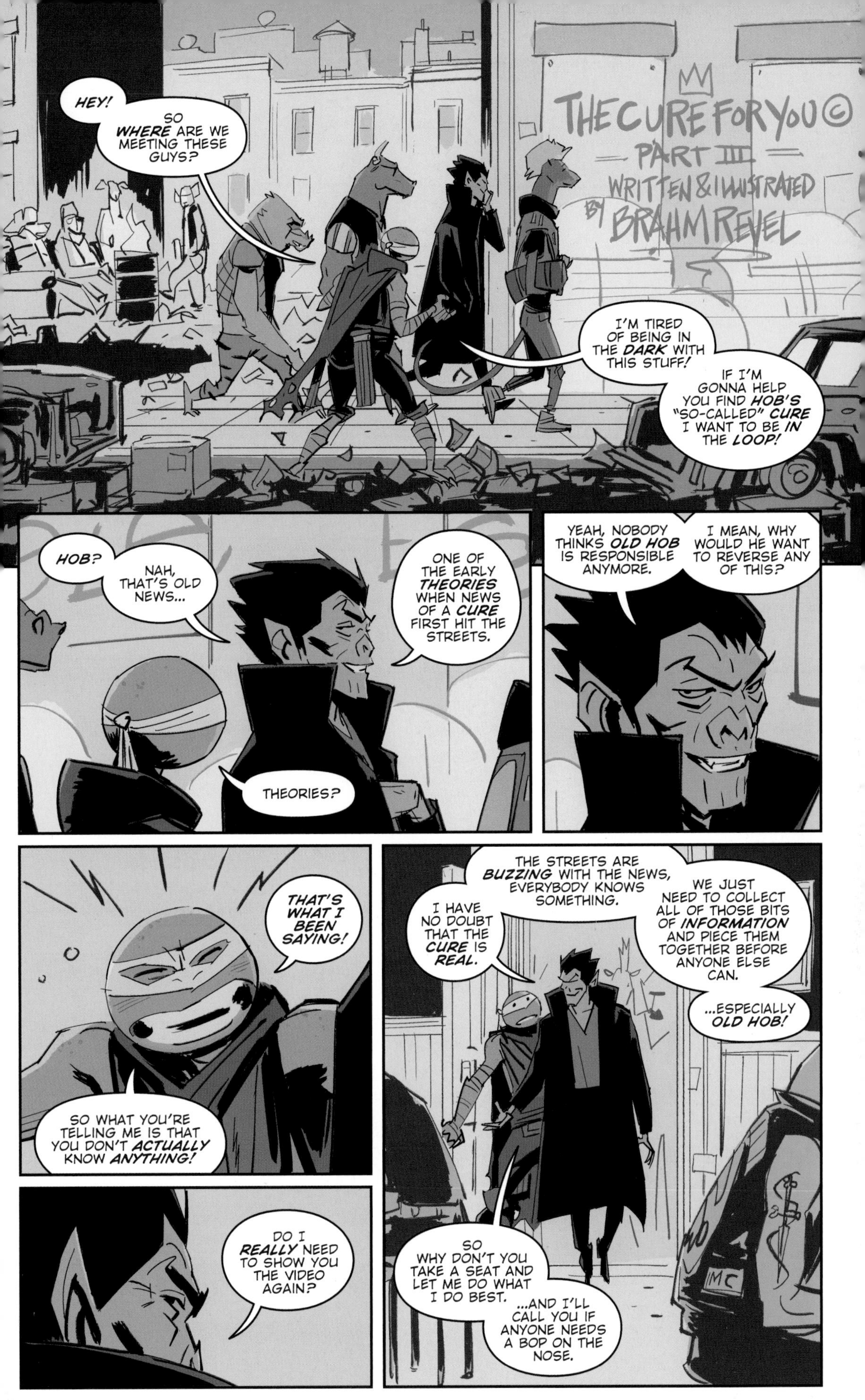
HEY!
SO WHERE ARE WE MEETING THESE GUYS?
THE CURE FOR YOU ©
PART III
WRITTEN & ILLUSTRATED BY BRAHM REVEL
I'M TIRED OF BEING IN THE DARK WITH THIS STUFF!
IF I'M GONNA HELP YOU FIND HOB'S "SO-CALLED" CURE I WANT TO BE IN THE LOOP!
HOB?
NAH, THAT'S OLD NEWS...
ONE OF THE EARLY THEORIES WHEN NEWS OF A CURE FIRST HIT THE STREETS.
THEORIES?
YEAH, NOBODY THINKS OLD HOB IS RESPONSIBLE ANYMORE.
I MEAN, WHY WOULD HE WANT TO REVERSE ANY OF THIS?
THAT'S WHAT I BEEN SAYING!
SO WHAT YOU'RE TELLING ME IS THAT YOU DON'T ACTUALLY KNOW ANYTHING!
DO I REALLY NEED TO SHOW YOU THE VIDEO AGAIN?
THE STREETS ARE BUZZING WITH THE NEWS, EVERYBODY KNOWS SOMETHING.
I HAVE NO DOUBT THAT THE CURE IS REAL.
WE JUST NEED TO COLLECT ALL OF THOSE BITS OF INFORMATION AND PIECE THEM TOGETHER BEFORE ANYONE ELSE CAN.
...ESPECIALLY OLD HOB!
SO WHY DON'T YOU TAKE A SEAT AND LET ME DO WHAT I DO BEST.
...AND I'LL CALL YOU IF ANYONE NEEDS A BOP ON THE NOSE.

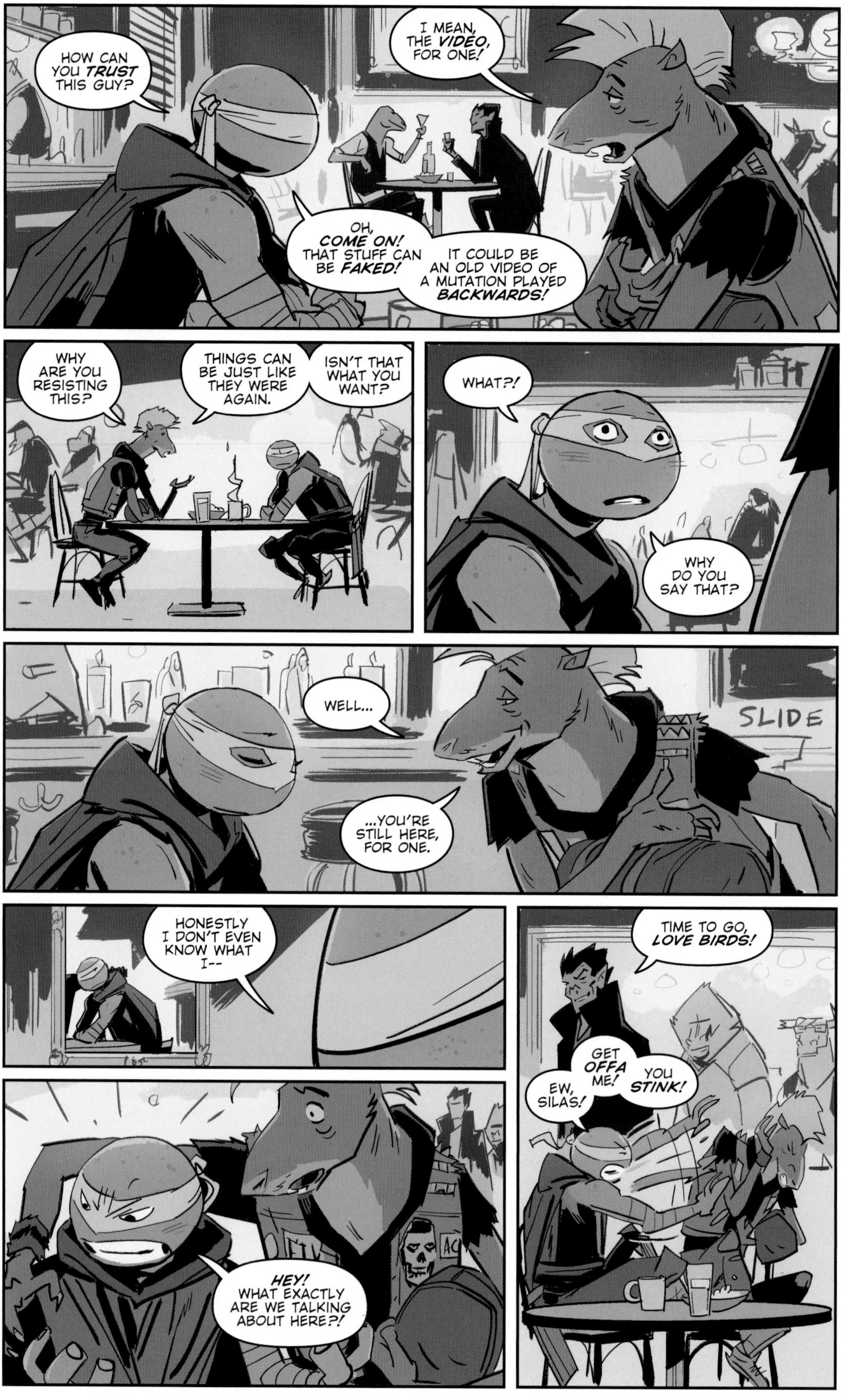
HOW CAN YOU TRUST THIS GUY?
I MEAN, THE VIDEO, FOR ONE!
OH, COME ON! THAT STUFF CAN BE FAKED!
IT COULD BE AN OLD VIDEO OF A MUTATION PLAYED BACKWARDS!
WHY ARE YOU RESISTING THIS?
THINGS CAN BE JUST LIKE THEY WERE AGAIN.
ISN'T THAT WHAT YOU WANT?
WHAT?!
WHY DO YOU SAY THAT?
WELL...
...YOU'RE STILL HERE, FOR ONE.
SLIDE
HONESTLY I DON'T EVEN KNOW WHAT I--
HEY! WHAT EXACTLY ARE WE TALKING ABOUT HERE?!
TIME TO GO, LOVE BIRDS!
EW, SILAS!
GET OFFA ME!
YOU STINK!

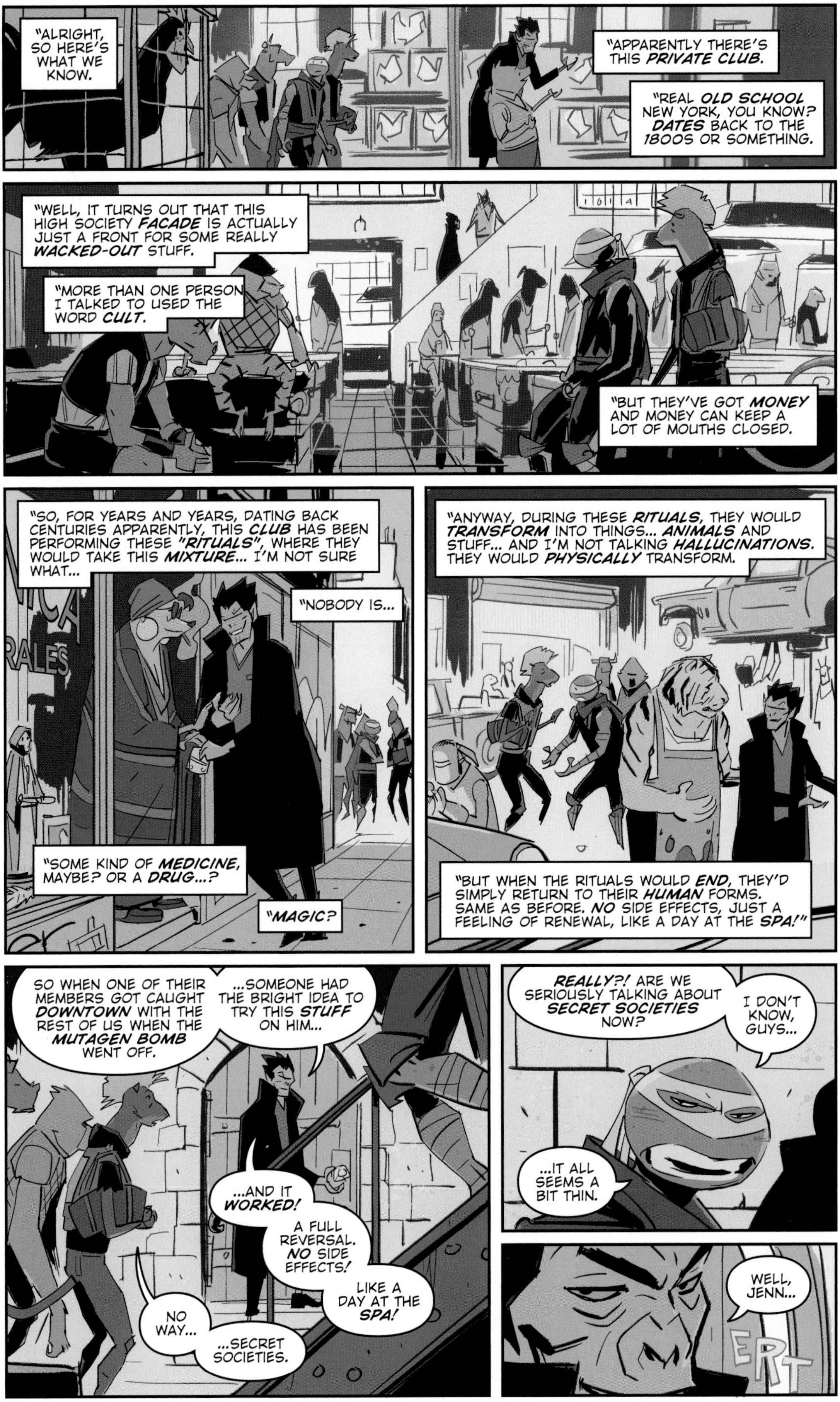
"ALRIGHT, SO HERE'S WHAT WE KNOW.
"APPARENTLY THERE'S THIS PRIVATE CLUB.
"REAL OLD SCHOOL NEW YORK, YOU KNOW? DATES BACK TO THE 1800S OR SOMETHING.
"WELL, IT TURNS OUT THAT THIS HIGH SOCIETY FACADE IS ACTUALLY JUST A FRONT FOR SOME REALLY WACKED-OUT STUFF.
"MORE THAN ONE PERSON I TALKED TO USED THE WORD CULT.
"BUT THEY'VE GOT MONEY AND MONEY CAN KEEP A LOT OF MOUTHS CLOSED.
"SO, FOR YEARS AND YEARS, DATING BACK CENTURIES APPARENTLY, THIS CLUB HAS BEEN PERFORMING THESE "RITUALS", WHERE THEY WOULD TAKE THIS MIXTURE... I'M NOT SURE WHAT...
"NOBODY IS...
"SOME KIND OF MEDICINE, MAYBE? OR A DRUG...?
"MAGIC?
"ANYWAY, DURING THESE RITUALS, THEY WOULD TRANSFORM INTO THINGS... ANIMALS AND STUFF... AND I'M NOT TALKING HALLUCINATIONS. THEY WOULD PHYSICALLY TRANSFORM.
"BUT WHEN THE RITUALS WOULD END, THEY'D SIMPLY RETURN TO THEIR HUMAN FORMS. SAME AS BEFORE. NO SIDE EFFECTS, JUST A FEELING OF RENEWAL, LIKE A DAY AT THE SPA!"
SO WHEN ONE OF THEIR MEMBERS GOT CAUGHT DOWNTOWN WITH THE REST OF US WHEN THE MUTAGEN BOMB WENT OFF.
...SOMEONE HAD THE BRIGHT IDEA TO TRY THIS STUFF ON HIM...
...AND IT WORKED!
A FULL REVERSAL. NO SIDE EFFECTS!
LIKE A DAY AT THE SPA!
NO WAY...
...SECRET SOCIETIES.
REALLY?! ARE WE SERIOUSLY TALKING ABOUT SECRET SOCIETIES NOW?
I DON'T KNOW, GUYS...
...IT ALL SEEMS A BIT THIN.
WELL, JENN...
ERT

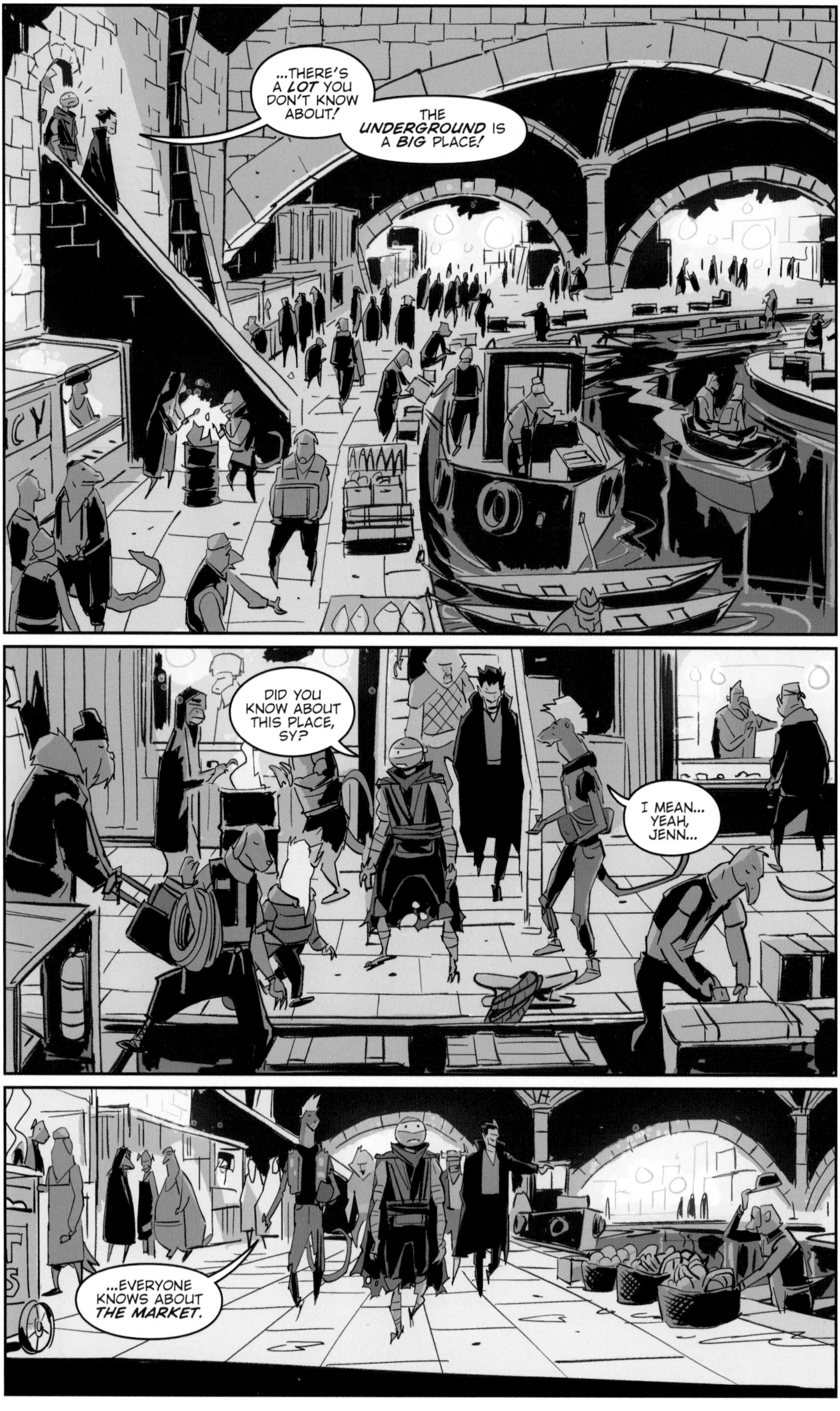
...THERE'S A *LOT* YOU DON'T KNOW ABOUT!
THE *UNDERGROUND* IS A *BIG* PLACE!
DID YOU KNOW ABOUT THIS PLACE, SY?
I MEAN... YEAH, JENN...
...EVERYONE KNOWS ABOUT *THE MARKET.*

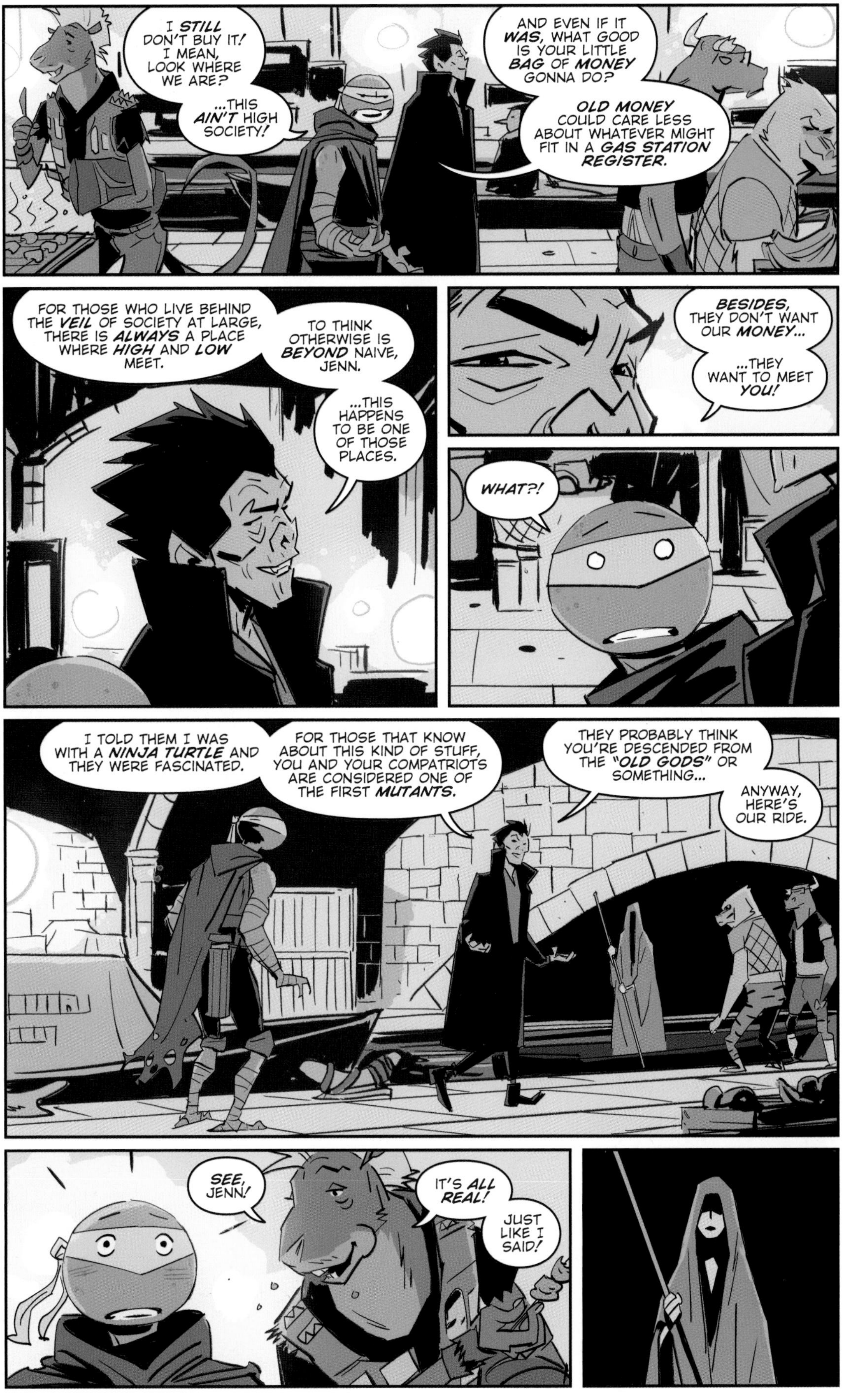

I STILL DON'T BUY IT! I MEAN, LOOK WHERE WE ARE?
...THIS AIN'T HIGH SOCIETY!
AND EVEN IF IT WAS, WHAT GOOD IS YOUR LITTLE BAG OF MONEY GONNA DO?
OLD MONEY COULD CARE LESS ABOUT WHATEVER MIGHT FIT IN A GAS STATION REGISTER.
FOR THOSE WHO LIVE BEHIND THE VEIL OF SOCIETY AT LARGE, THERE IS ALWAYS A PLACE WHERE HIGH AND LOW MEET.
TO THINK OTHERWISE IS BEYOND NAIVE, JENN.
...THIS HAPPENS TO BE ONE OF THOSE PLACES.
BESIDES, THEY DON'T WANT OUR MONEY...
...THEY WANT TO MEET YOU!
WHAT?!
I TOLD THEM I WAS WITH A NINJA TURTLE AND THEY WERE FASCINATED.
FOR THOSE THAT KNOW ABOUT THIS KIND OF STUFF, YOU AND YOUR COMPATRIOTS ARE CONSIDERED ONE OF THE FIRST MUTANTS.
THEY PROBABLY THINK YOU'RE DESCENDED FROM THE "OLD GODS" OR SOMETHING...
ANYWAY, HERE'S OUR RIDE.
SEE, JENN!
IT'S ALL REAL!
JUST LIKE I SAID!

IT'S YOU, ISN'T IT?

...FROM THE *VIDEO*?

YES.

THEN IT'S *TRUE*...?

...IT REALLY WORKS?

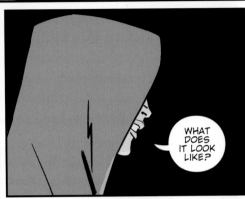

WHAT DOES IT LOOK LIKE?

SO...

...ARE YOU *HAPPY* TO BE BACK TO *NORMAL*?

AND WHY WOULDN'T I BE?

HA HA HA HA HA HA

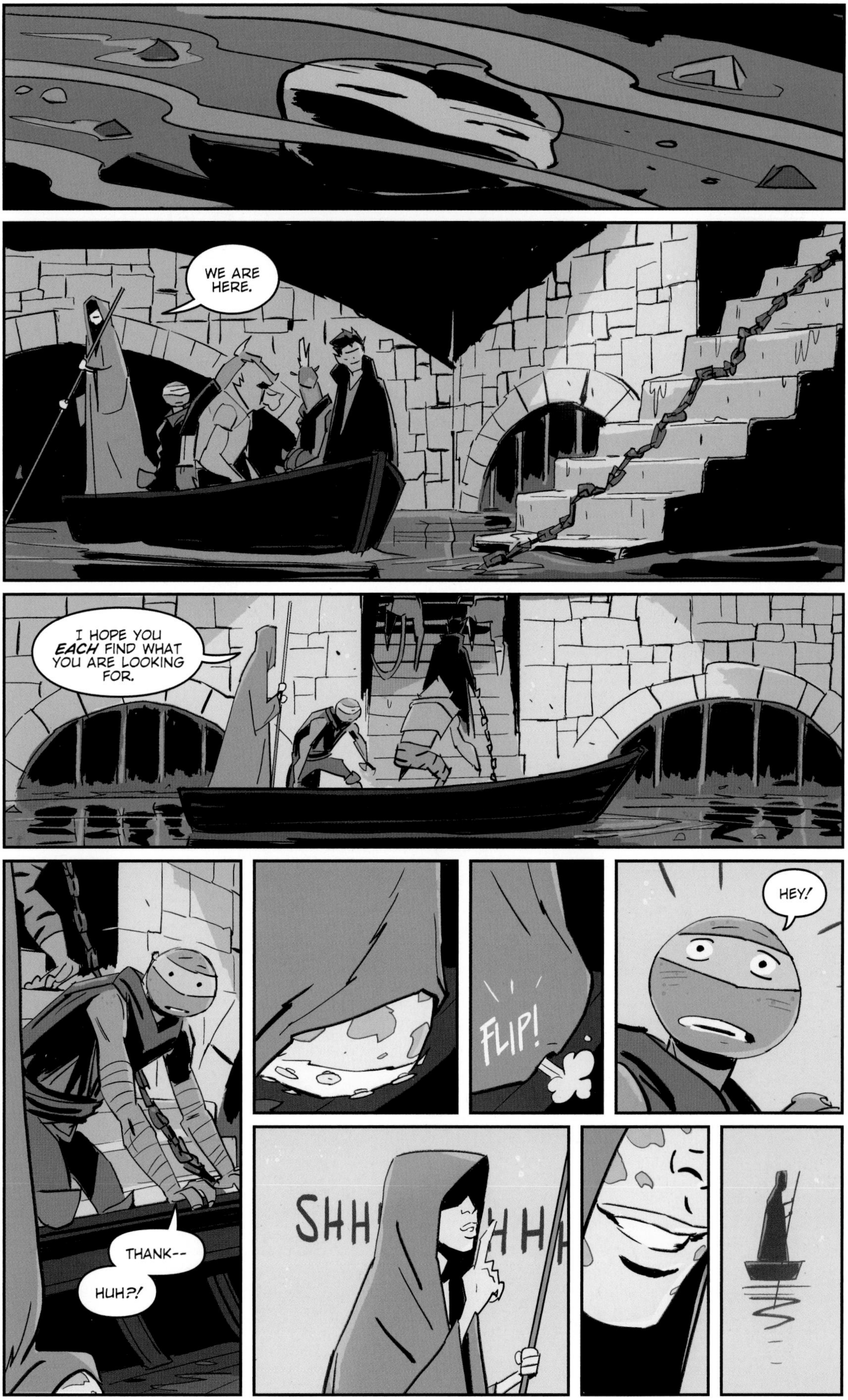
WE ARE HERE.
I HOPE YOU EACH FIND WHAT YOU ARE LOOKING FOR.
THANK--
HUH?!
FLIP!
HEY!
SHHHHHH

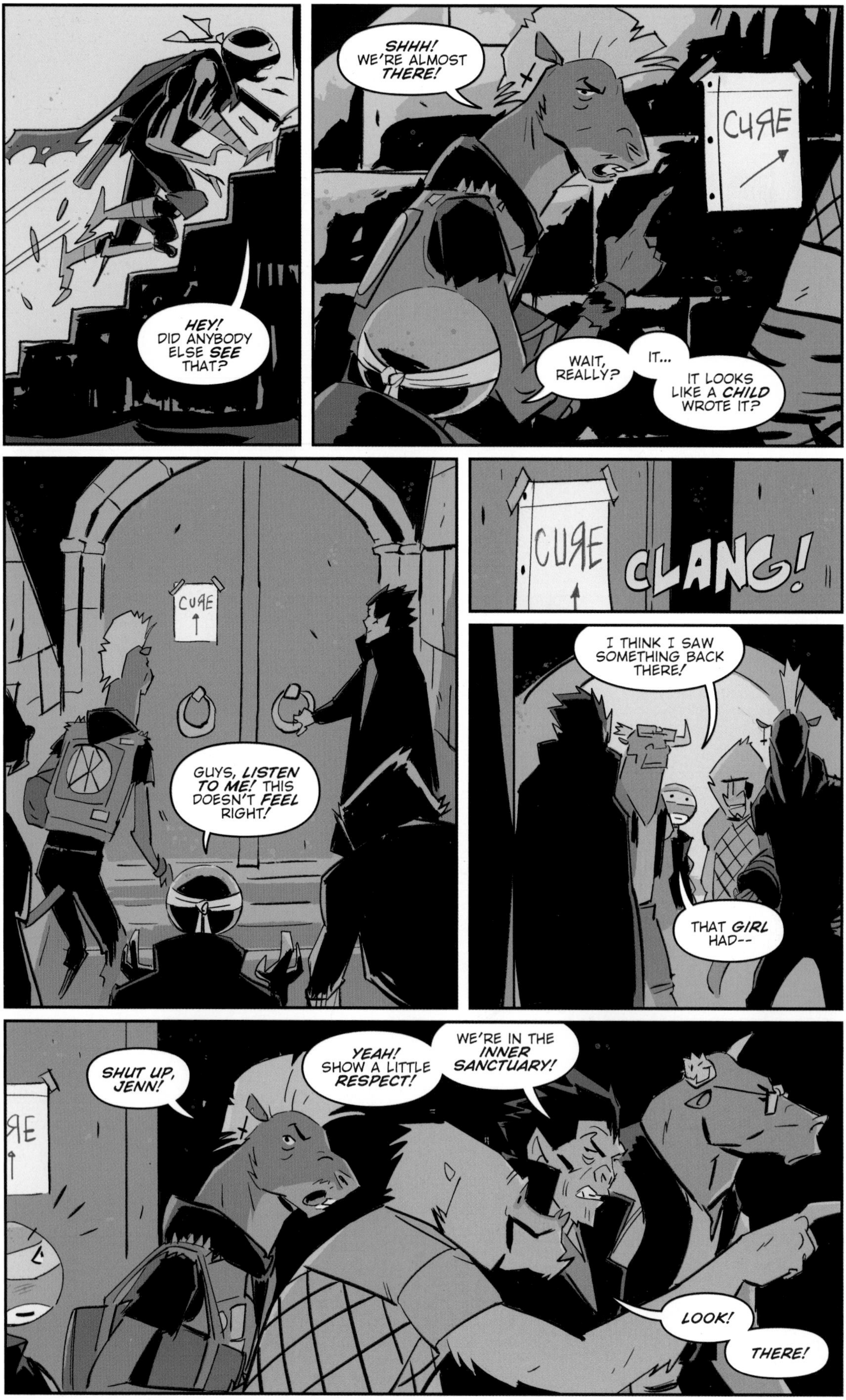
HEY! DID ANYBODY ELSE SEE THAT?
SHHH! WE'RE ALMOST THERE!
CURE
WAIT, REALLY?
IT... IT LOOKS LIKE A CHILD WROTE IT?
CURE
GUYS, LISTEN TO ME! THIS DOESN'T FEEL RIGHT!
CURE
CLANG!
I THINK I SAW SOMETHING BACK THERE!
THAT GIRL HAD--
SHUT UP, JENN!
YEAH! SHOW A LITTLE RESPECT!
WE'RE IN THE INNER SANCTUARY!
LOOK!
THERE!

HERE IT IS.

FINALLY...

SERIOUSLY?!

THIS DOESN'T FEEL *WRONG* TO ANYBODY ELSE?

WOOSH

WOOSH

WOOSH

HELLO?

WE, UH... BID YOU FINE *GENTLEMEN* A GOOD EVENING.

WAIT A MINUTE... THIS PLACE LOOKS *FAMILIAR*...

OH, NO...

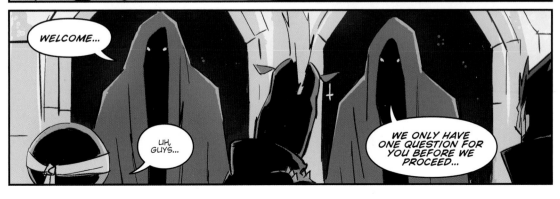

WELCOME...

UH, GUYS...

WE ONLY HAVE ONE QUESTION FOR YOU BEFORE WE PROCEED...

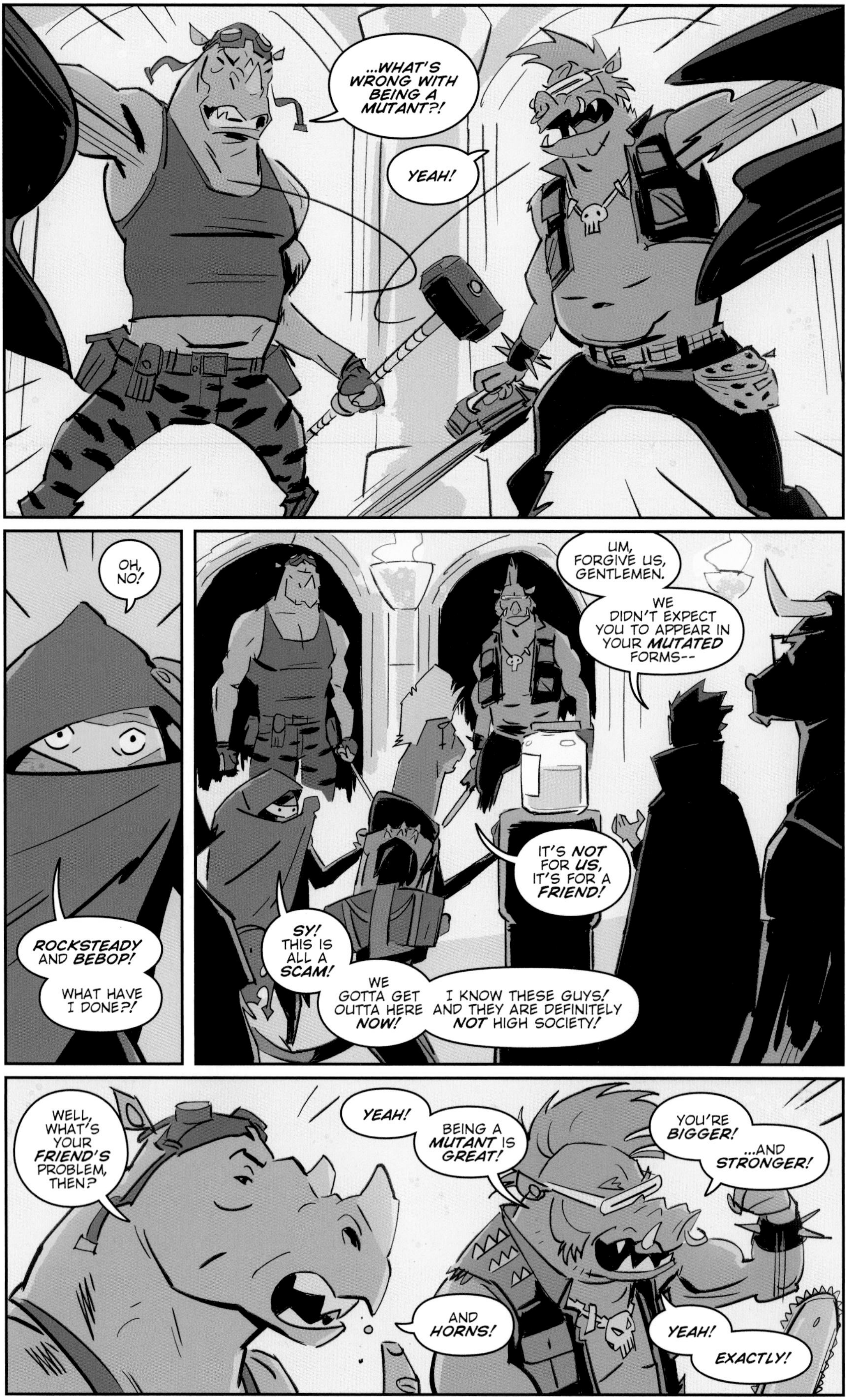
...WHAT'S WRONG WITH BEING A MUTANT?!
YEAH!
OH, NO!
ROCKSTEADY AND BEBOP!
WHAT HAVE I DONE?!
UM, FORGIVE US, GENTLEMEN.
WE DIDN'T EXPECT YOU TO APPEAR IN YOUR MUTATED FORMS--
IT'S NOT FOR US, IT'S FOR A FRIEND!
SY! THIS IS ALL A SCAM!
WE GOTTA GET OUTTA HERE NOW!
I KNOW THESE GUYS! AND THEY ARE DEFINITELY NOT HIGH SOCIETY!
WELL, WHAT'S YOUR FRIEND'S PROBLEM, THEN?
YEAH!
BEING A MUTANT IS GREAT!
YOU'RE BIGGER!
...AND STRONGER!
AND HORNS!
YEAH!
EXACTLY!

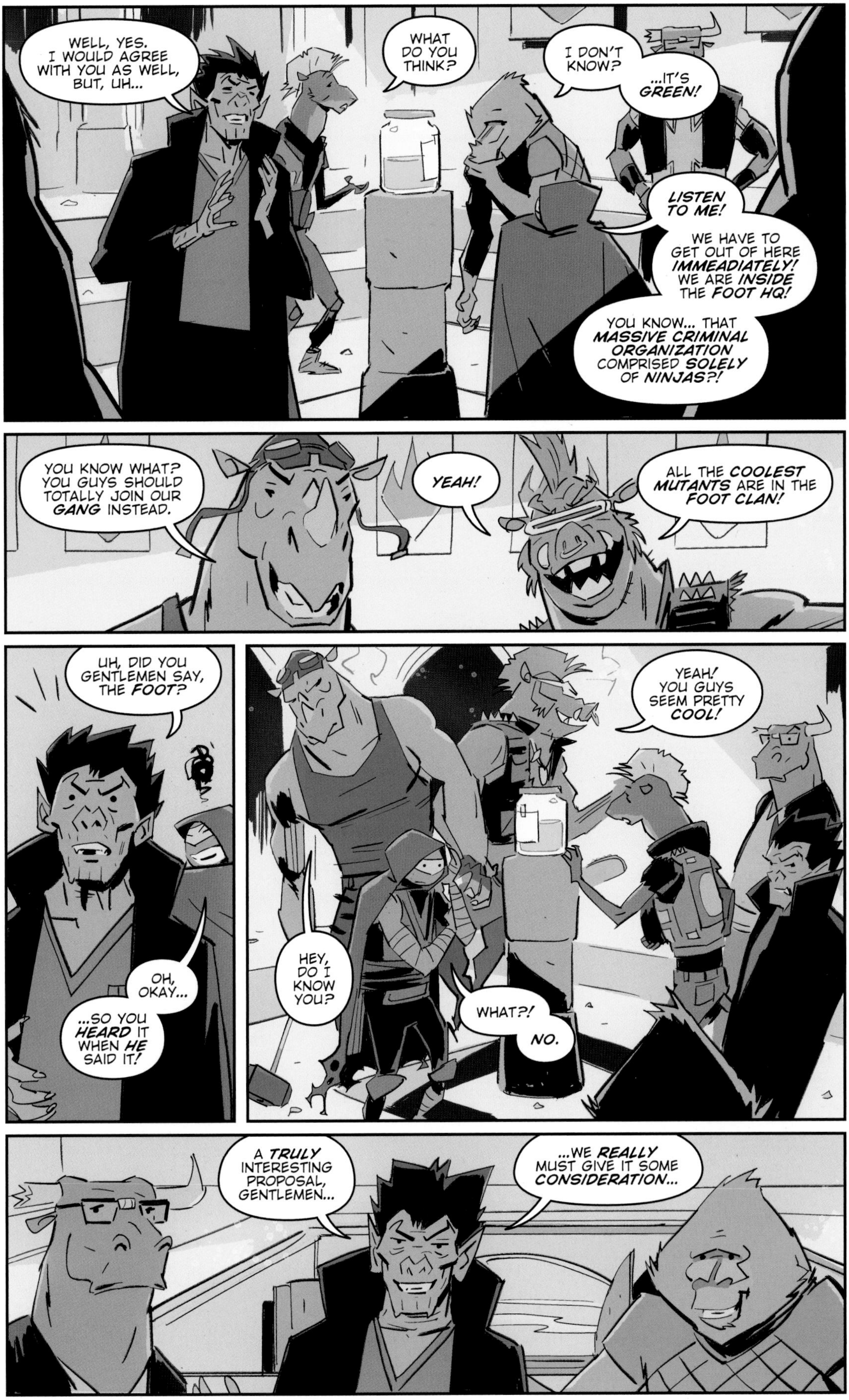
WELL, YES. I WOULD AGREE WITH YOU AS WELL, BUT, UH...
WHAT DO YOU THINK?
I DON'T KNOW?
...IT'S GREEN!
LISTEN TO ME!
WE HAVE TO GET OUT OF HERE IMMEADIATELY! WE ARE INSIDE THE FOOT HQ!
YOU KNOW... THAT MASSIVE CRIMINAL ORGANIZATION COMPRISED SOLELY OF NINJAS?!
YOU KNOW WHAT? YOU GUYS SHOULD TOTALLY JOIN OUR GANG INSTEAD.
YEAH!
ALL THE COOLEST MUTANTS ARE IN THE FOOT CLAN!
UH, DID YOU GENTLEMEN SAY, THE FOOT?
OH, OKAY...
...SO YOU HEARD IT WHEN HE SAID IT!
YEAH! YOU GUYS SEEM PRETTY COOL!
HEY, DO I KNOW YOU?
WHAT?!
NO.
A TRULY INTERESTING PROPOSAL, GENTLEMEN...
...WE REALLY MUST GIVE IT SOME CONSIDERATION...

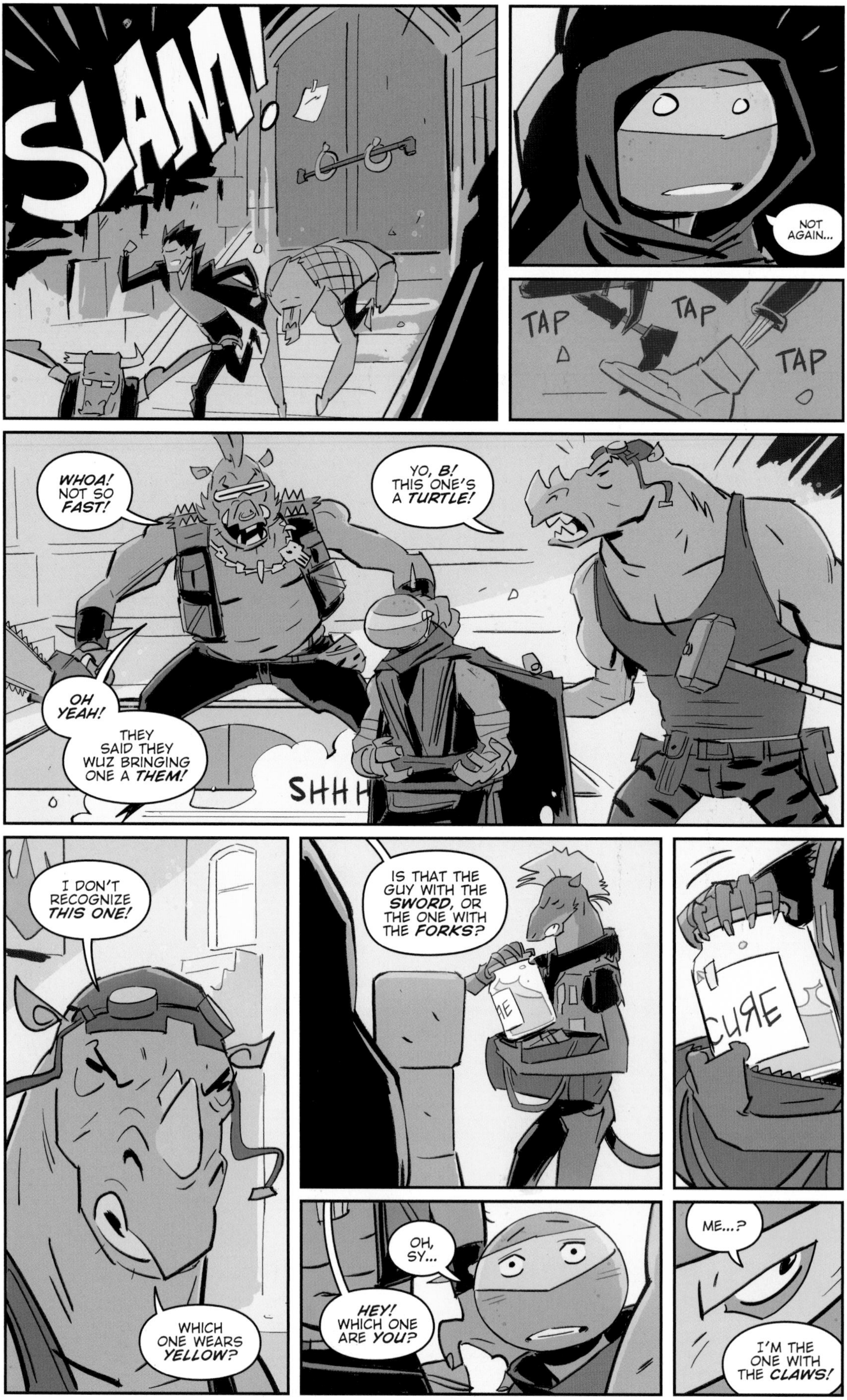
SLAM!
NOT AGAIN...
TAP
TAP
TAP
WHOA! NOT SO FAST!
YO, B! THIS ONE'S A TURTLE!
OH YEAH!
THEY SAID THEY WUZ BRINGING ONE A THEM!
SHHH
I DON'T RECOGNIZE THIS ONE!
WHICH ONE WEARS YELLOW?
IS THAT THE GUY WITH THE SWORD, OR THE ONE WITH THE FORKS?
CURE
OH, SY...
HEY! WHICH ONE ARE YOU?
ME...?
I'M THE ONE WITH THE CLAWS!

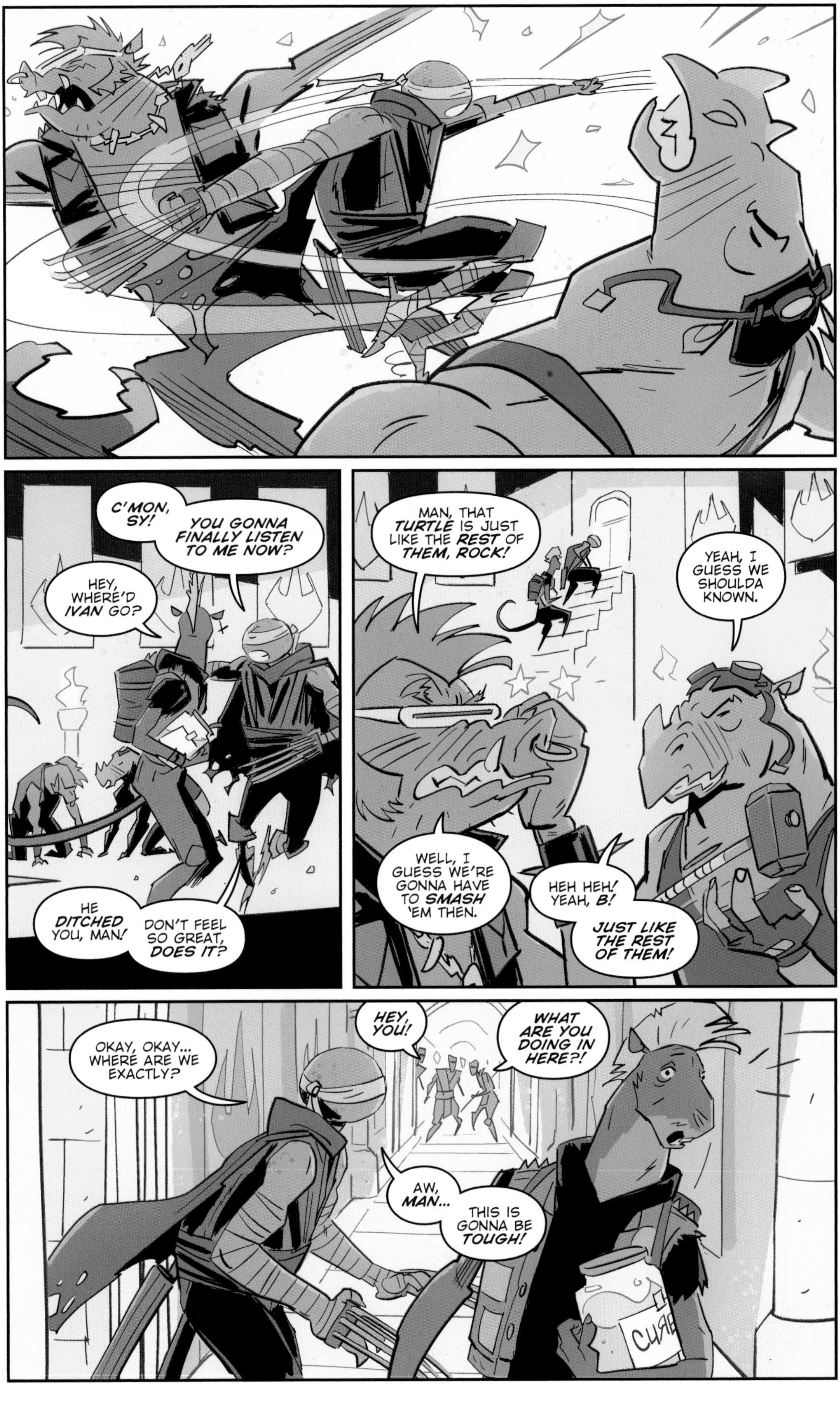
C'MON, SY!
YOU GONNA FINALLY LISTEN TO ME NOW?
HEY, WHERE'D IVAN GO?
HE DITCHED YOU, MAN!
DON'T FEEL SO GREAT, DOES IT?
MAN, THAT TURTLE IS JUST LIKE THE REST OF THEM, ROCK!
YEAH, I GUESS WE SHOULDA KNOWN.
WELL, I GUESS WE'RE GONNA HAVE TO SMASH 'EM THEN.
HEH HEH! YEAH, B!
JUST LIKE THE REST OF THEM!
OKAY, OKAY... WHERE ARE WE EXACTLY?
HEY, YOU!
WHAT ARE YOU DOING IN HERE?!
AW, MAN...
THIS IS GONNA BE TOUGH!

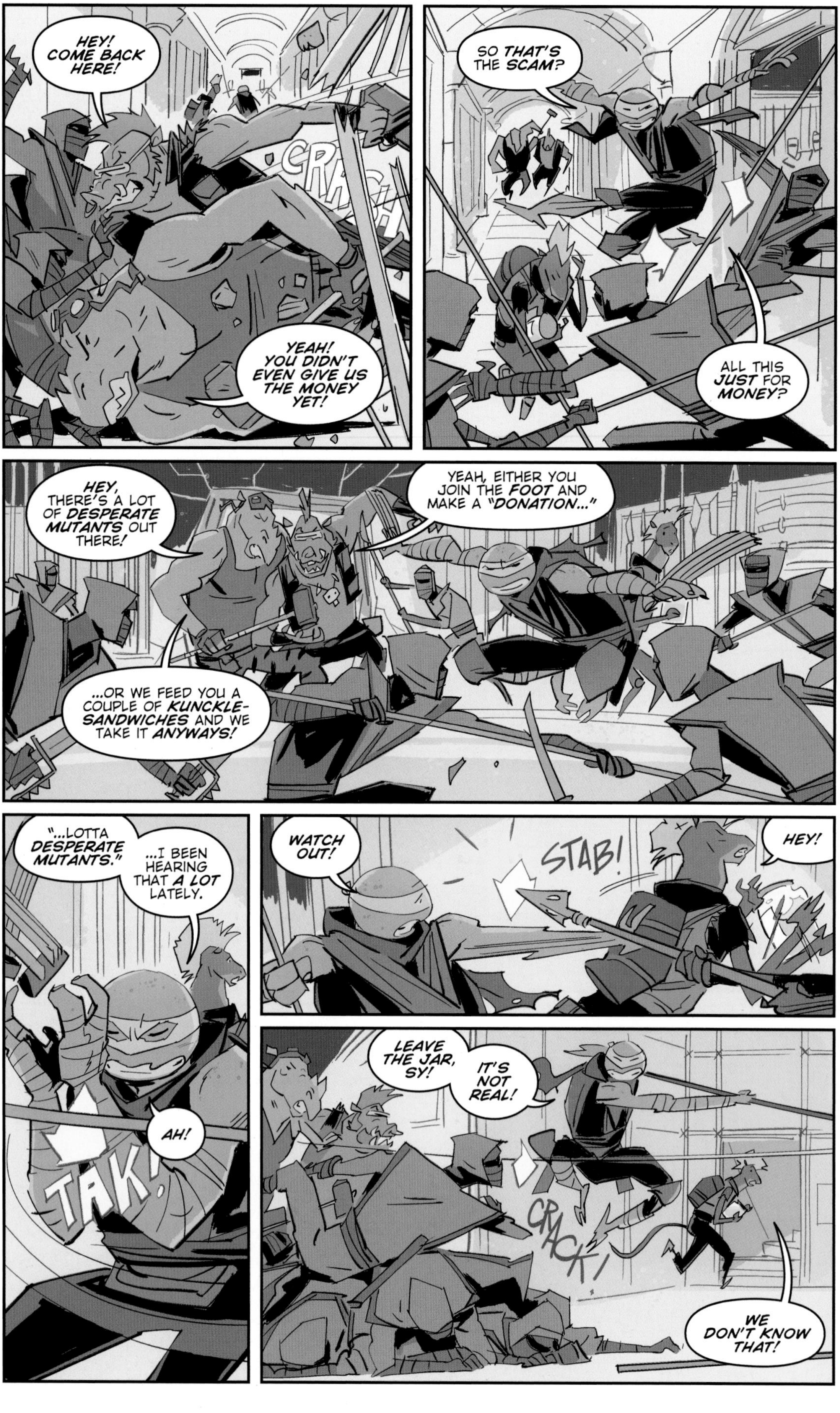
HEY! COME BACK HERE!
CRAASH
YEAH! YOU DIDN'T EVEN GIVE US THE MONEY YET!
SO THAT'S THE SCAM?
ALL THIS JUST FOR MONEY?
HEY, THERE'S A LOT OF DESPERATE MUTANTS OUT THERE!
YEAH, EITHER YOU JOIN THE FOOT AND MAKE A "DONATION..."
...OR WE FEED YOU A COUPLE OF KUNCKLE-SANDWICHES AND WE TAKE IT ANYWAYS!
"...LOTTA DESPERATE MUTANTS."
...I BEEN HEARING THAT A LOT LATELY.
AH!
TAK!
WATCH OUT!
STAB!
HEY!
LEAVE THE JAR, SY!
IT'S NOT REAL!
CRACK!
WE DON'T KNOW THAT!

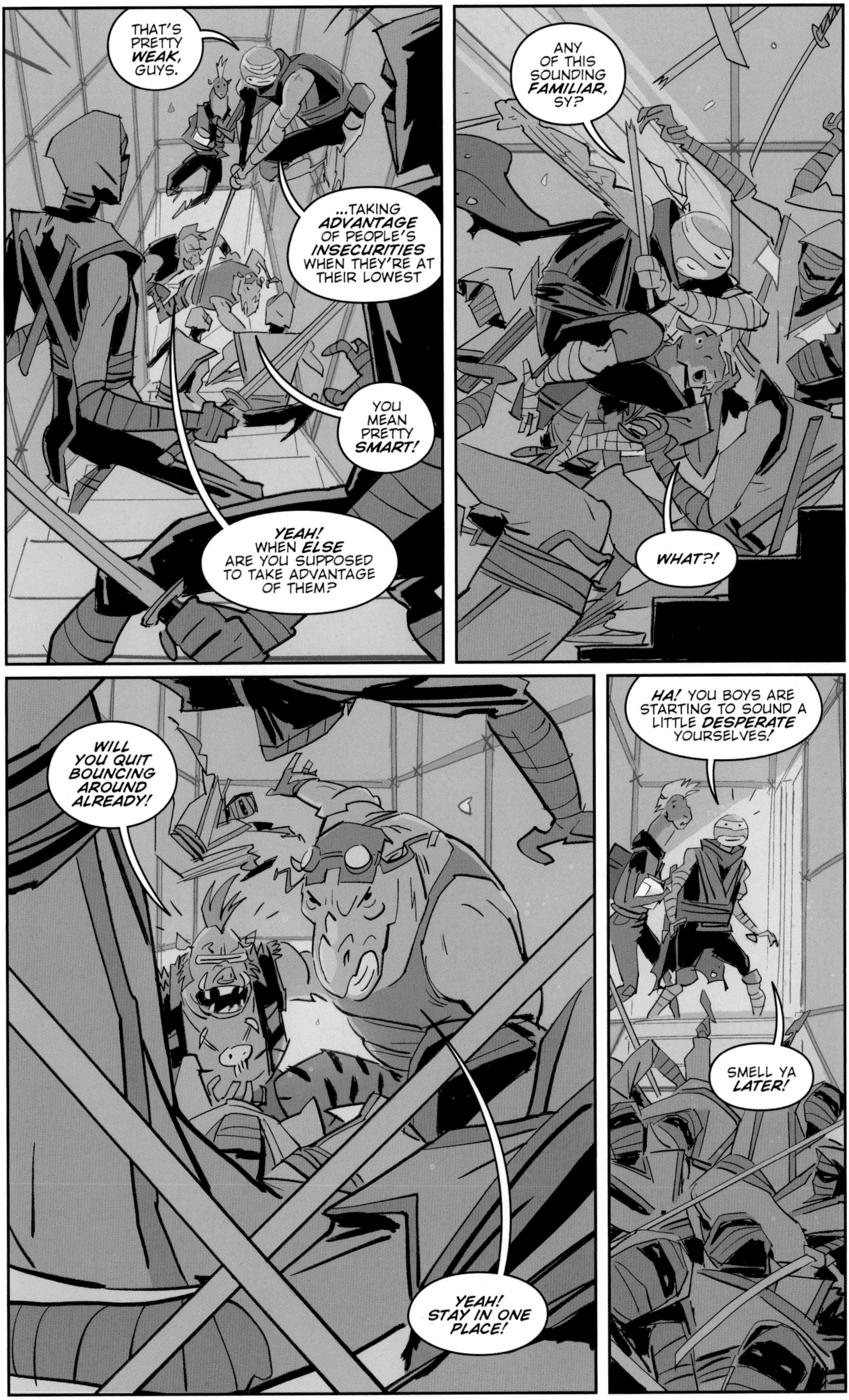
THAT'S PRETTY WEAK, GUYS.
...TAKING ADVANTAGE OF PEOPLE'S INSECURITIES WHEN THEY'RE AT THEIR LOWEST
YOU MEAN PRETTY SMART!
YEAH! WHEN ELSE ARE YOU SUPPOSED TO TAKE ADVANTAGE OF THEM?
ANY OF THIS SOUNDING FAMILIAR, SY?
WHAT?!
WILL YOU QUIT BOUNCING AROUND ALREADY!
YEAH! STAY IN ONE PLACE!
HA! YOU BOYS ARE STARTING TO SOUND A LITTLE DESPERATE YOURSELVES!
SMELL YA LATER!

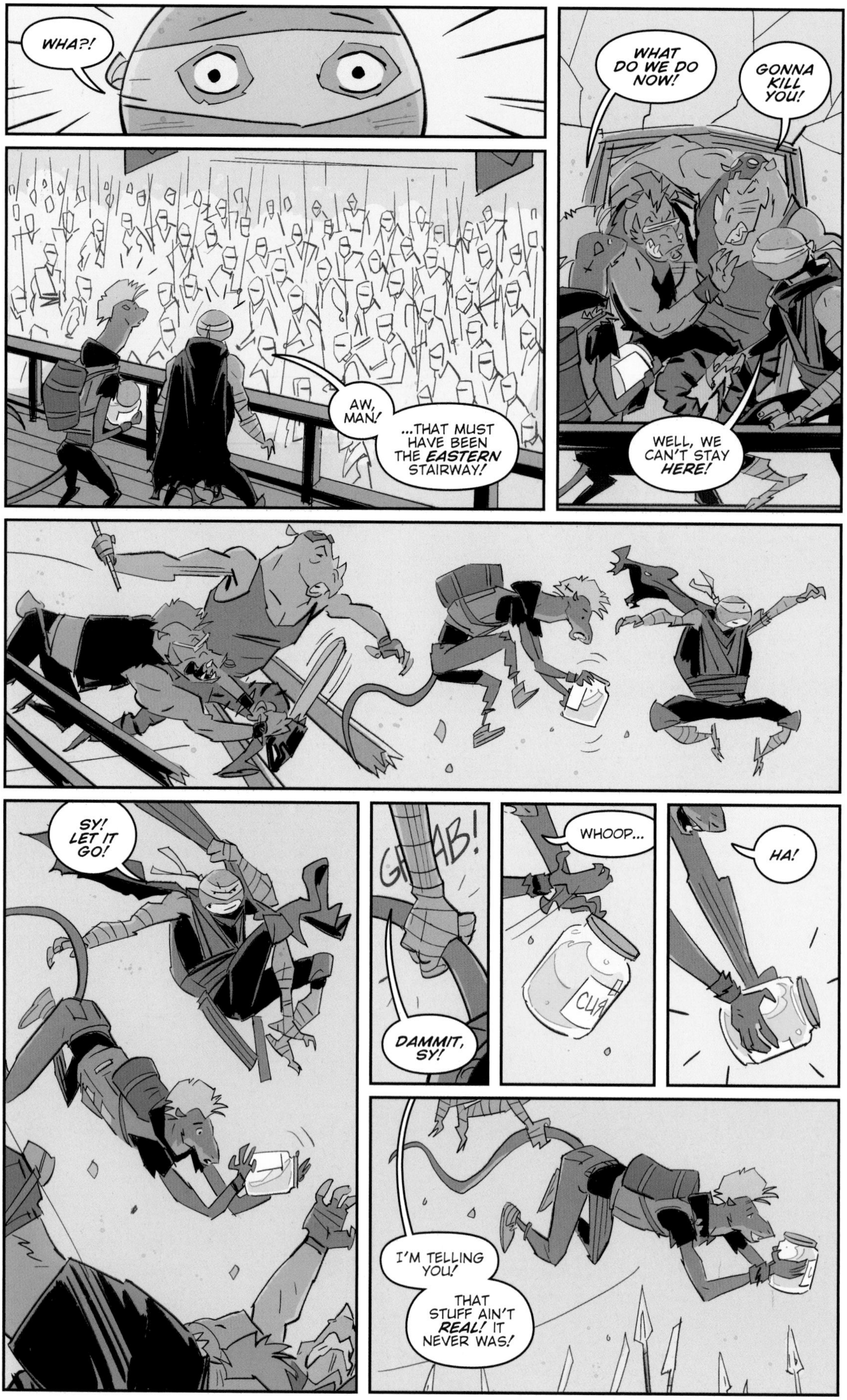
WHA?!
AW, MAN!
...THAT MUST HAVE BEEN THE EASTERN STAIRWAY!
WHAT DO WE DO NOW!
GONNA KILL YOU!
WELL, WE CAN'T STAY HERE!
SY! LET IT GO!
GRAB!
DAMMIT, SY!
WHOOP...
HA!
I'M TELLING YOU!
THAT STUFF AIN'T REAL! IT NEVER WAS!

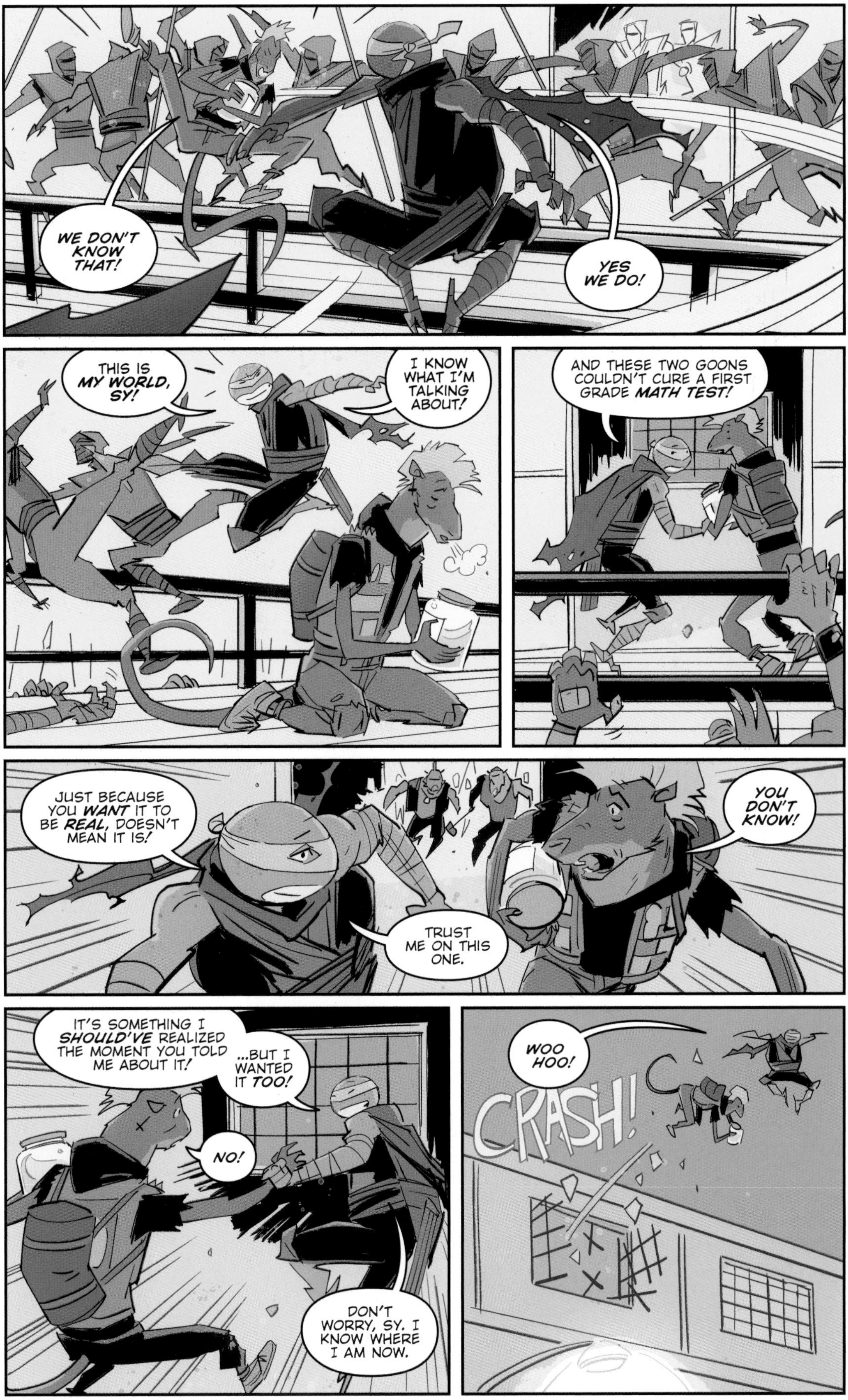

WE DON'T KNOW THAT!
YES WE DO!
THIS IS MY WORLD, SY!
I KNOW WHAT I'M TALKING ABOUT!
AND THESE TWO GOONS COULDN'T CURE A FIRST GRADE MATH TEST!
JUST BECAUSE YOU WANT IT TO BE REAL, DOESN'T MEAN IT IS!
YOU DON'T KNOW!
TRUST ME ON THIS ONE.
IT'S SOMETHING I SHOULD'VE REALIZED THE MOMENT YOU TOLD ME ABOUT IT!
...BUT I WANTED IT TOO!
NO!
DON'T WORRY, SY. I KNOW WHERE I AM NOW.
WOO HOO!
CRASH!

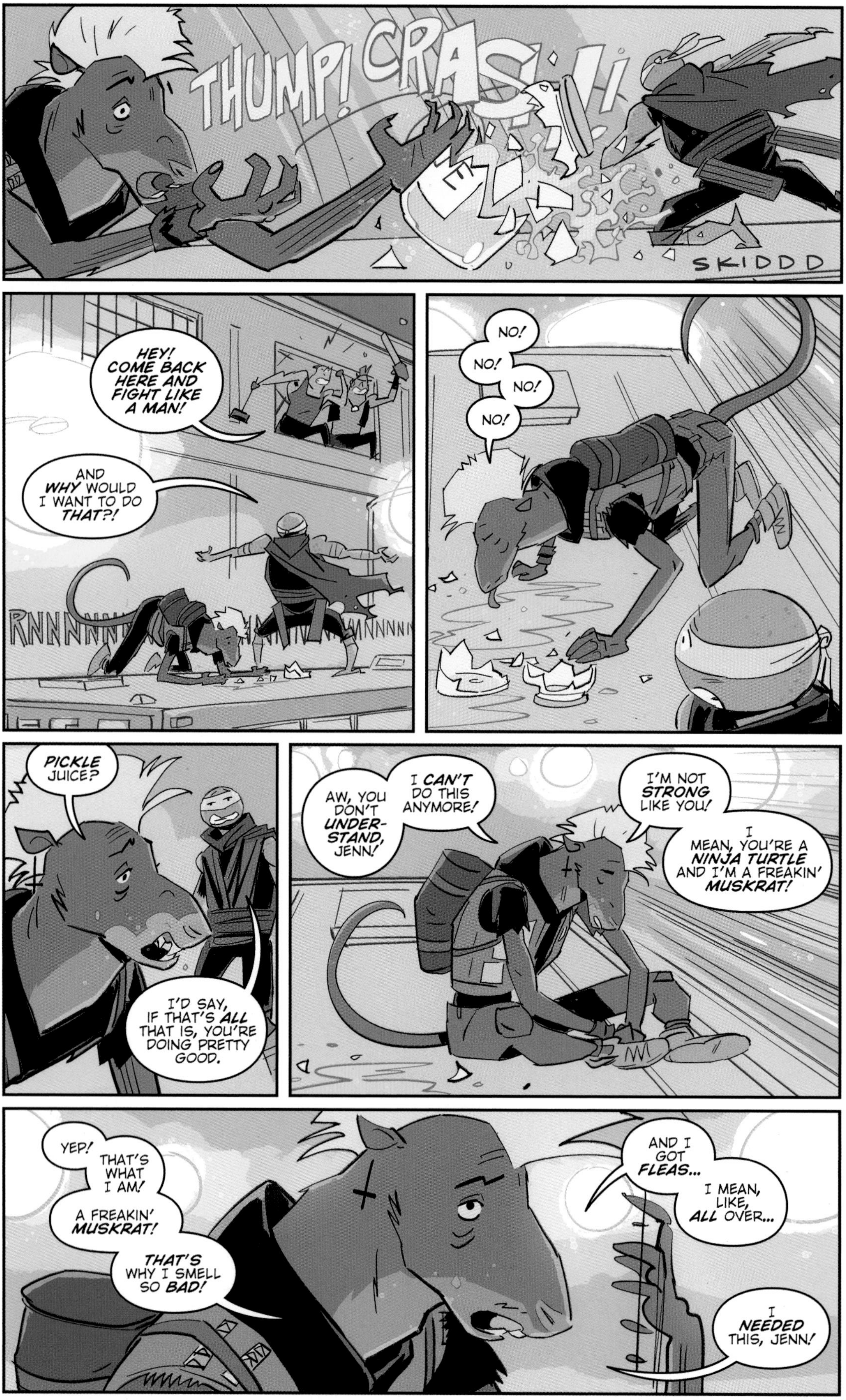
THUMP! CRASH!!
SKIDDD
HEY! COME BACK HERE AND FIGHT LIKE A MAN!
AND WHY WOULD I WANT TO DO THAT?!
RNNNNNNNNNNNNNN
NO!
NO!
NO!
NO!
PICKLE JUICE?
I'D SAY, IF THAT'S ALL THAT IS, YOU'RE DOING PRETTY GOOD.
AW, YOU DON'T UNDER-STAND, JENN!
I CAN'T DO THIS ANYMORE!
I'M NOT STRONG LIKE YOU!
I MEAN, YOU'RE A NINJA TURTLE AND I'M A FREAKIN' MUSKRAT!
YEP!
THAT'S WHAT I AM!
A FREAKIN' MUSKRAT!
THAT'S WHY I SMELL SO BAD!
AND I GOT FLEAS...
I MEAN, LIKE, ALL OVER...
I NEEDED THIS, JENN!

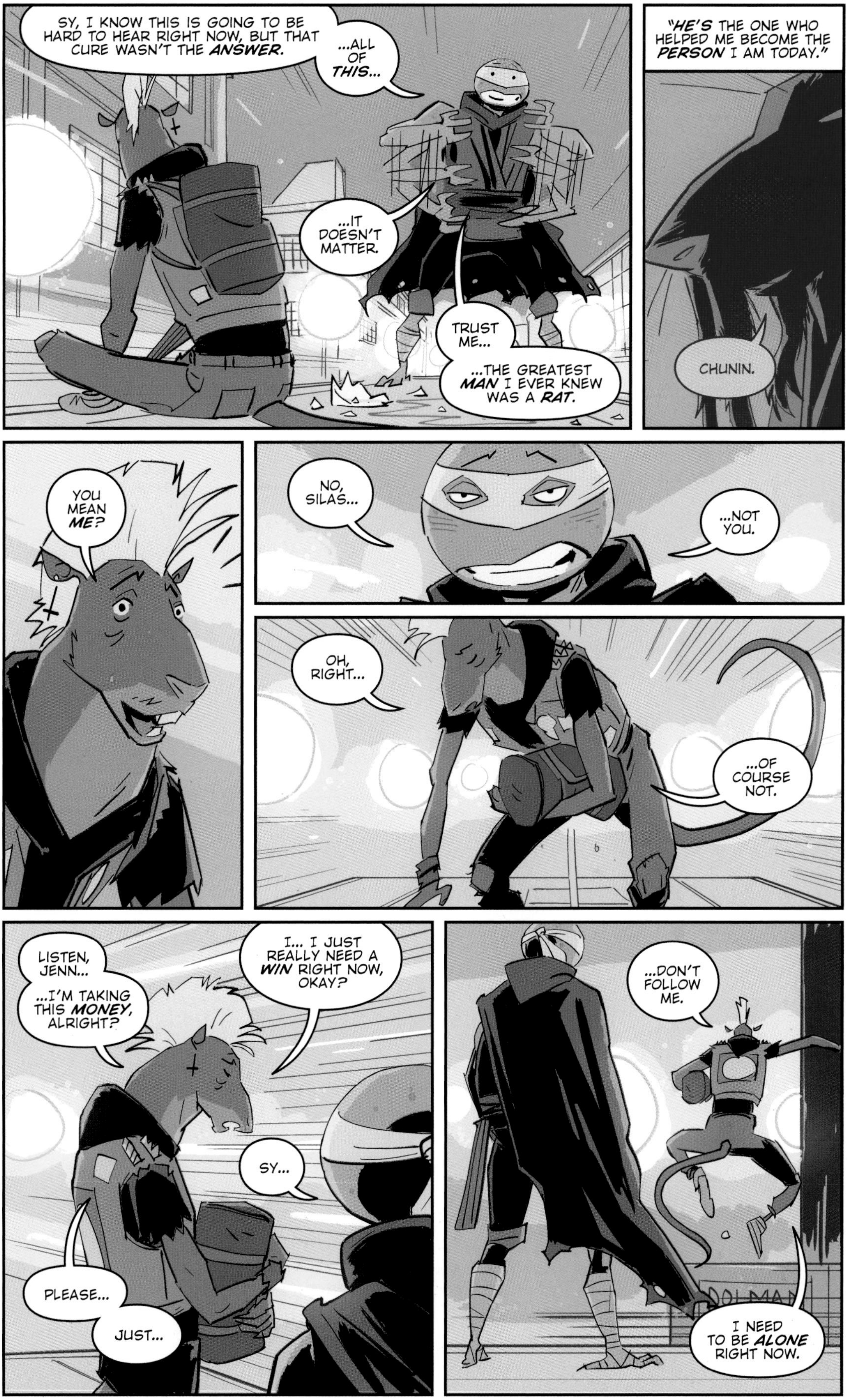
SY, I KNOW THIS IS GOING TO BE HARD TO HEAR RIGHT NOW, BUT THAT CURE WASN'T THE ANSWER.
...ALL OF THIS...
...IT DOESN'T MATTER.
TRUST ME...
...THE GREATEST MAN I EVER KNEW WAS A RAT.
"HE'S THE ONE WHO HELPED ME BECOME THE PERSON I AM TODAY."
CHUNIN.
YOU MEAN ME?
NO, SILAS...
...NOT YOU.
OH, RIGHT...
...OF COURSE NOT.
LISTEN, JENN...
...I'M TAKING THIS MONEY, ALRIGHT?
I... I JUST REALLY NEED A WIN RIGHT NOW, OKAY?
SY...
PLEASE...
JUST...
...DON'T FOLLOW ME.
I NEED TO BE ALONE RIGHT NOW.

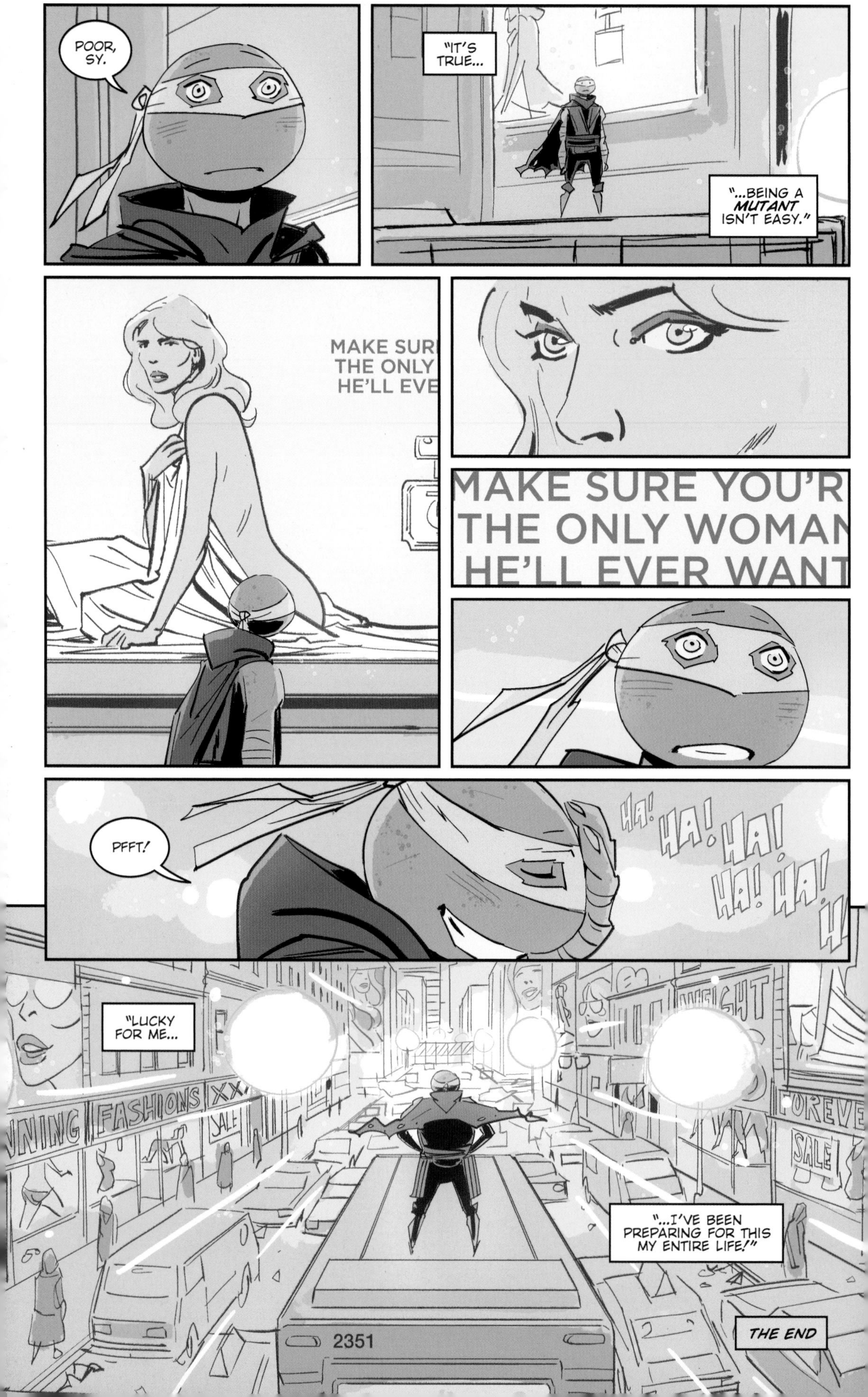

POOR, SY.
"IT'S TRUE...
"...BEING A MUTANT ISN'T EASY."
MAKE SURE THE ONLY HE'LL EVE
MAKE SURE YOU'R THE ONLY WOMAN HE'LL EVER WANT
PFFT!
HA! HA! HA! HA! HA! H
"LUCKY FOR ME...
FASHIONS
SALE
FOREVE
SALE
"...I'VE BEEN PREPARING FOR THIS MY ENTIRE LIFE!"
2351
THE END

Art by Peach Momoko

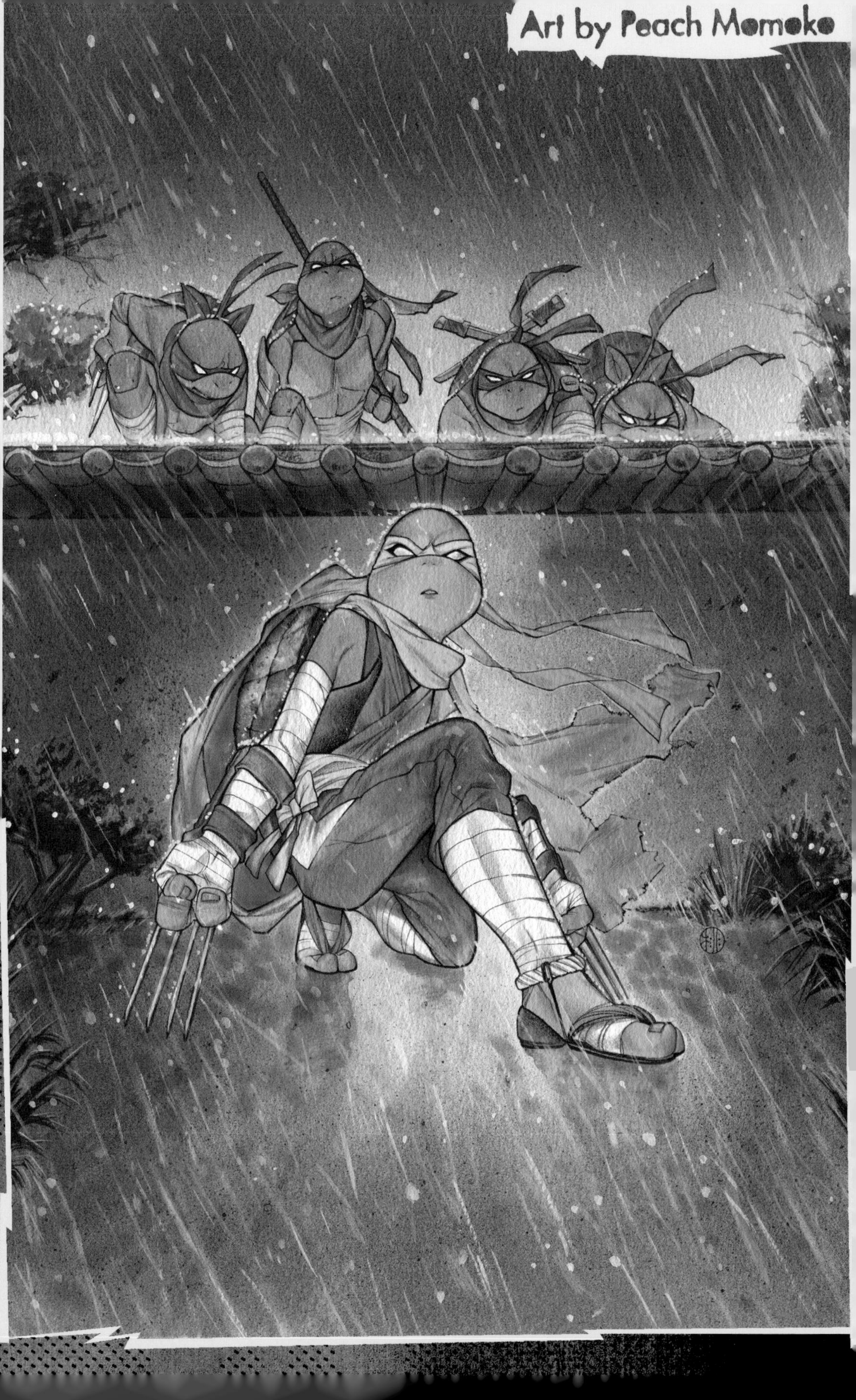

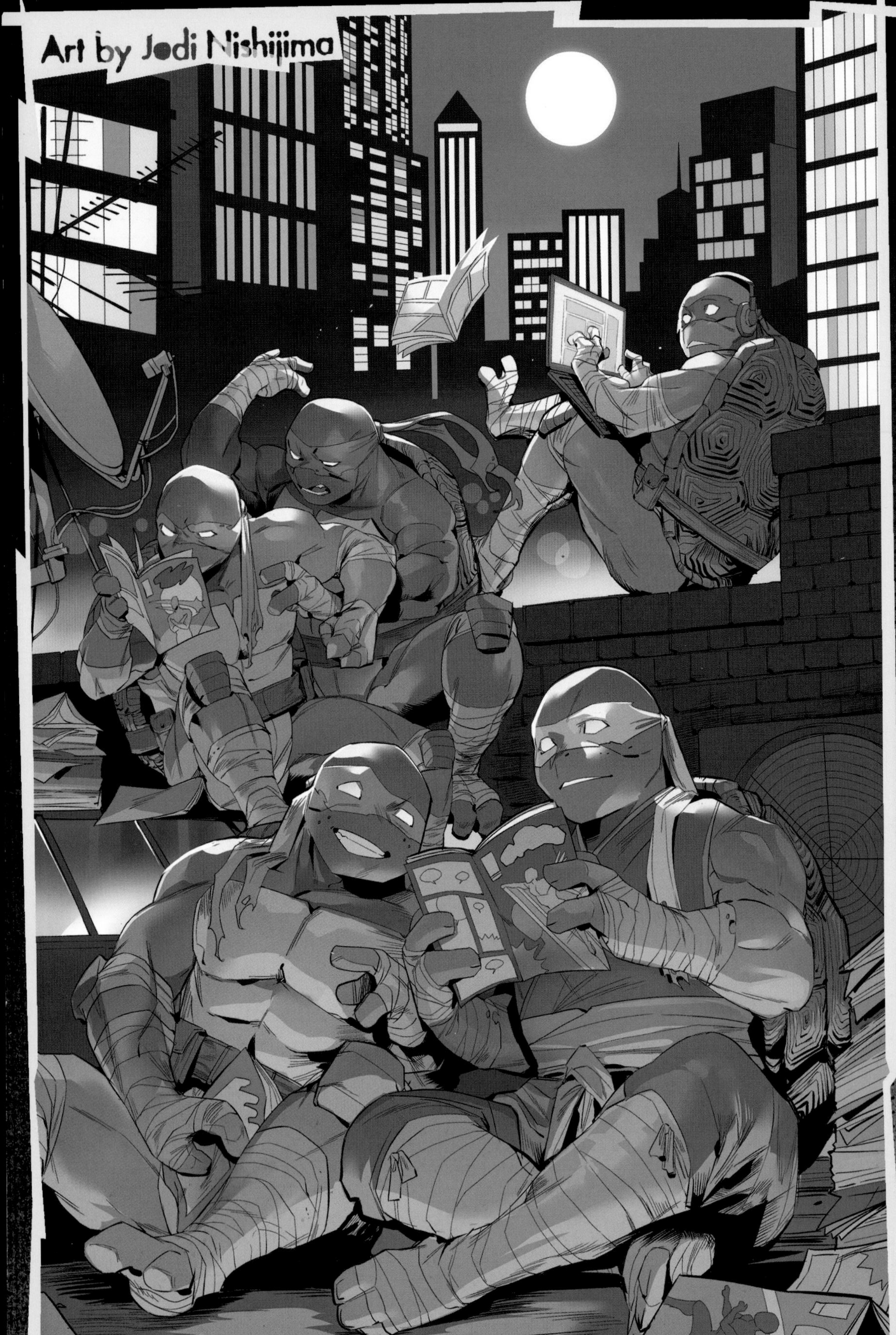

Art by Jodi Nishijima

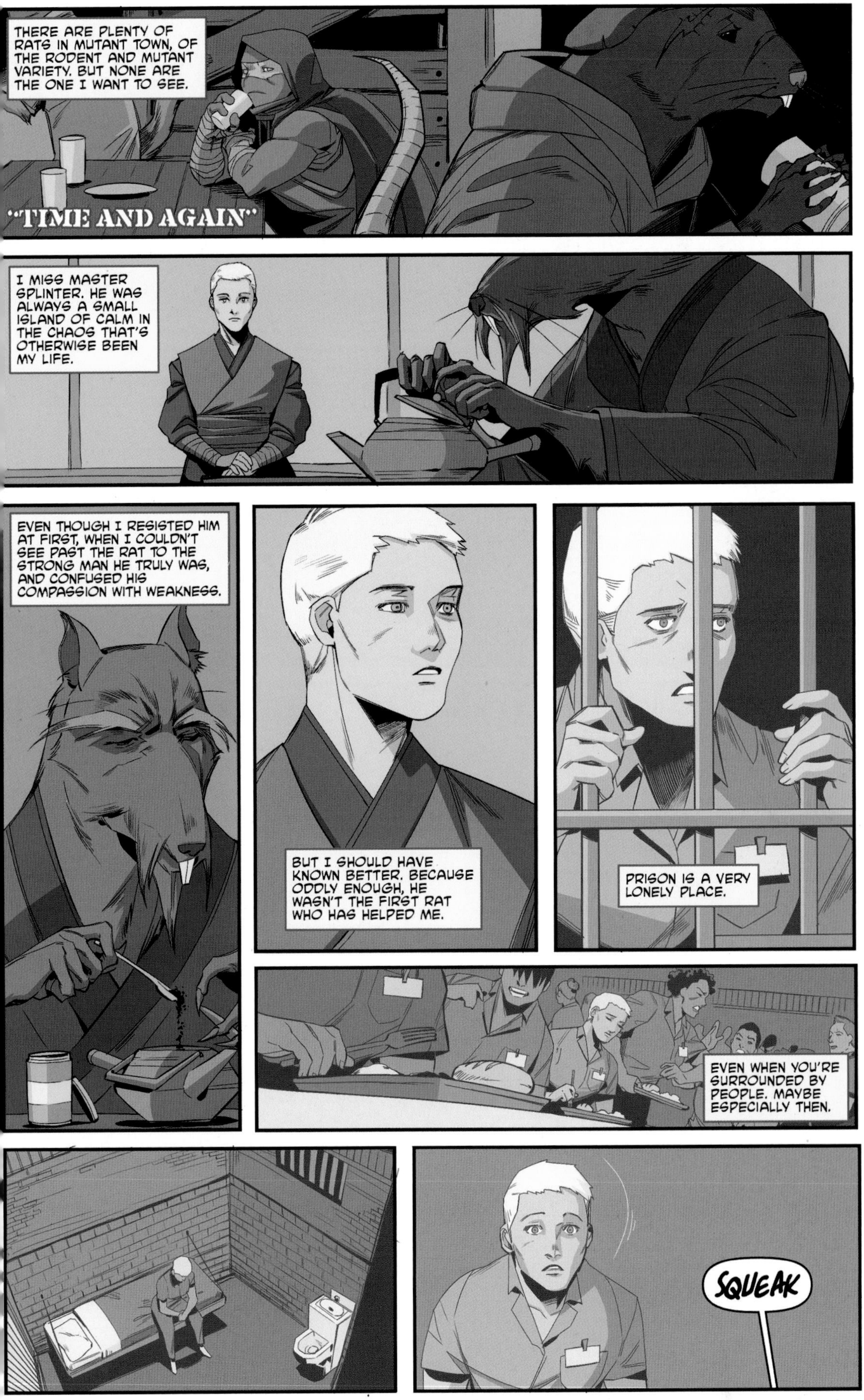

THERE ARE PLENTY OF RATS IN MUTANT TOWN, OF THE RODENT AND MUTANT VARIETY. BUT NONE ARE THE ONE I WANT TO SEE.
"TIME AND AGAIN"
I MISS MASTER SPLINTER. HE WAS ALWAYS A SMALL ISLAND OF CALM IN THE CHAOS THAT'S OTHERWISE BEEN MY LIFE.
EVEN THOUGH I RESISTED HIM AT FIRST, WHEN I COULDN'T SEE PAST THE RAT TO THE STRONG MAN HE TRULY WAS, AND CONFUSED HIS COMPASSION WITH WEAKNESS.
BUT I SHOULD HAVE KNOWN BETTER. BECAUSE ODDLY ENOUGH, HE WASN'T THE FIRST RAT WHO HAS HELPED ME.
PRISON IS A VERY LONELY PLACE.
EVEN WHEN YOU'RE SURROUNDED BY PEOPLE. MAYBE ESPECIALLY THEN.
SQUEAK

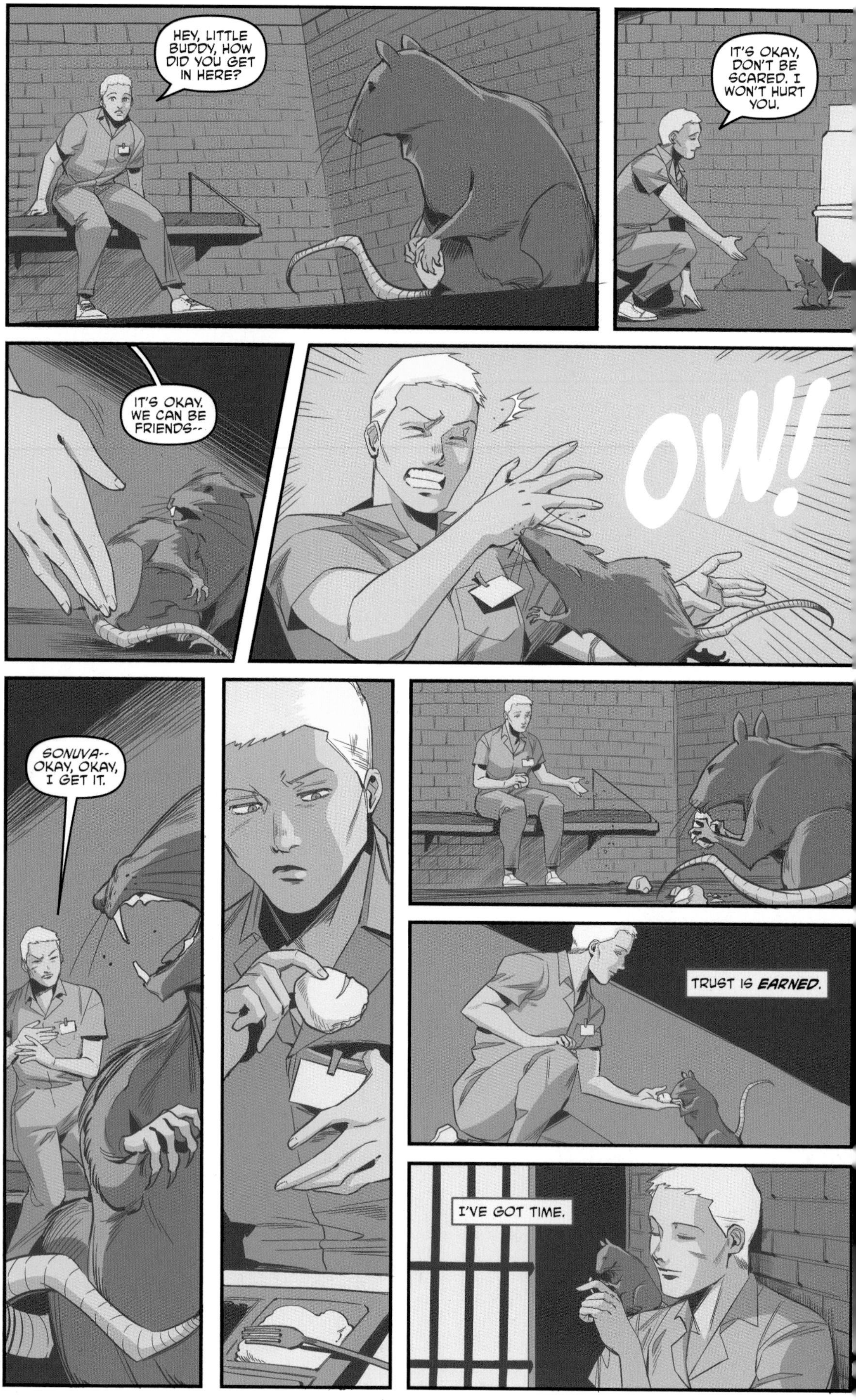
HEY, LITTLE BUDDY, HOW DID YOU GET IN HERE?
IT'S OKAY, DON'T BE SCARED. I WON'T HURT YOU.
IT'S OKAY. WE CAN BE FRIENDS--
OW!
SONUVA-- OKAY, OKAY, I GET IT.
TRUST IS EARNED.
I'VE GOT TIME.

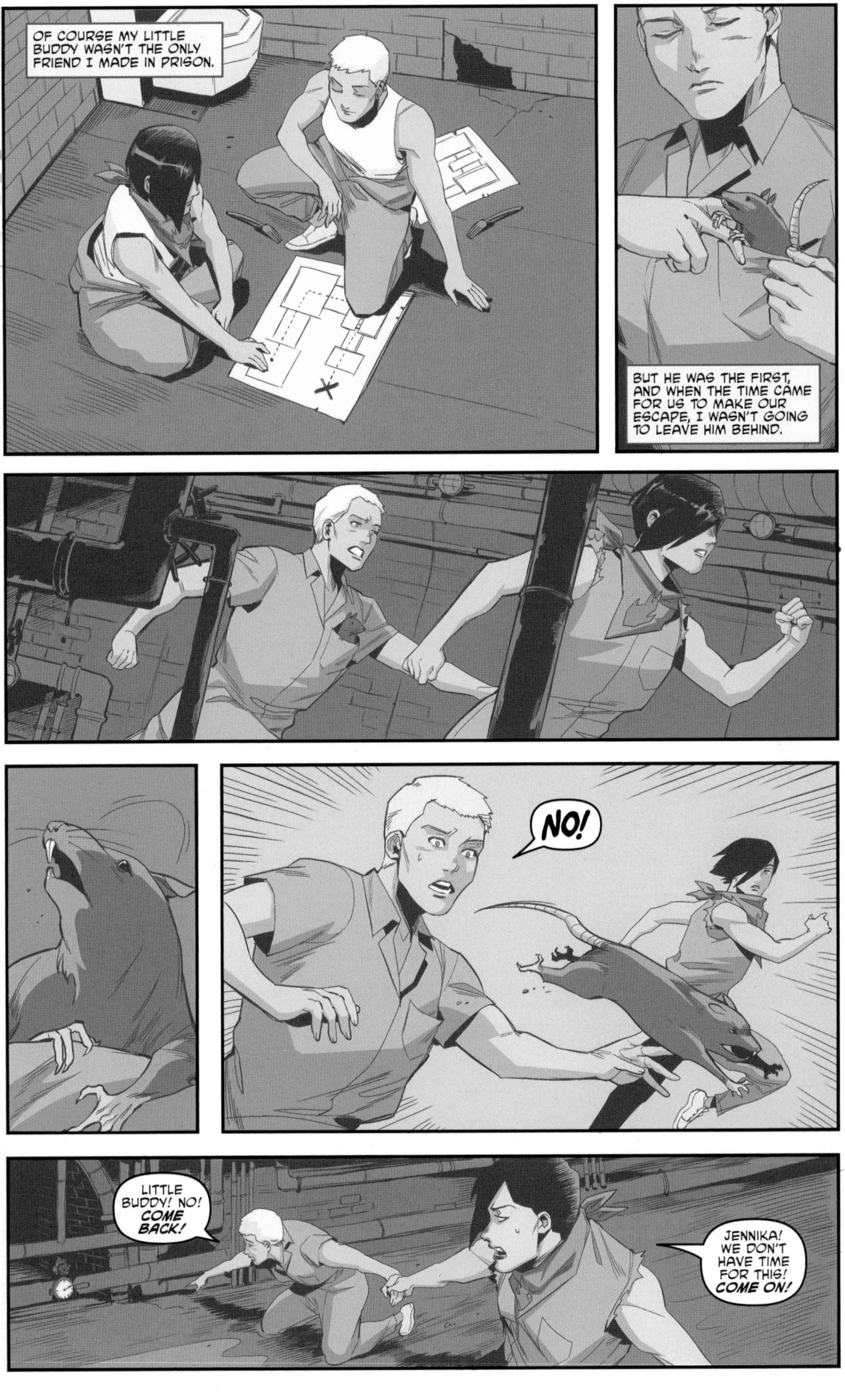
OF COURSE MY LITTLE BUDDY WASN'T THE ONLY FRIEND I MADE IN PRISON.
BUT HE WAS THE FIRST, AND WHEN THE TIME CAME FOR US TO MAKE OUR ESCAPE, I WASN'T GOING TO LEAVE HIM BEHIND.
NO!
LITTLE BUDDY! NO! COME BACK!
JENNIKA! WE DON'T HAVE TIME FOR THIS! COME ON!

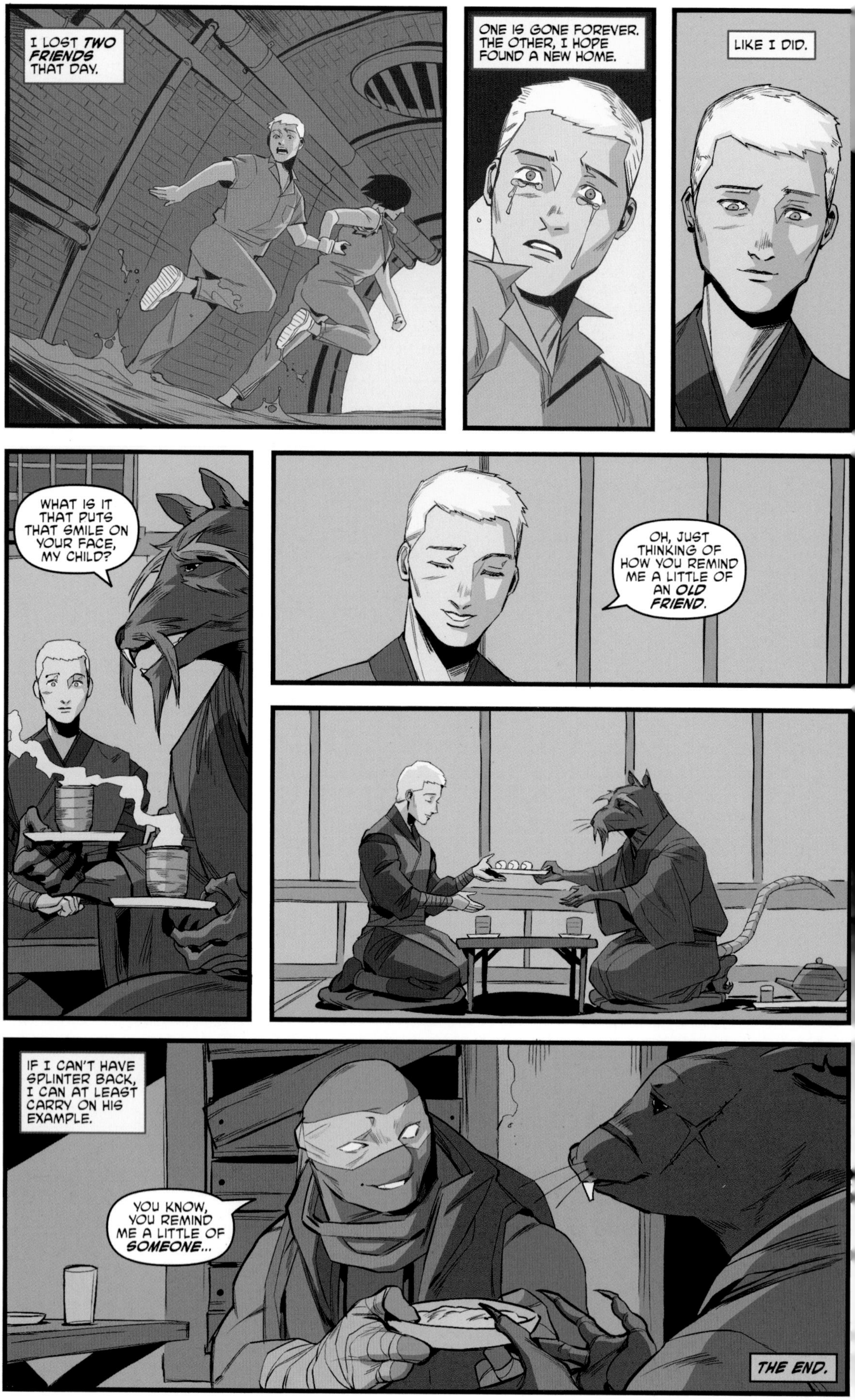
I LOST TWO FRIENDS THAT DAY.
ONE IS GONE FOREVER. THE OTHER, I HOPE FOUND A NEW HOME.
LIKE I DID.
WHAT IS IT THAT PUTS THAT SMILE ON YOUR FACE, MY CHILD?
OH, JUST THINKING OF HOW YOU REMIND ME A LITTLE OF AN OLD FRIEND.
IF I CAN'T HAVE SPLINTER BACK, I CAN AT LEAST CARRY ON HIS EXAMPLE.
YOU KNOW, YOU REMIND ME A LITTLE OF SOMEONE...
THE END.

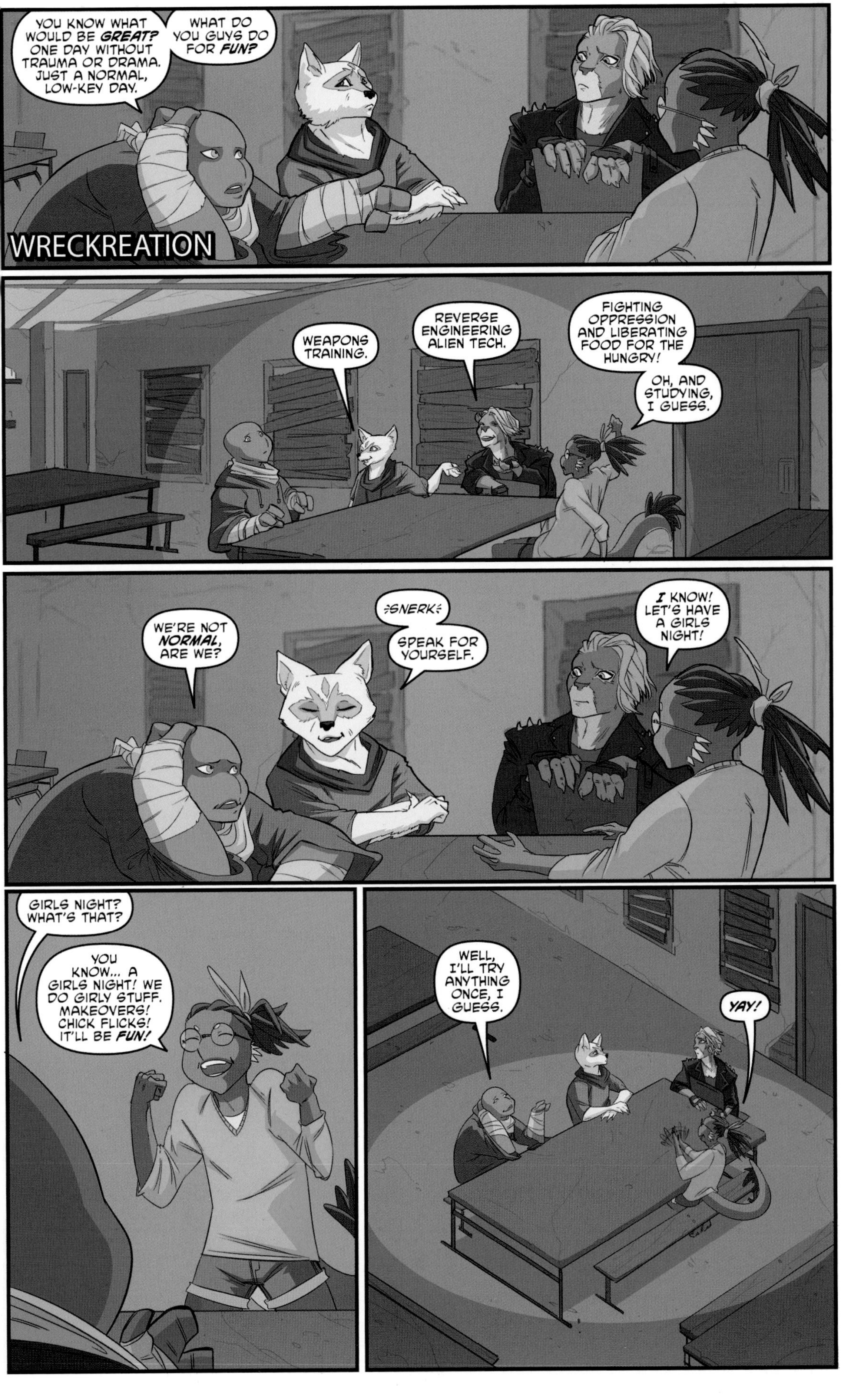
YOU KNOW WHAT WOULD BE GREAT? ONE DAY WITHOUT TRAUMA OR DRAMA. JUST A NORMAL, LOW-KEY DAY.
WHAT DO YOU GUYS DO FOR FUN?
WRECKREATION
WEAPONS TRAINING.
REVERSE ENGINEERING ALIEN TECH.
FIGHTING OPPRESSION AND LIBERATING FOOD FOR THE HUNGRY!
OH, AND STUDYING, I GUESS.
WE'RE NOT NORMAL, ARE WE?
SNERK
SPEAK FOR YOURSELF.
I KNOW! LET'S HAVE A GIRLS NIGHT!
GIRLS NIGHT? WHAT'S THAT?
YOU KNOW... A GIRLS NIGHT! WE DO GIRLY STUFF. MAKEOVERS! CHICK FLICKS! IT'LL BE FUN!
WELL, I'LL TRY ANYTHING ONCE, I GUESS.
YAY!

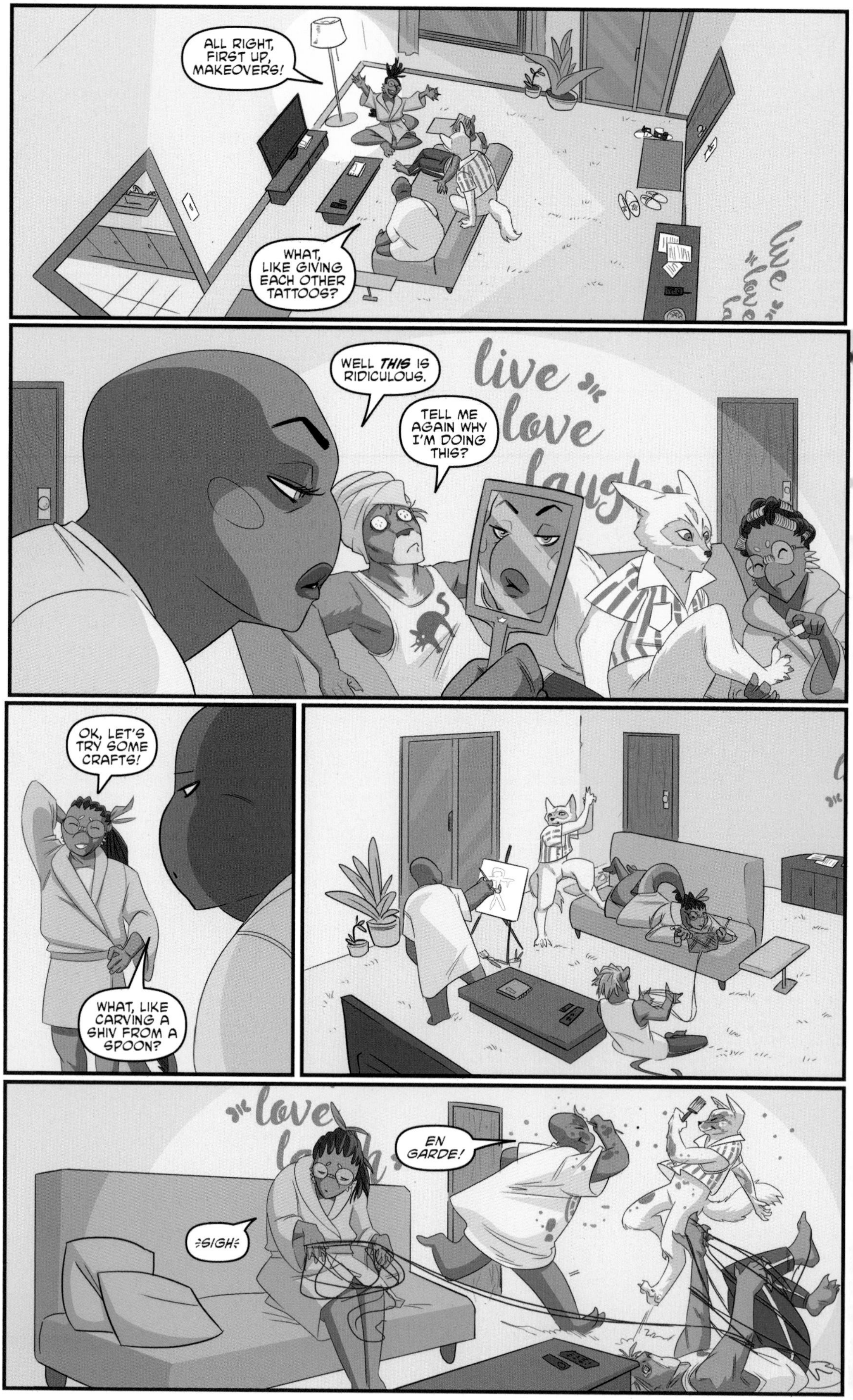

ALL RIGHT, FIRST UP, MAKEOVERS!
WHAT, LIKE GIVING EACH OTHER TATTOOS?
WELL *THIS* IS RIDICULOUS.
live love laugh
TELL ME AGAIN WHY I'M DOING THIS?
OK, LET'S TRY SOME CRAFTS!
WHAT, LIKE CARVING A SHIV FROM A SPOON?
EN GARDE!
SIGH

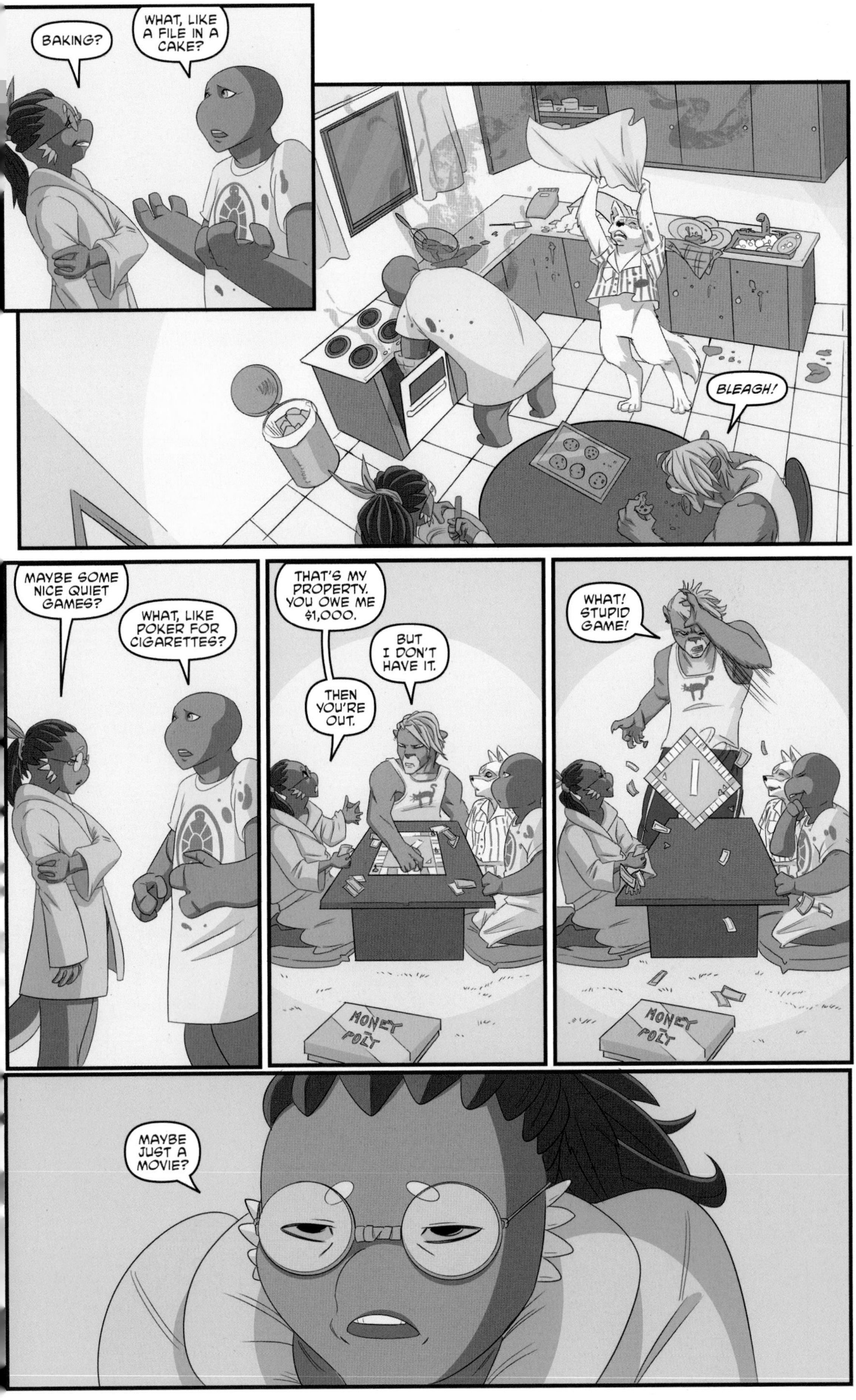

BAKING?
WHAT, LIKE A FILE IN A CAKE?
BLEAGH!
MAYBE SOME NICE QUIET GAMES?
WHAT, LIKE POKER FOR CIGARETTES?
THAT'S MY PROPERTY. YOU OWE ME $1,000.
BUT I DON'T HAVE IT.
THEN YOU'RE OUT.
MONEY POLY
WHAT! STUPID GAME!
MONEY POLY
MAYBE JUST A MOVIE?

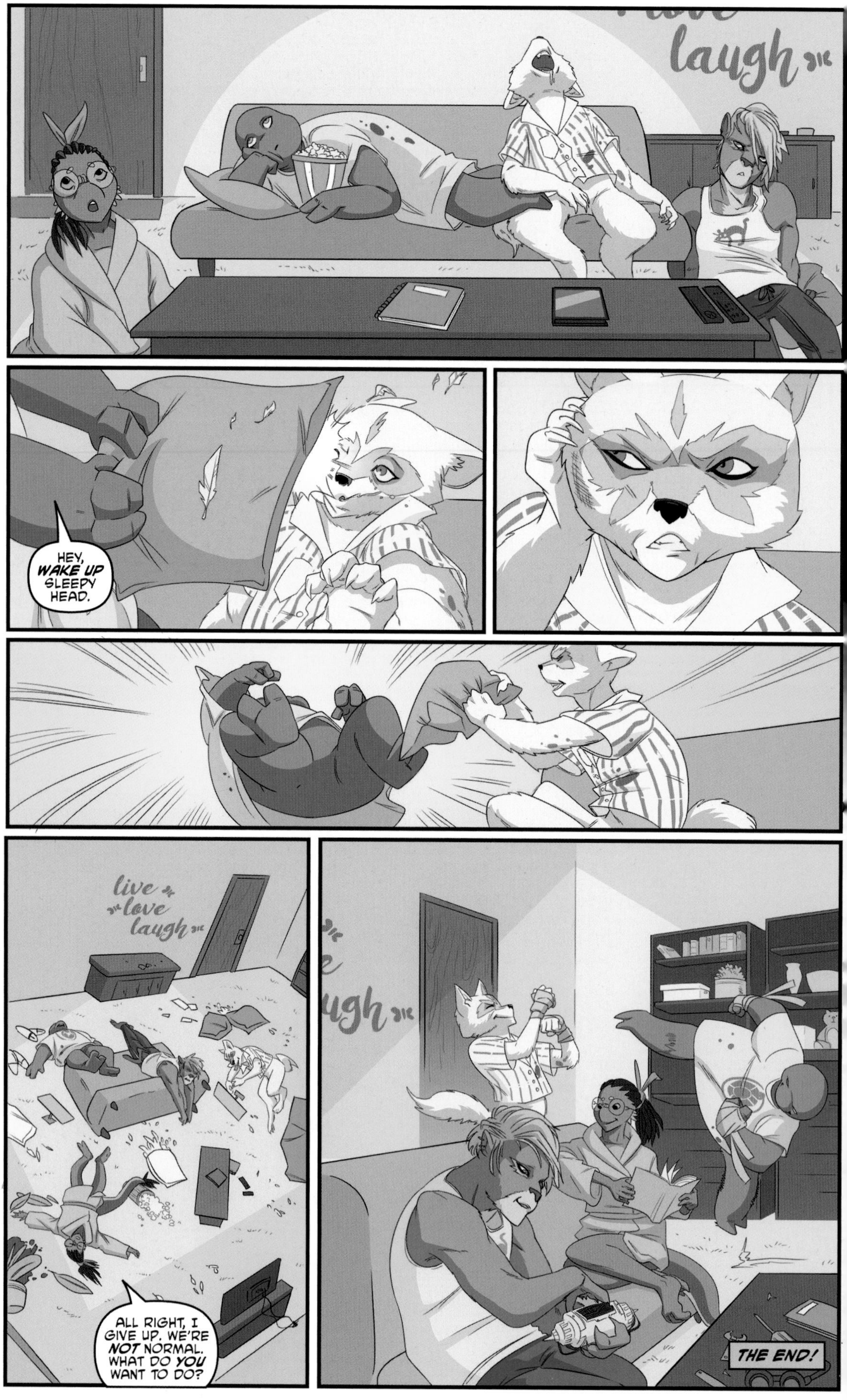
love
laugh
HEY, WAKE UP SLEEPY HEAD.
live
love
laugh
ugh
ALL RIGHT, I GIVE UP. WE'RE NOT NORMAL. WHAT DO YOU WANT TO DO?
THE END!

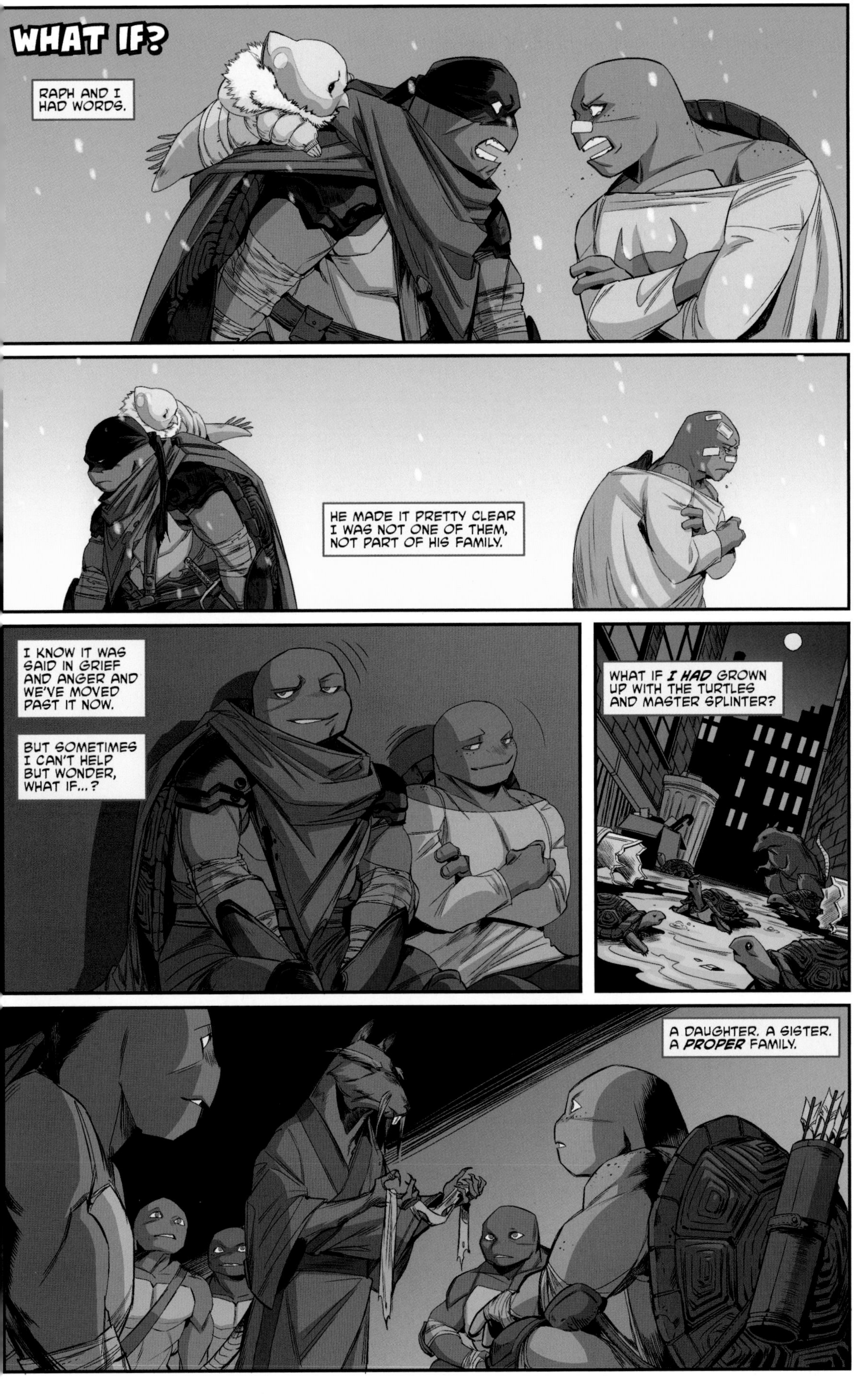
WHAT IF?
RAPH AND I HAD WORDS.
HE MADE IT PRETTY CLEAR I WAS NOT ONE OF THEM, NOT PART OF HIS FAMILY.
I KNOW IT WAS SAID IN GRIEF AND ANGER AND WE'VE MOVED PAST IT NOW.
BUT SOMETIMES I CAN'T HELP BUT WONDER, WHAT IF...?
WHAT IF I HAD GROWN UP WITH THE TURTLES AND MASTER SPLINTER?
A DAUGHTER. A SISTER. A PROPER FAMILY.

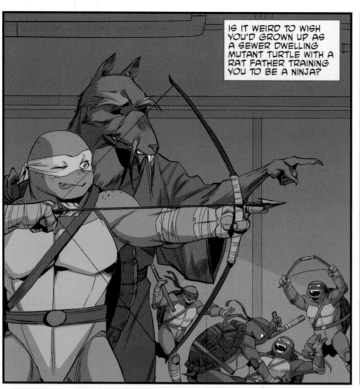

IS IT WEIRD TO WISH YOU'D GROWN UP AS A SEWER DWELLING MUTANT TURTLE WITH A RAT FATHER TRAINING YOU TO BE A NINJA?

OR STRANGER STILL, A REINCARNATED FAMILY WITH MEMORIES OF ANOTHER ERA. IMAGINE, THE LOVE OF *TWO* LIFETIMES.

AND THE TRAGEDY.

WHAT WOULD MY ROLE HAVE BEEN IN THAT FAMILY? WOULD I HAVE BEEN LIKE MY BROTHERS?

IF I HAD BEEN THE STOLEN TURTLE, STARTING LIFE ALONE, WOULD I HAVE MADE THE SAME CHOICES AS RAPH?

WOULD I HAVE FALLEN FOR CASEY, JUST THE SAME?

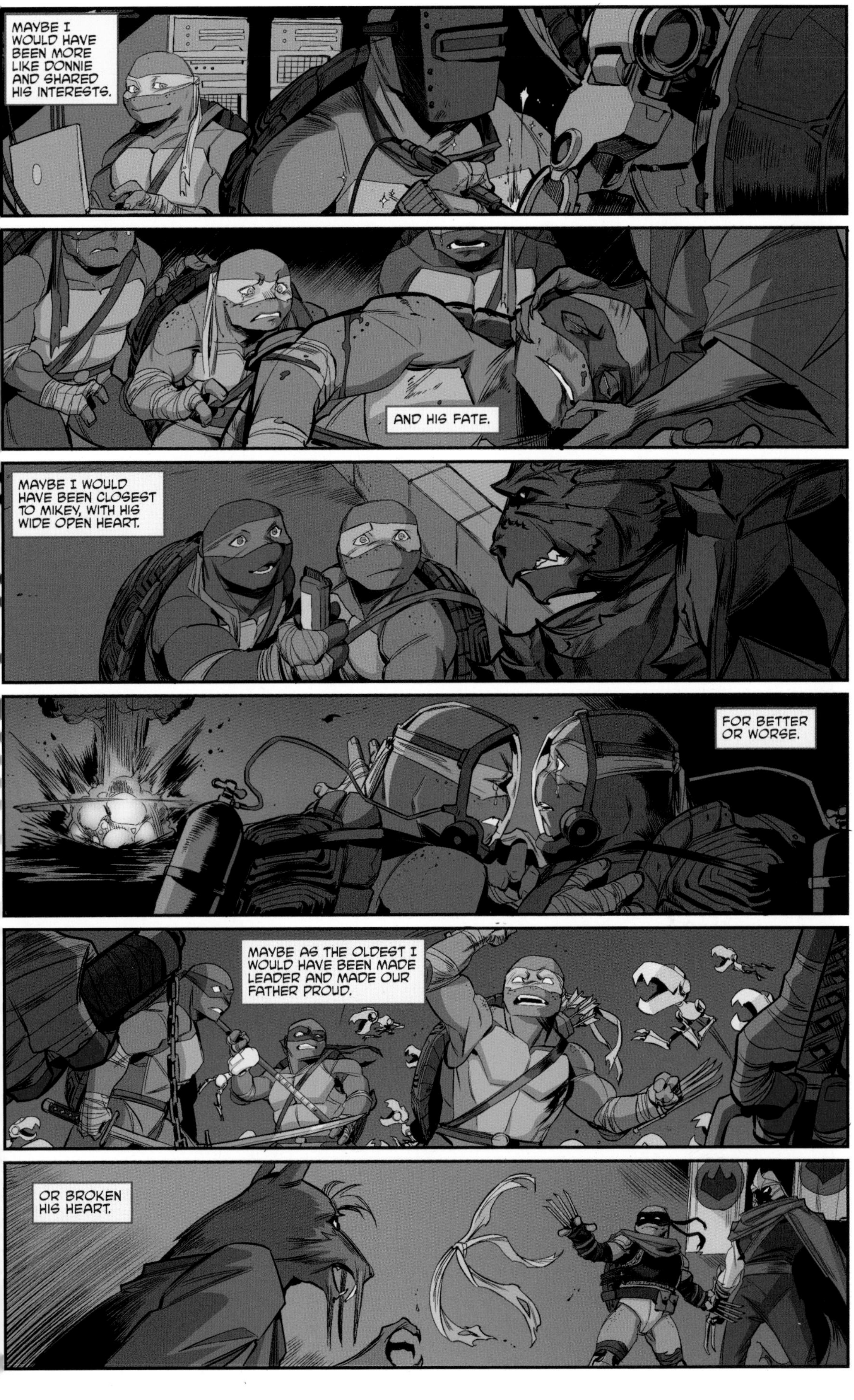
MAYBE I WOULD HAVE BEEN MORE LIKE DONNIE AND SHARED HIS INTERESTS.
AND HIS FATE.
MAYBE I WOULD HAVE BEEN CLOSEST TO MIKEY, WITH HIS WIDE OPEN HEART.
FOR BETTER OR WORSE.
MAYBE AS THE OLDEST I WOULD HAVE BEEN MADE LEADER AND MADE OUR FATHER PROUD.
OR BROKEN HIS HEART.

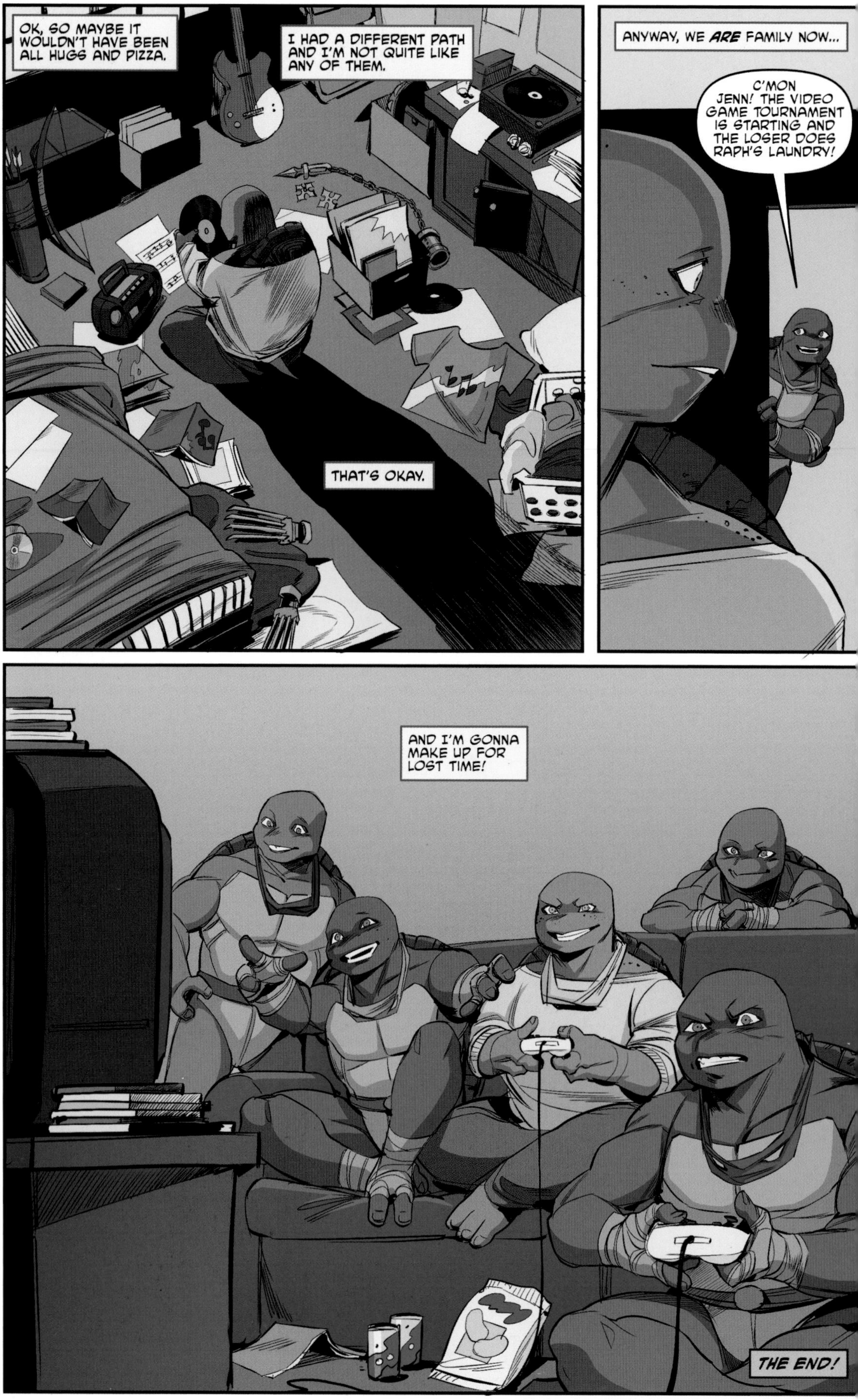
OK, SO MAYBE IT WOULDN'T HAVE BEEN ALL HUGS AND PIZZA.
I HAD A DIFFERENT PATH AND I'M NOT QUITE LIKE ANY OF THEM.
THAT'S OKAY.
ANYWAY, WE ARE FAMILY NOW...
C'MON JENN! THE VIDEO GAME TOURNAMENT IS STARTING AND THE LOSER DOES RAPH'S LAUNDRY!
AND I'M GONNA MAKE UP FOR LOST TIME!
THE END!

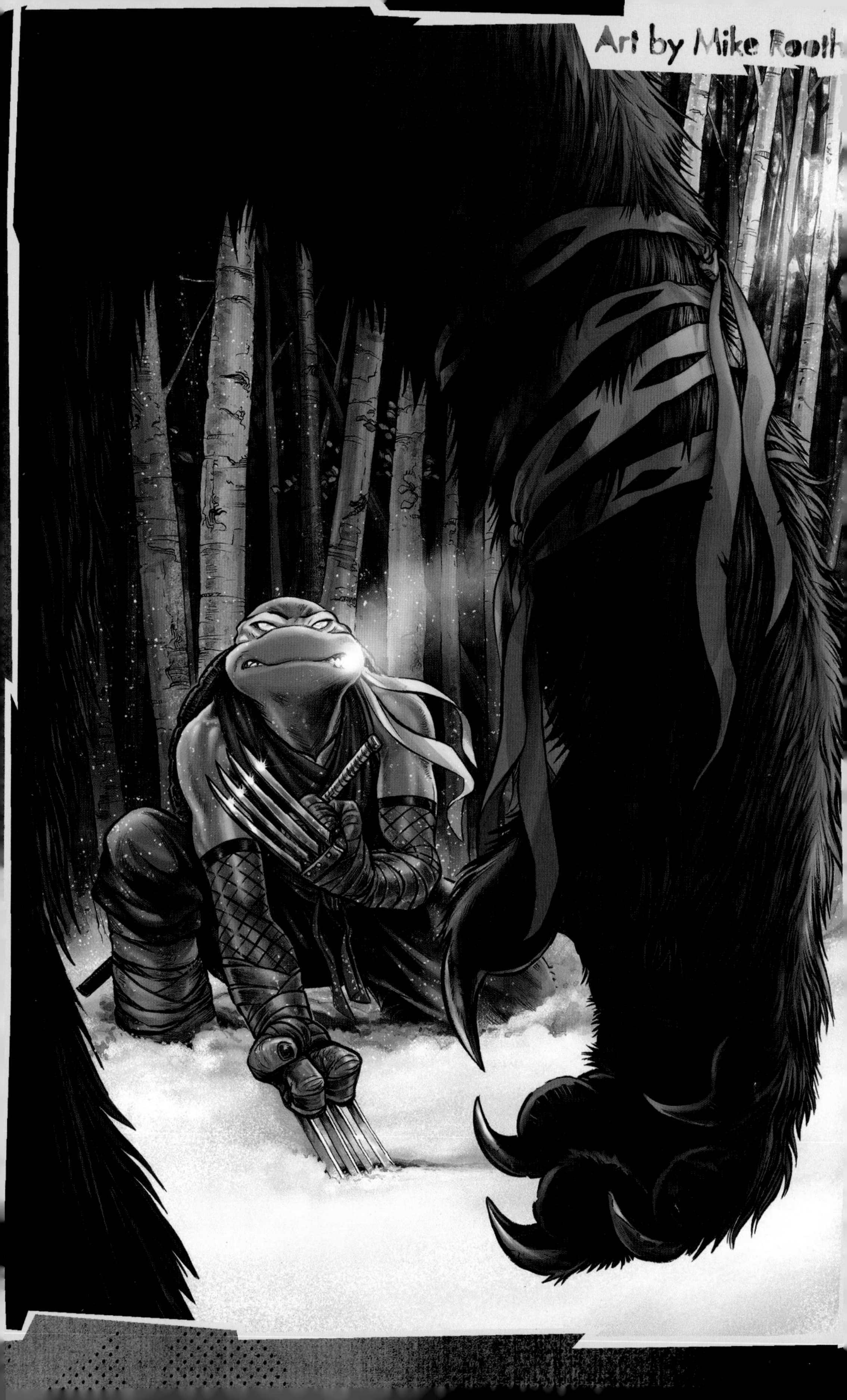
Art by Mike Rooth

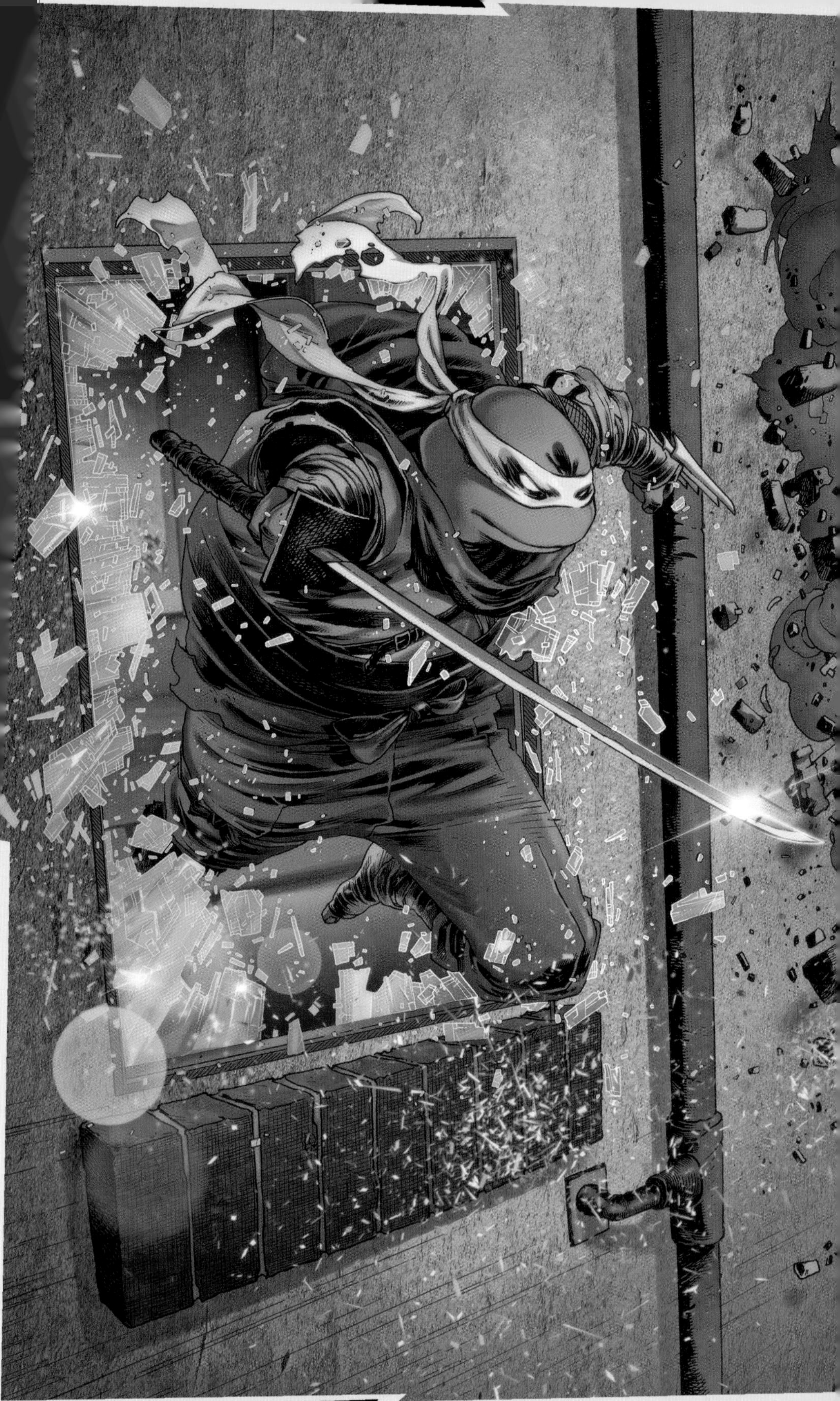

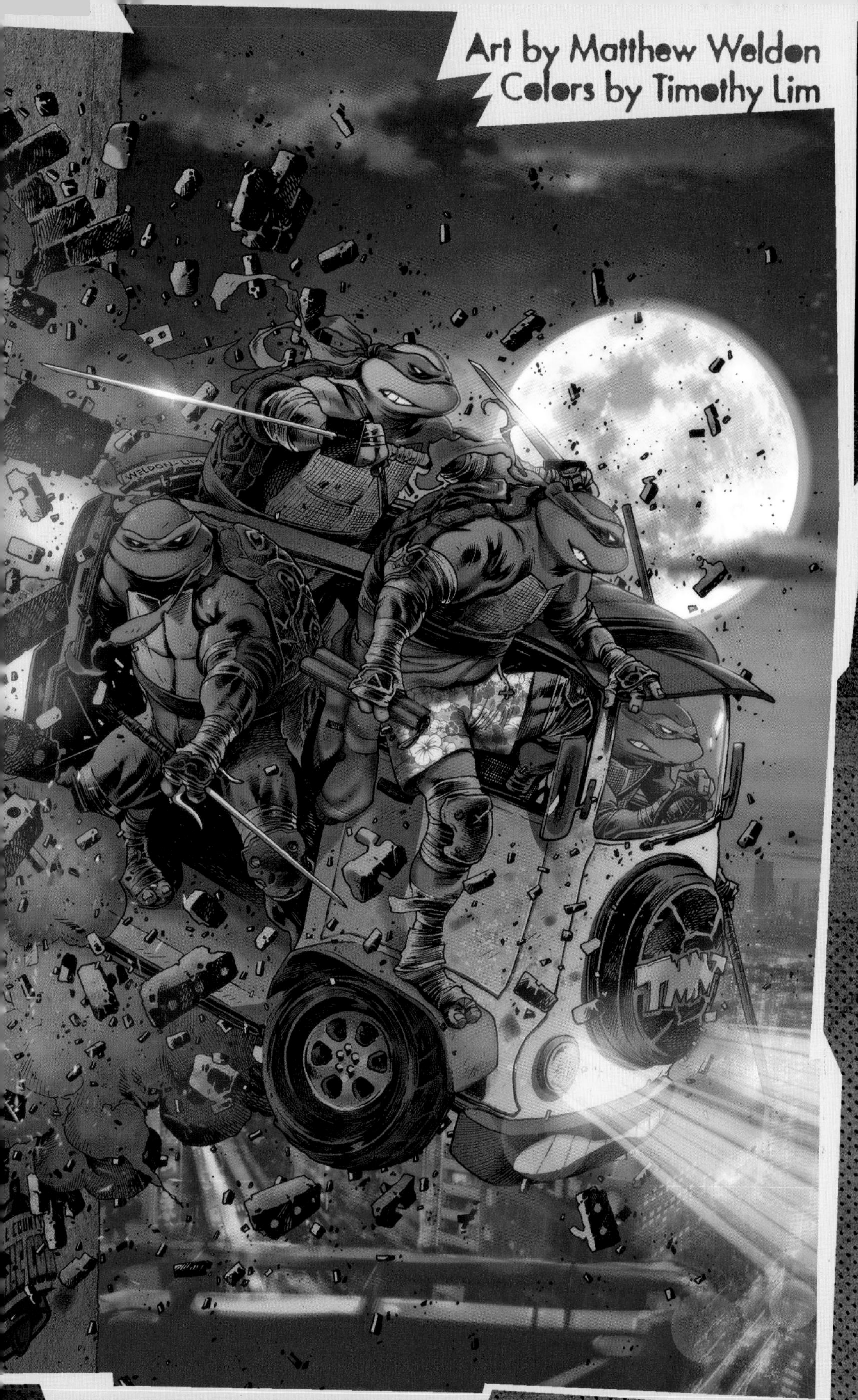

Art by Matthew Weldon
Colors by Timothy Lim

Art by Kael Ngu

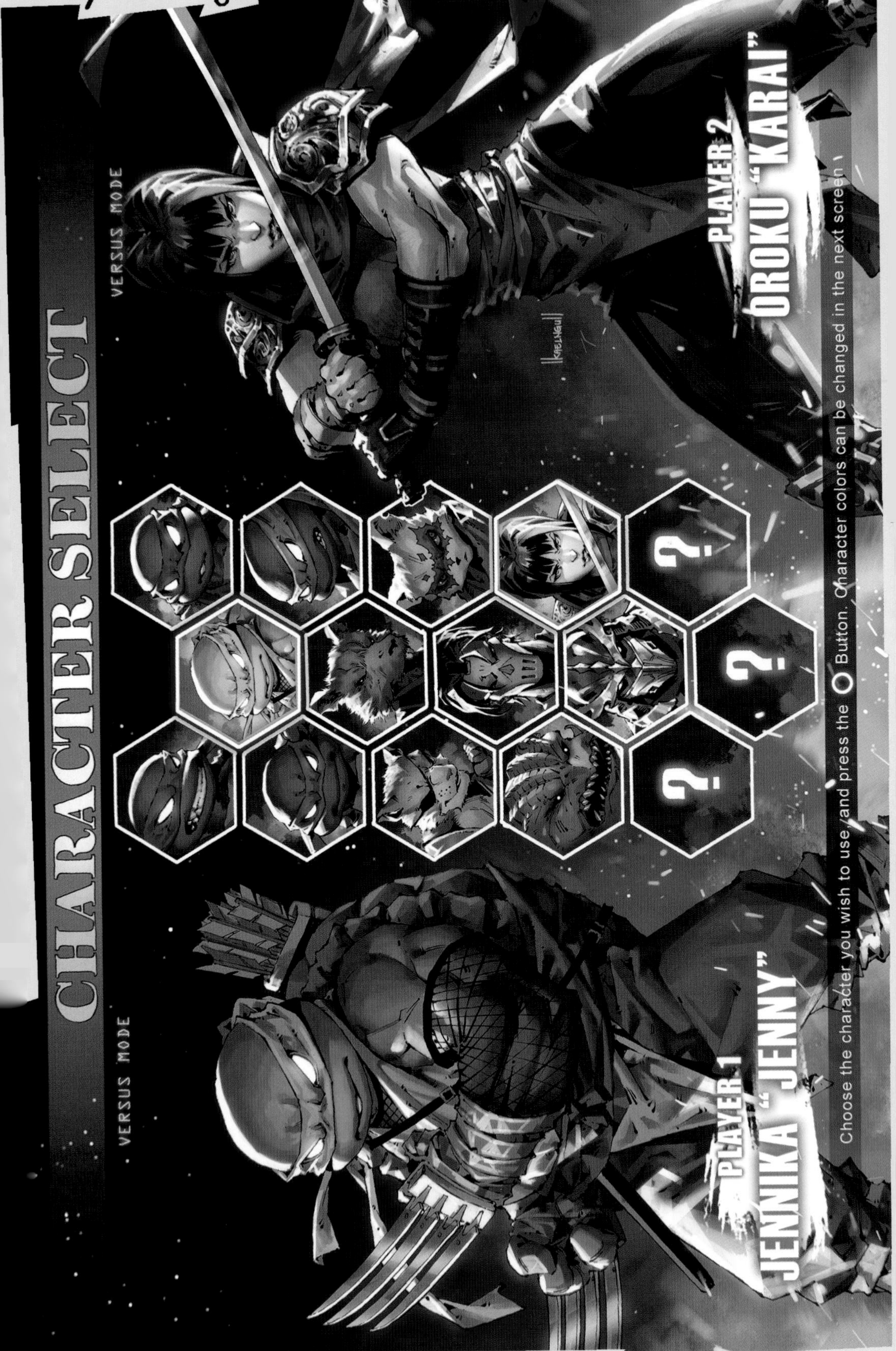
CHARACTER SELECT
VERSUS MODE
VERSUS MODE
PLAYER 1
JENNIKA "JENNY"
PLAYER 2
OROKU "KARAI"
Choose the character you wish to use and press the ◯ Button. Character colors can be changed in the next screen
KAELNGU

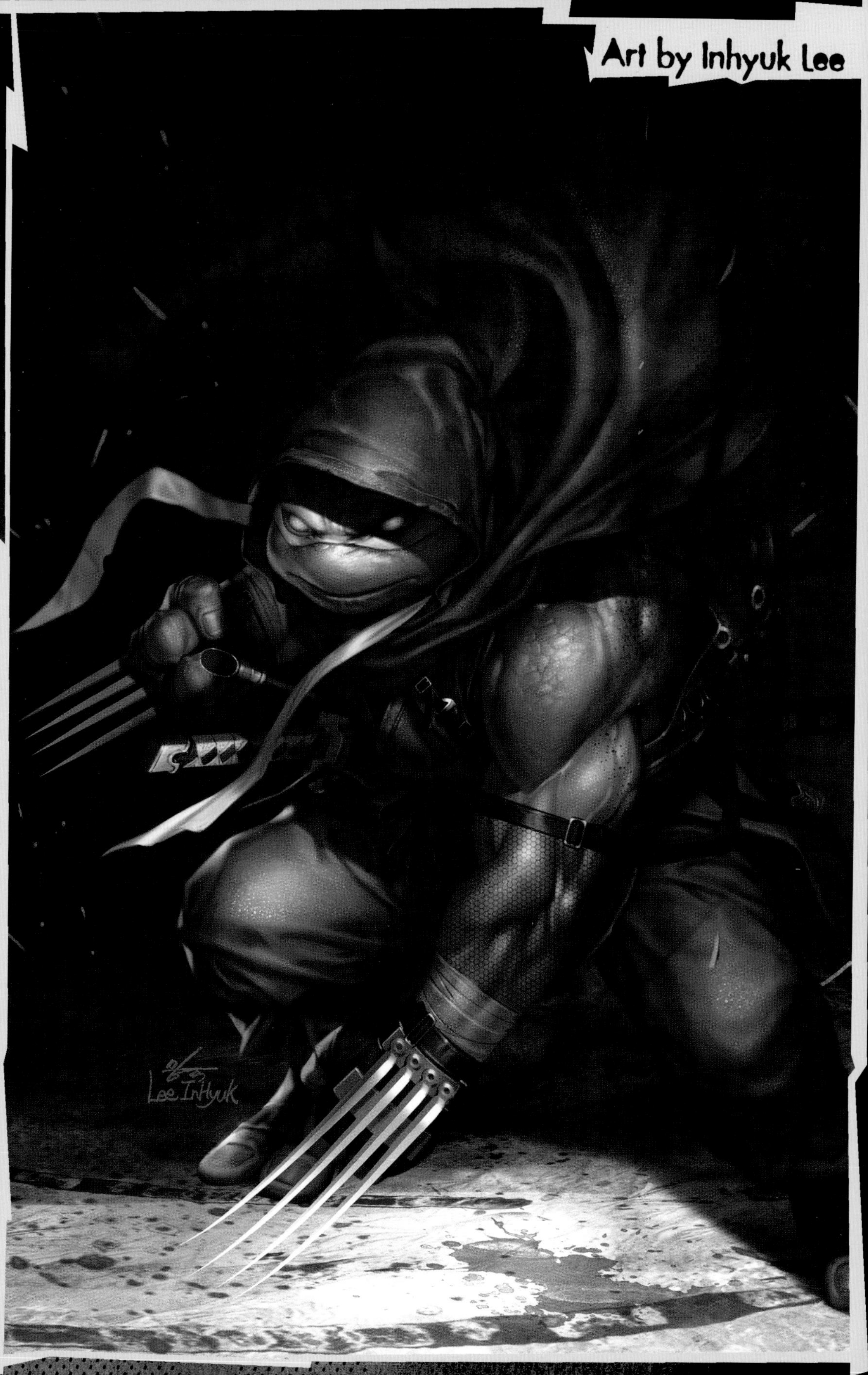
Lee InHyuk
Art by Inhyuk Lee

Art by Tyler Kirkham

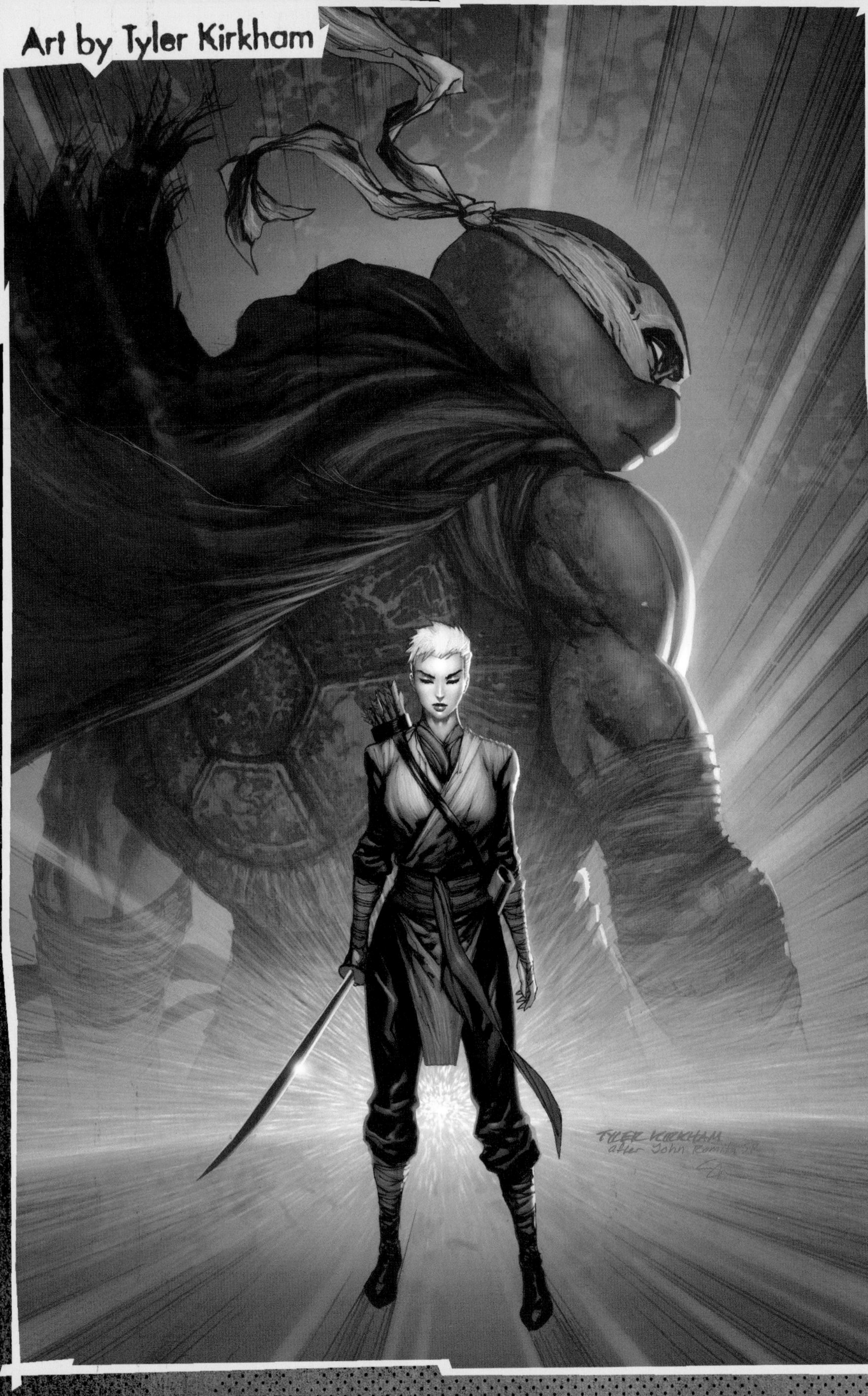
TYLER KIRKHAM
after John Romita

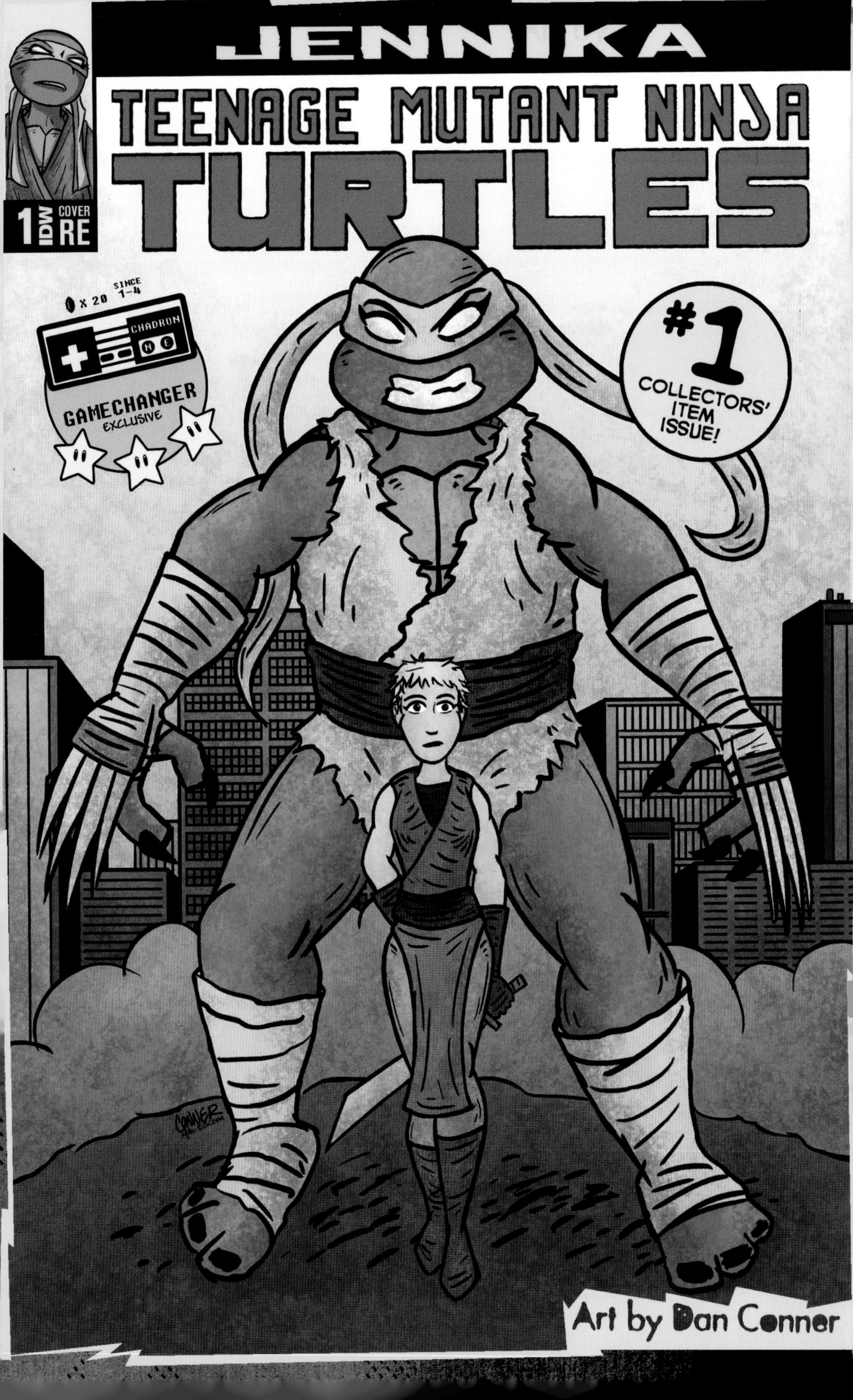
JENNIKA
TEENAGE MUTANT NINJA
TURTLES
1 IDW COVER RE
x 20 SINCE 1-4
CHADRON
GAMECHANGER EXCLUSIVE
#1 COLLECTORS' ITEM ISSUE!
Art by Dan Conner

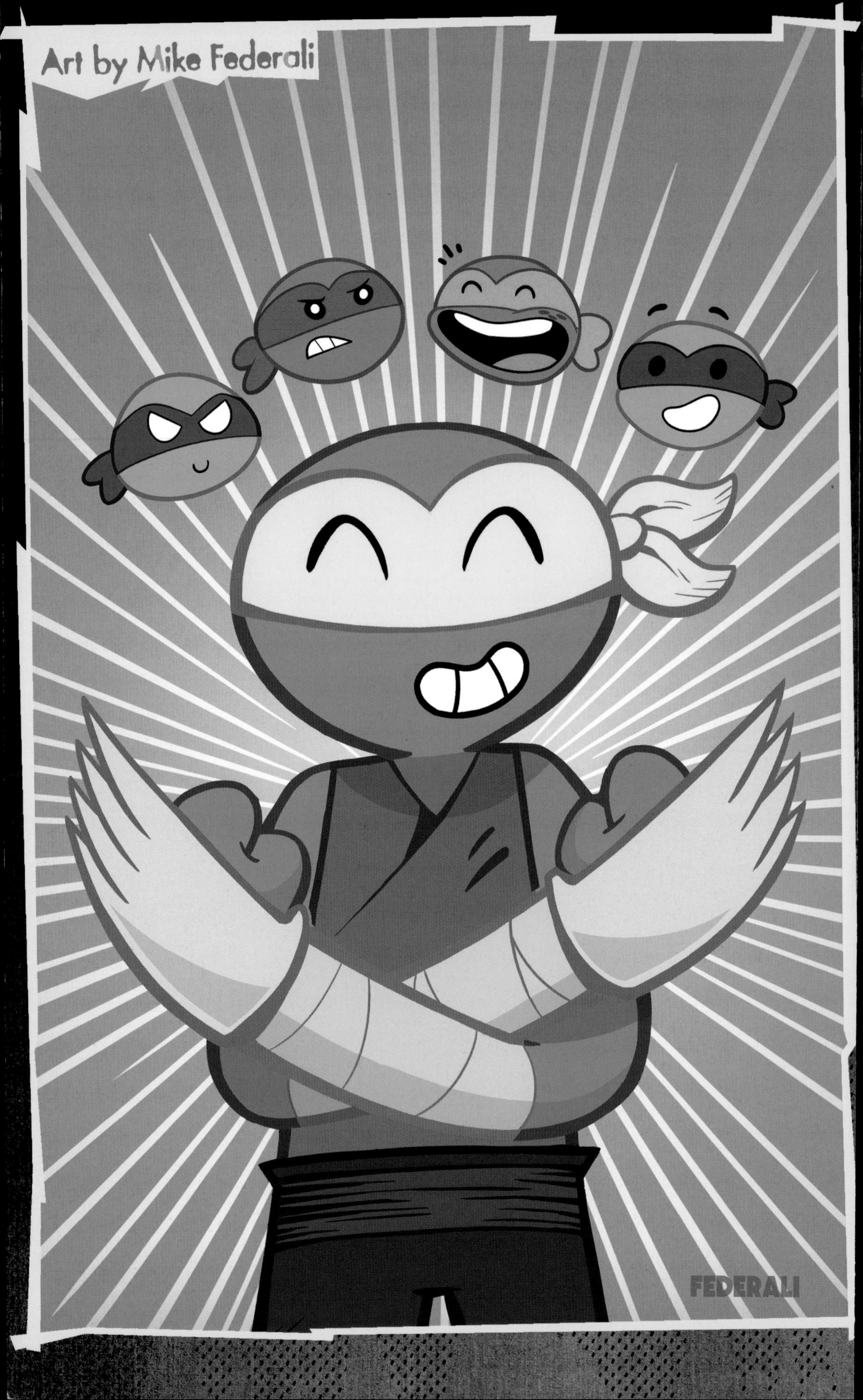
Art by Mike Federali
FEDERALI

Art by Kevin Eastman

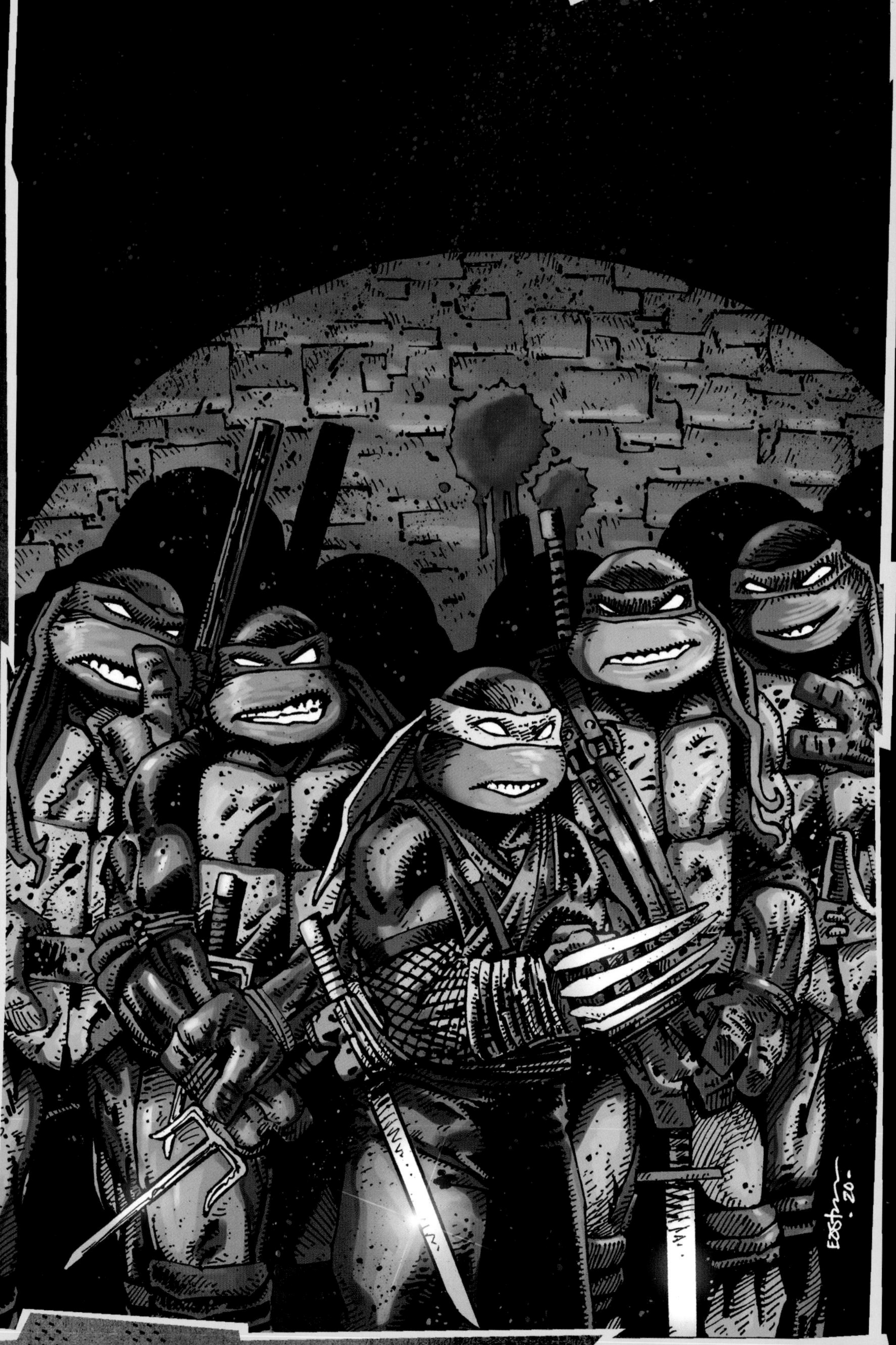

Art by Alan Quah

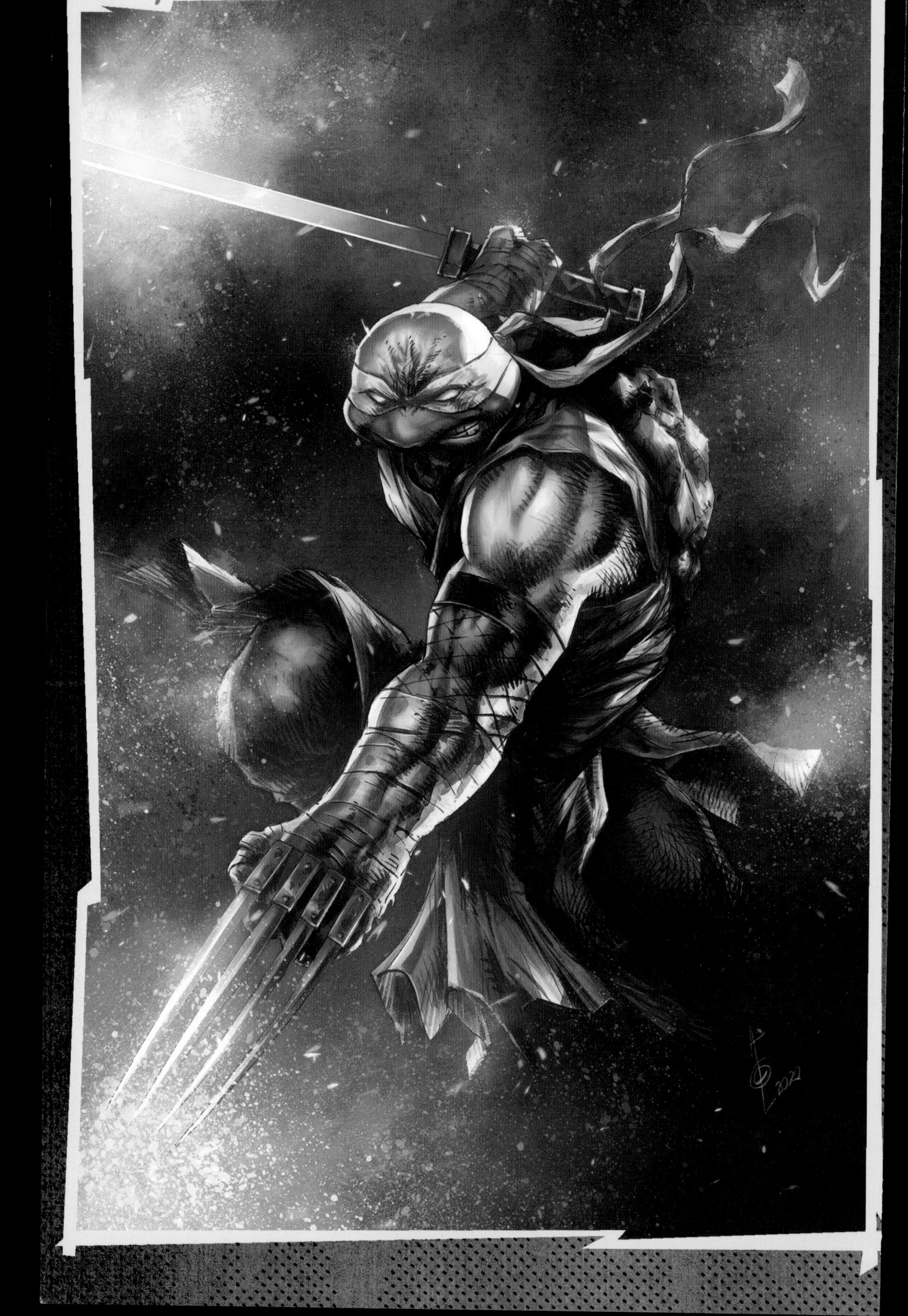

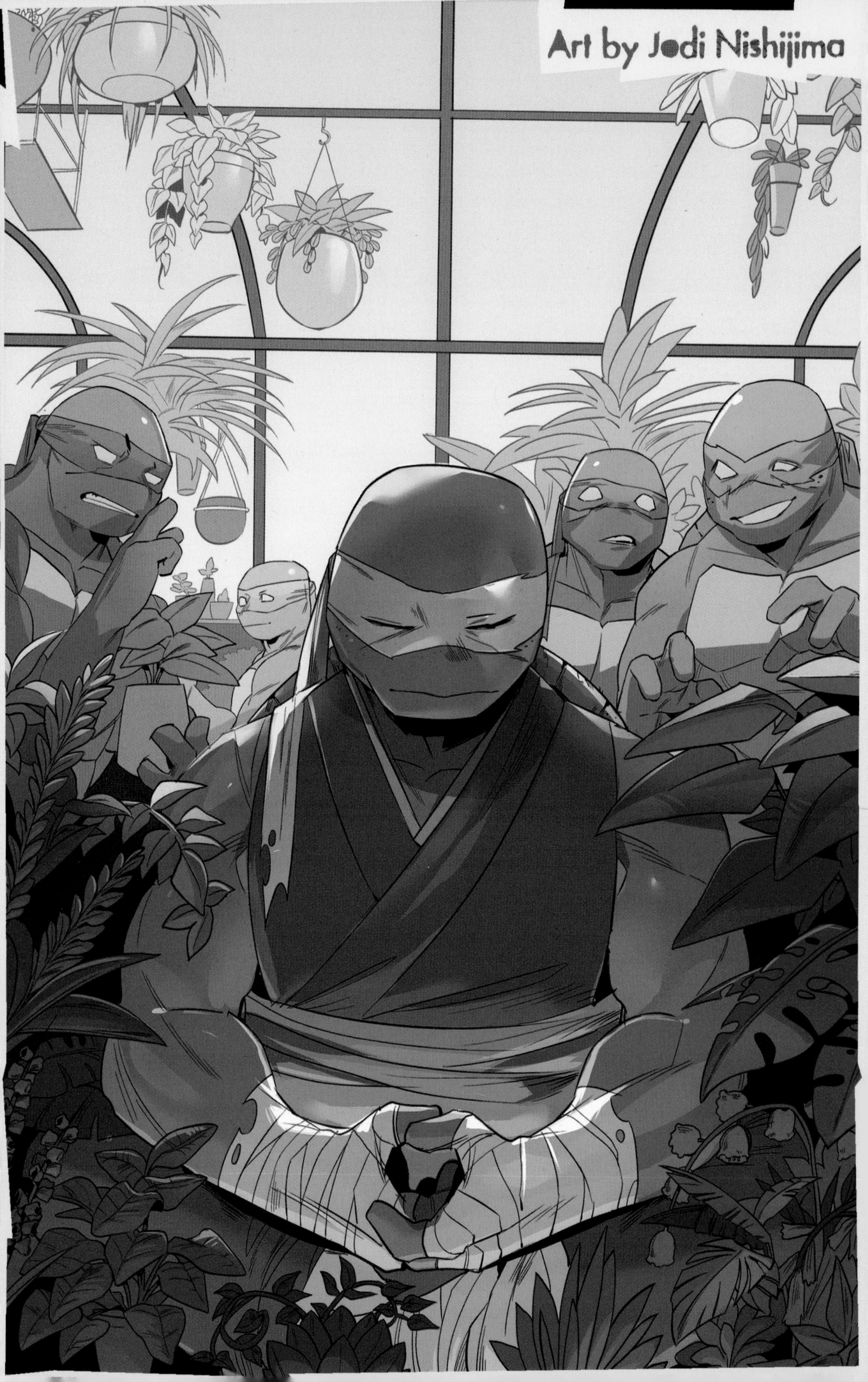

Art by Jodi Nishijima

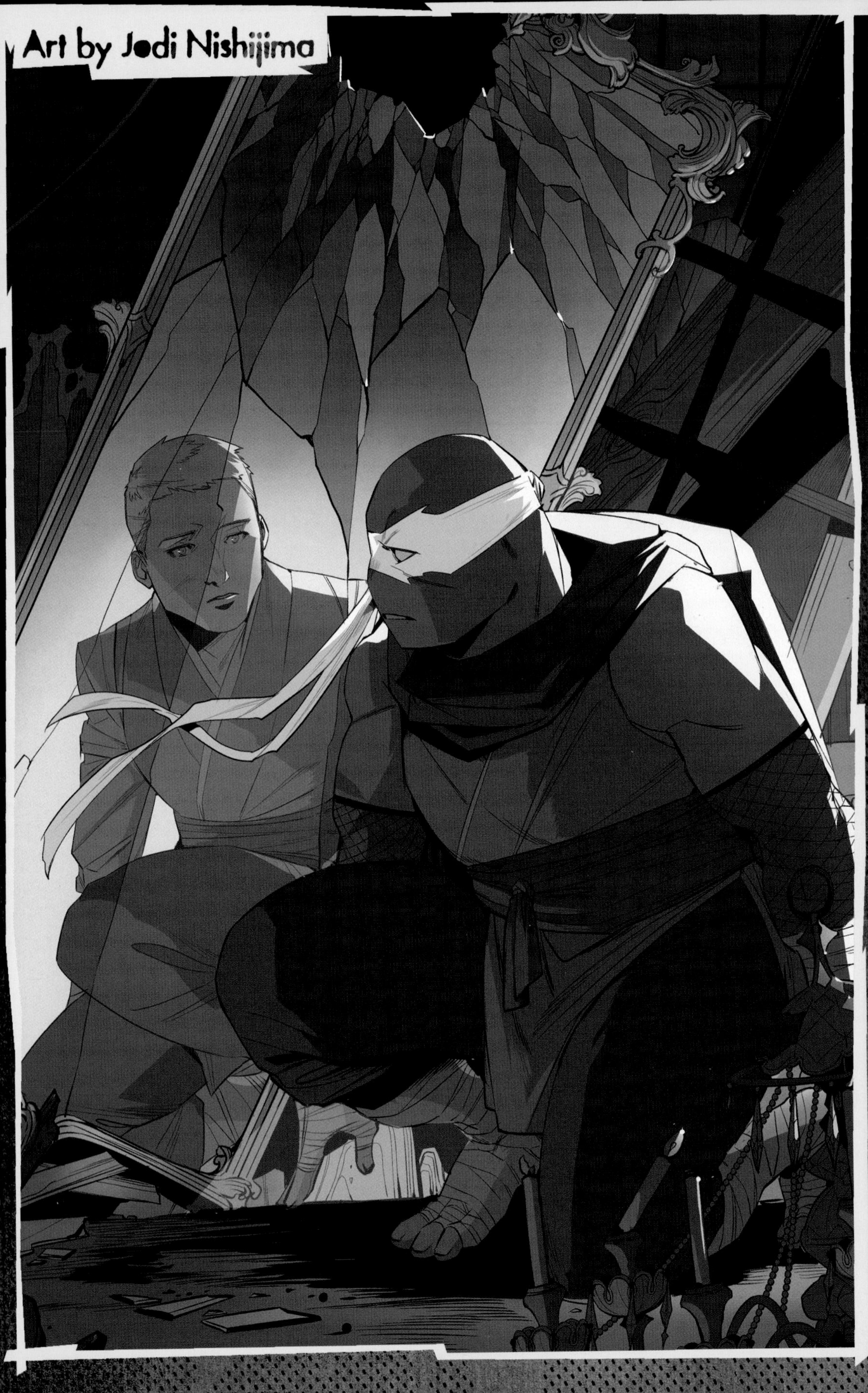

Art by Jodi Nishijima

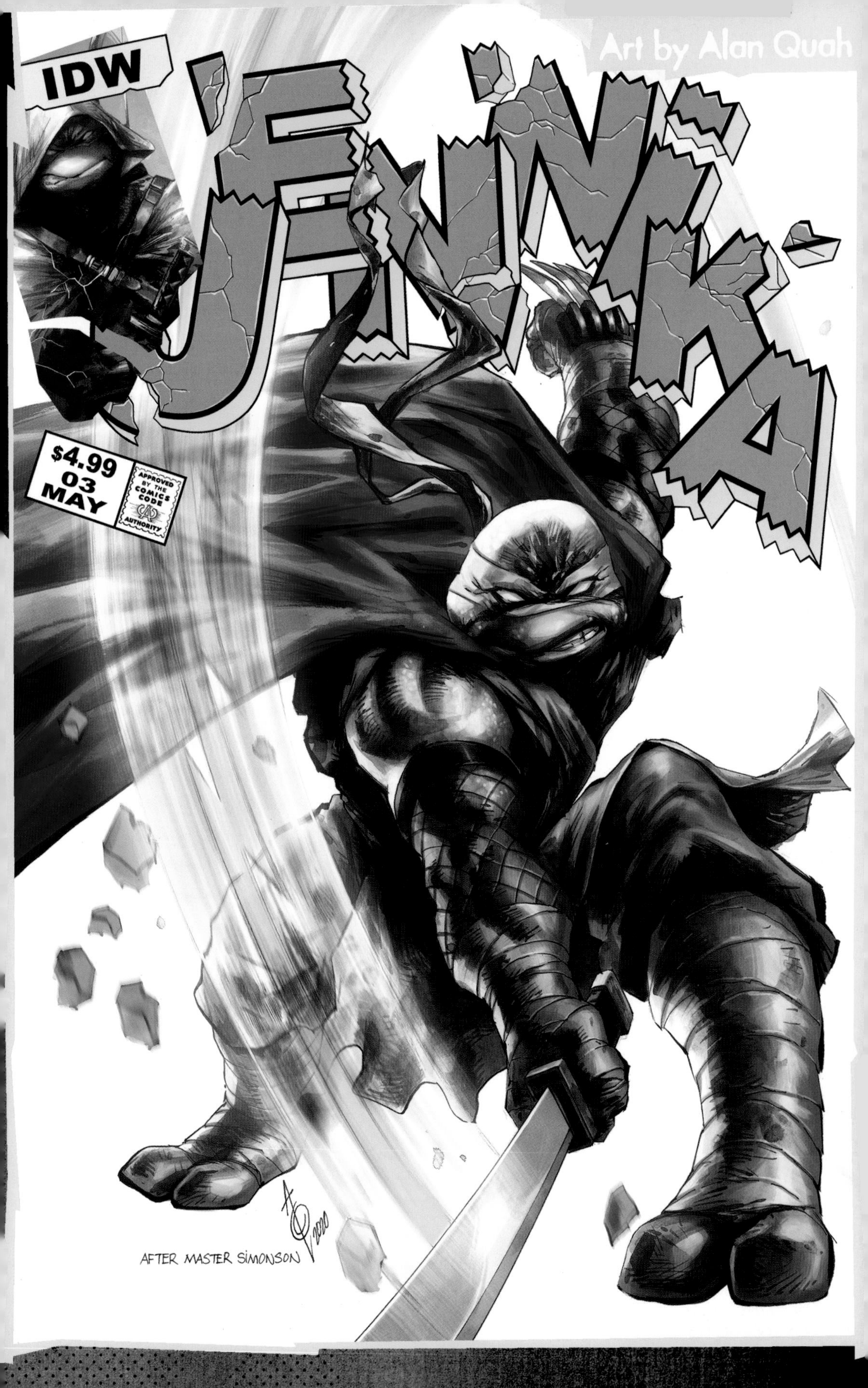
IDW
JENNIKA
$4.99
03
MAY
APPROVED BY THE COMICS CODE AUTHORITY
AFTER MASTER SIMONSON

Art by Alan Quah

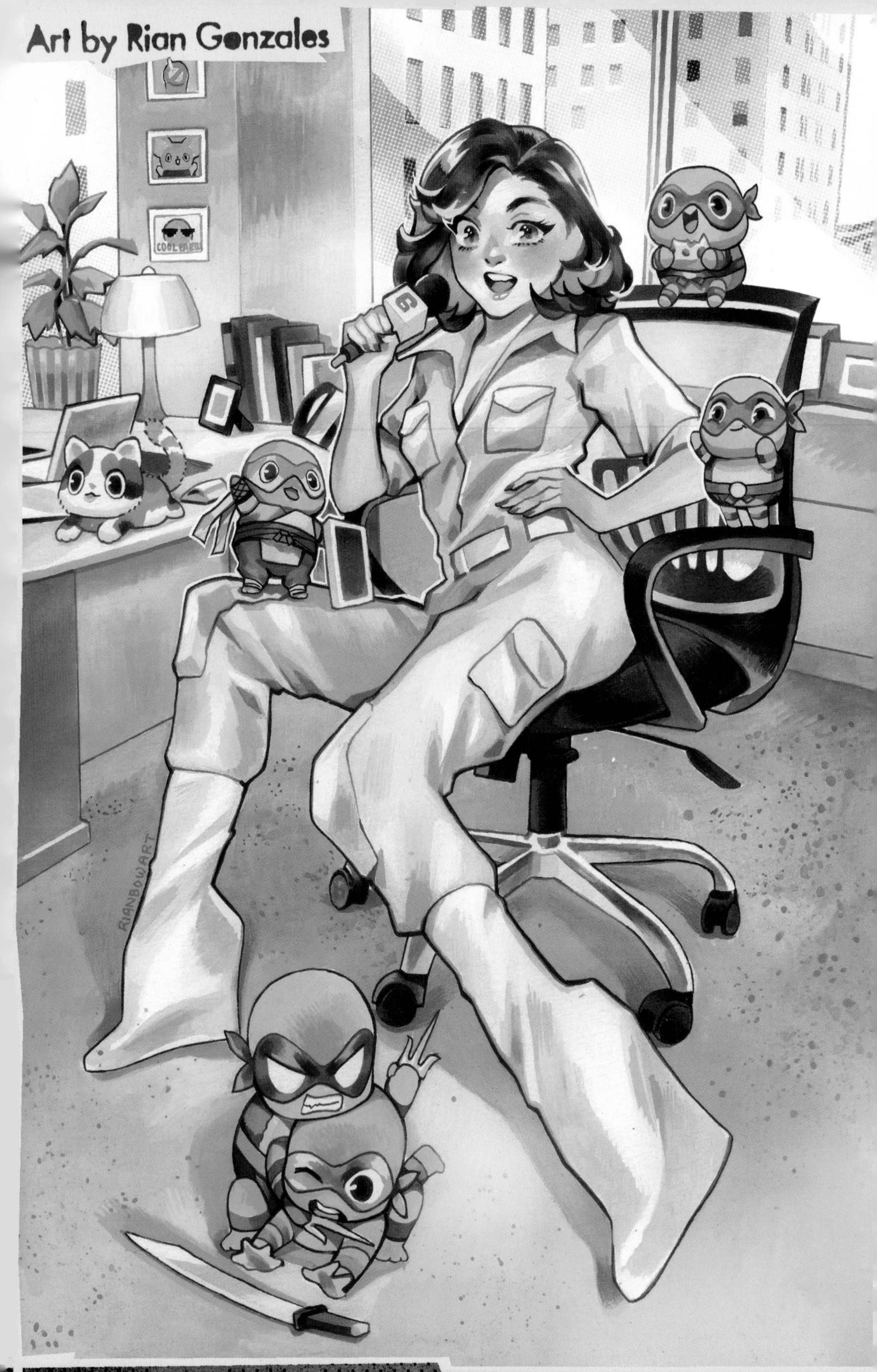
RIANBOWART
Art by Rian Gonzales

concept art by BRAHM REVEL

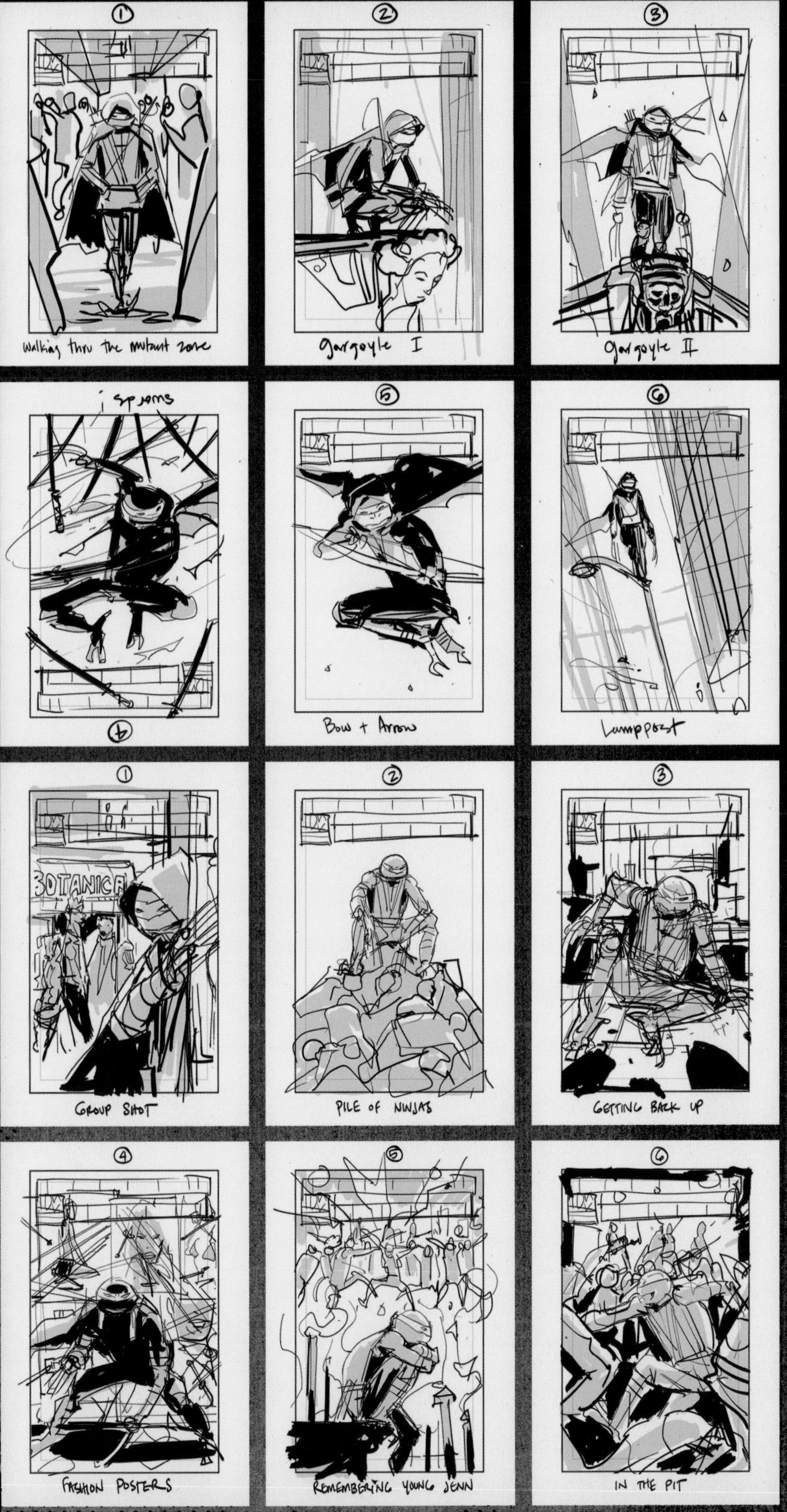
1
walking thru the mutant zone
2
Gargoyle I
3
Gargoyle II
i spears
4
5
Bow + Arrow
6
Lamppost
1
BOTANICA
GROUP SHOT
2
PILE OF NINJAS
3
GETTING BACK UP
4
FASHION POSTERS
5
REMEMBERING YOUNG JENN
6
IN THE PIT

art by **BRAHM REVEL**

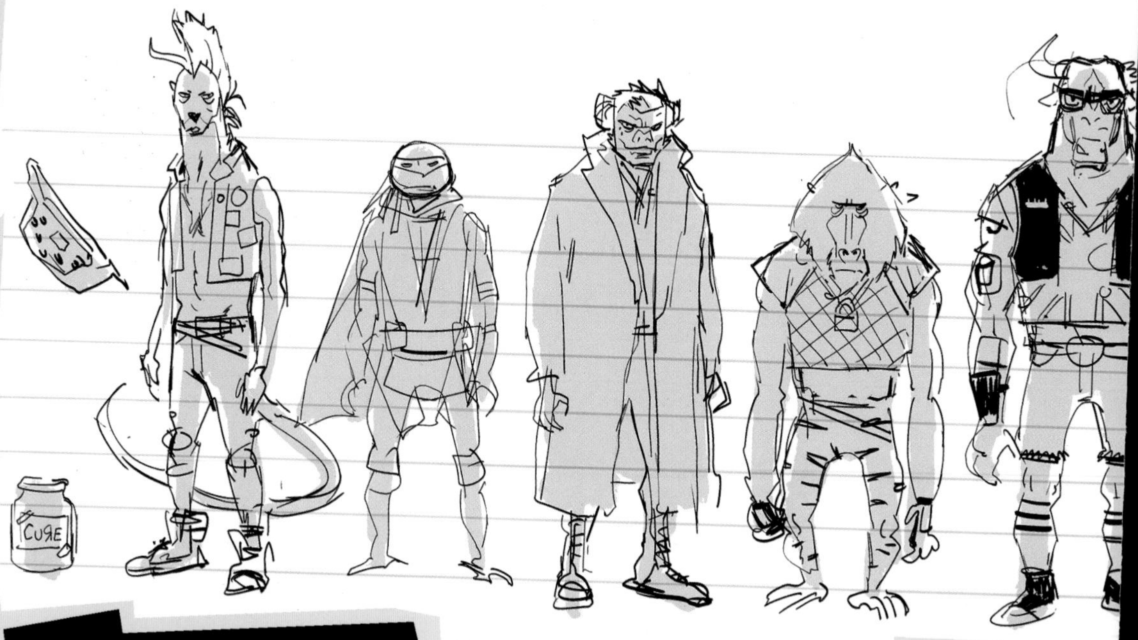
CURE

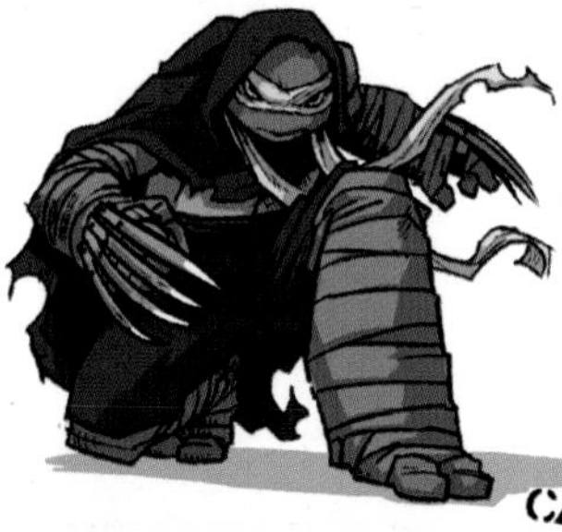

JENNIKA
"JENNY"

art by
SOPHIE CAMPBELL

art by **MICHAEL DIALYNAS**

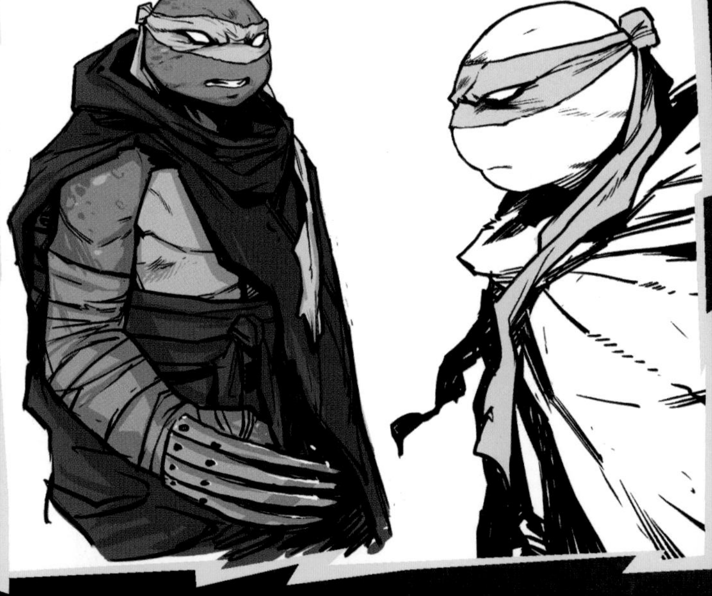

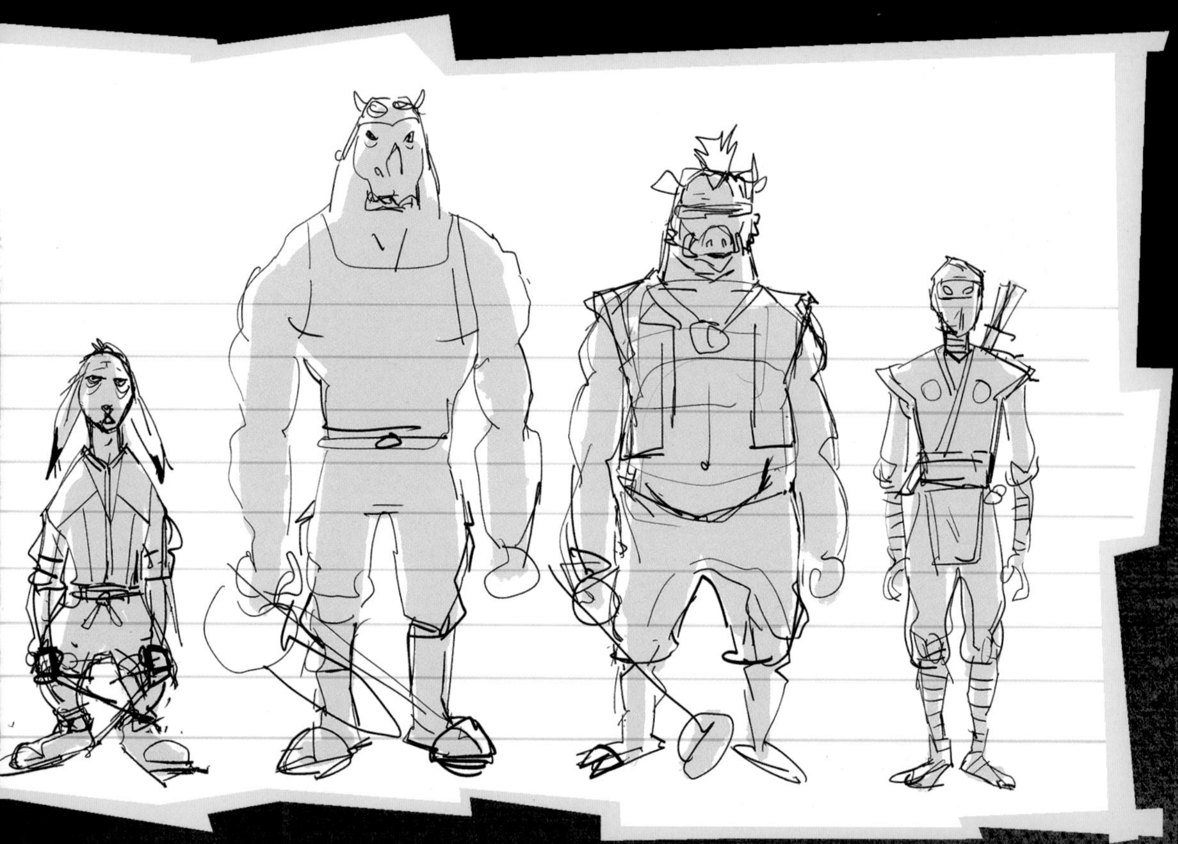

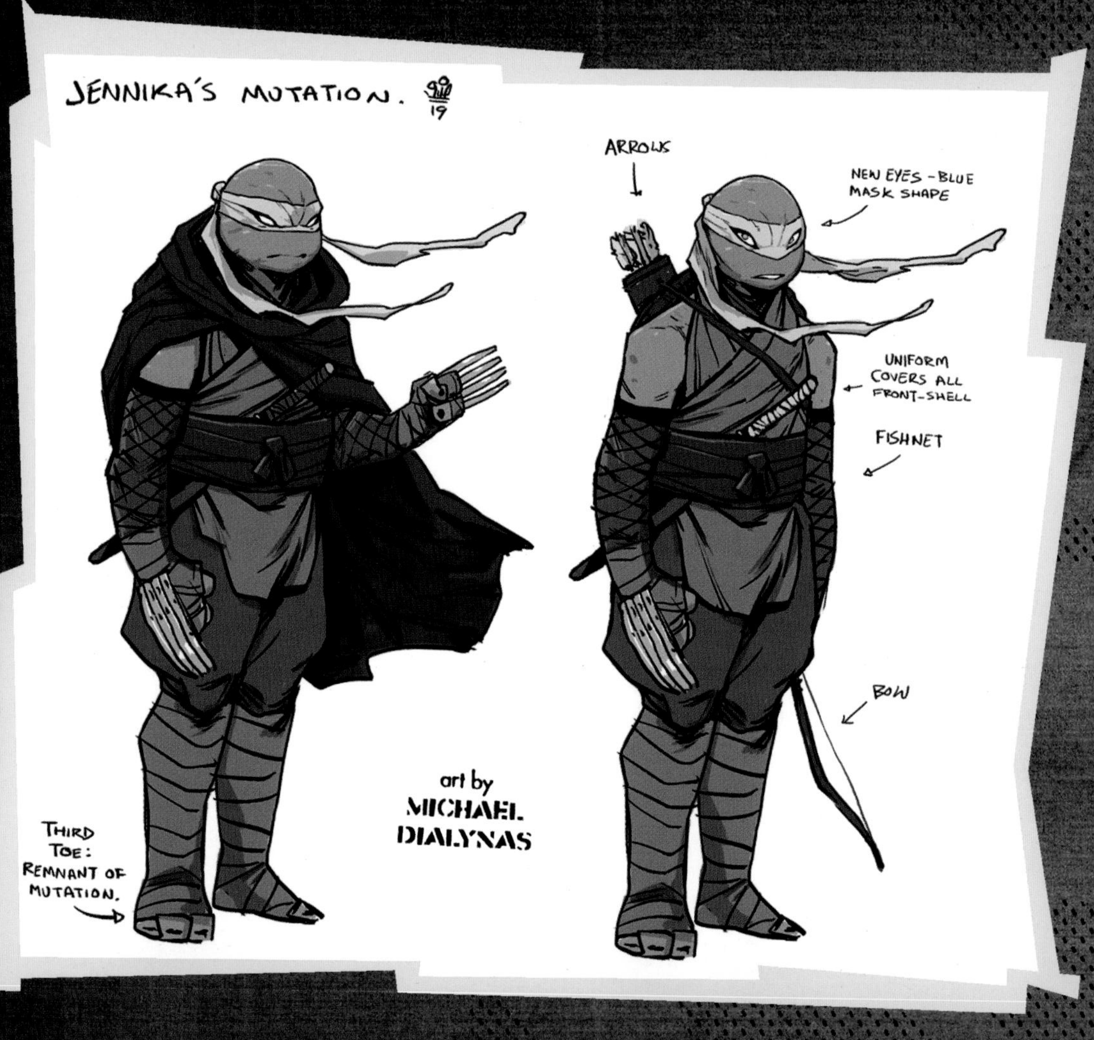
JENNIKA'S MUTATION.
ARROWS
NEW EYES - BLUE
MASK SHAPE
UNIFORM
COVERS ALL
FRONT-SHELL
FISHNET
BOW
THIRD
TOE:
REMNANT OF
MUTATION.
art by
MICHAEL
DIALYNAS

A TIMELINE OF IMPORTANT MOMENTS IN JENNIKA'S HISTORY

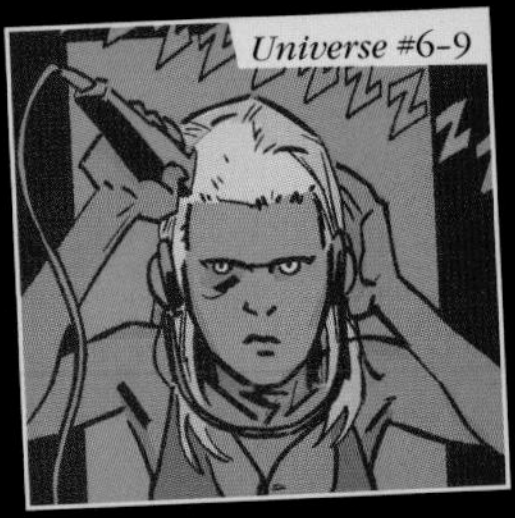
Universe #6-9

Jennika's difficult upbringing and early adulthood

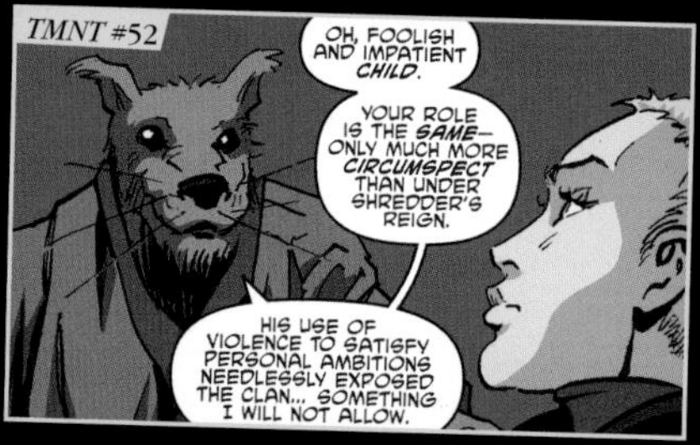

OH, FOOLISH AND IMPATIENT CHILD.
YOUR ROLE IS THE SAME— ONLY MUCH MORE CIRCUMSPECT THAN UNDER SHREDDER'S REIGN.
HIS USE OF VIOLENCE TO SATISFY PERSONAL AMBITIONS NEEDLESSLY EXPOSED THE CLAN... SOMETHING I WILL NOT ALLOW.

TMNT #52

Defeated and forgiven by Splinter

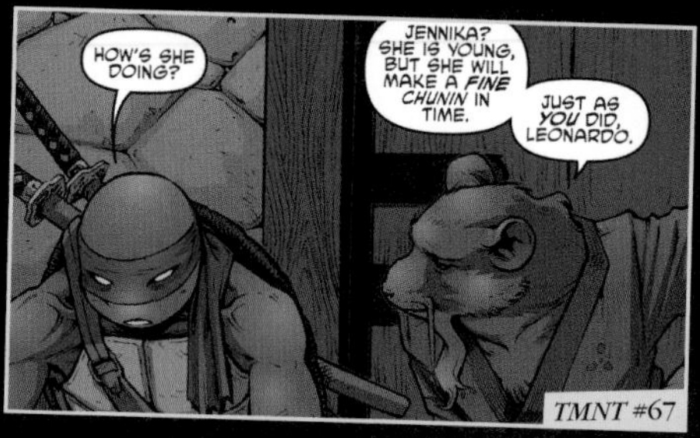

HOW'S SHE DOING?
JENNIKA? SHE IS YOUNG, BUT SHE WILL MAKE A FINE CHUNIN IN TIME.
JUST AS YOU DID, LEONARDO.

TMNT #67

Becomes Chunin of the Foot Clan under Splinter

Rebels against Splinter's leadership of the Foot Clan

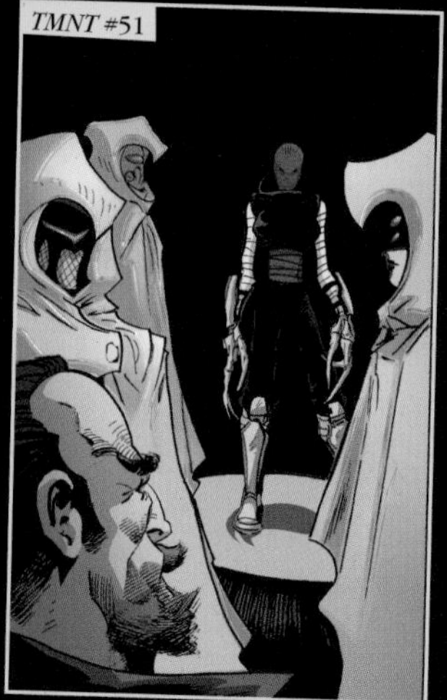
TMNT #51

Kills Darius Dun at Splinter's request

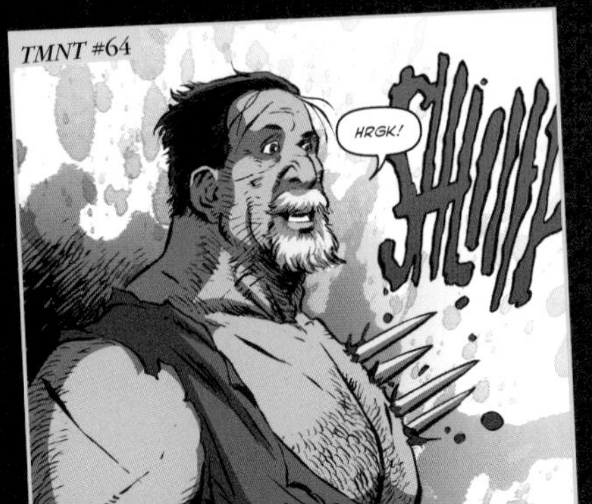

HRGK!

TMNT #64

TMNT #90
HERE— YOU'RE GONNA NEED THIS.
IS THIS YOUR MOTORCYCLE?

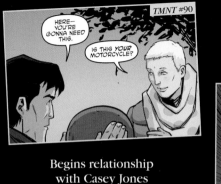

Begins relationship with Casey Jones

TMNT #93

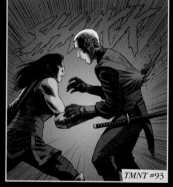

Stabbed by Karai

Mutated into a Turtle

TMNT #95

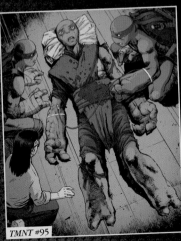

Fights against the Invasion of the Triceratons

TMNT #75
THIS CITY BELONGS TO THE FOOT CLAN.

Becomes an active citizen in Mutant Town

WHAT'S ALL THIS FOOD YOU GOT, ANYWAY?
OH! I'M BRINGING IT TO THE SHELTER, YOU KNOW WHERE THAT IS? THERE'S A CUTE SNOW FOX NAMED ALOPEX THERE.
TMNT #101

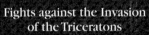

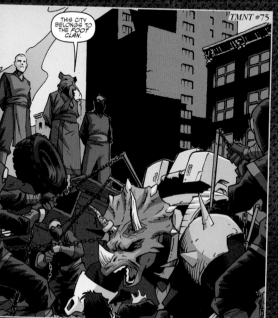

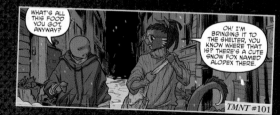

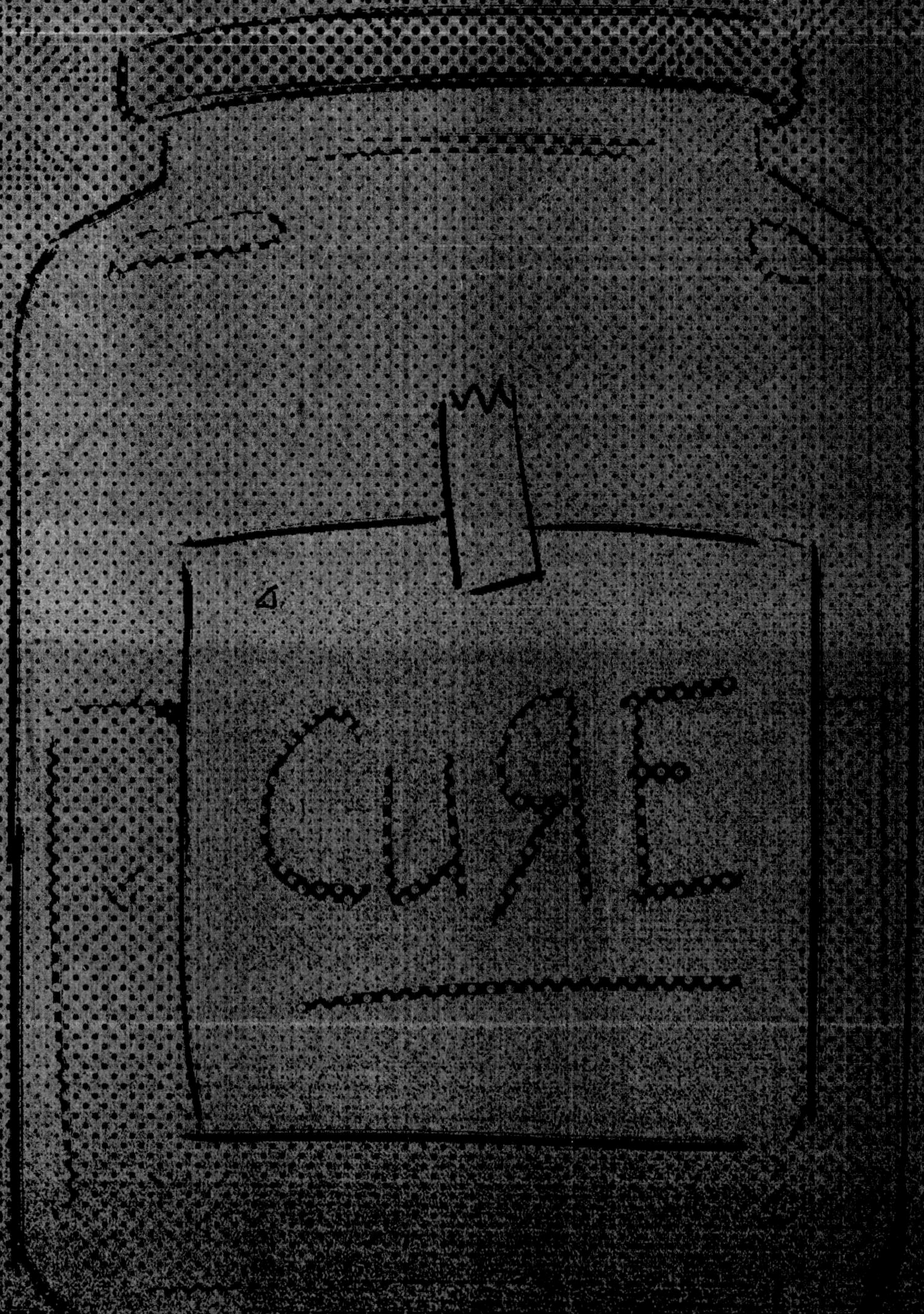
CURE